BRITAIN SINCE 1789
A CONCISE HISTORY

Britain since 1789
A Concise History

Martin Pugh

St. Martin's Press
New York

BRITAIN SINCE 1789

English language edition copyright © 1999 by Martin Pugh

First published as *Storia Della Gran Bretagna, 1789–1990* © 1997 by La Nuova Italia Scientifica, Roma

All rights reserved. No part of this book may be used or reproduced in any manner whatsoever without written permission except in the case of brief quotations embodied in critical articles or reviews. For information, address:

St. Martin's Press, Scholarly and Reference Division, 175 Fifth Avenue, New York, N.Y. 10010

First published in English in the United States of America in 1999

English language edition arranged through the mediation of Eulama Literary Agency.

This book is printed on paper suitable for recycling and made from fully managed and sustained forest sources.

Printed in Great Britain

ISBN 0–312–22358–7 clothbound
ISBN 0–312–22359–5 paperback

Library of Congress Cataloging-in-Publication Data
Pugh, Martin.
Britain since 1789 : a concise history / Martin Pugh.
p. cm.
Includes bibliographical references (p.   ) and index.
ISBN 0–312–22358–7 (cloth). — ISBN 0–312–22359–5 (pbk.)
1. Great Britain—History—19th century.   2. Great Britain–
–History—20th century.   3. Great Britain—History—1789–1820.
I. Title.
DA530.P84   1999
941.07—dc21   99–18933
                                                        CIP

For Alastair

Contents

List of Maps		ix
Preface		x
1	British Society and Economy in the Eighteenth Century	1
2	British Politics and the Political System in the Eighteenth Century	8
3	The Impact of the French Revolution, 1789–1815	19
4	The Industrial Revolution and the British People	28
5	Reaction and Radicalism, 1815–27	38
6	The Era of Reform, 1828–41	46
7	The Condition of England Question, 1832–48	54
8	The Triumph of Free Trade	63
9	Mid-Victorian Britain: Progress and Prosperity	71
10	Pax Britannica	83
11	Mid-Victorian Politics, 1846–65	91
12	The Era of Gladstonian Liberalism, 1865–85	98

13 The Age of Conservatism, 1886–1905   107

14 British Society in Decline, 1873–1902   114

15 The Working Class and Socialist Revival   122

16 The New Imperialism   129

17 The Emergence of the Interventionist State, 1905–14   137

18 The Edwardian Crisis   145

19 The Continental Commitment, 1890–1914   154

20 The Impact of the Great War   163

21 The Inter-War Economic Depression   172

22 The Rise of Labour, 1918–29   179

23 Political Stability in the 1930s   187

24 The Era of Appeasement   195

25 The Impact of the Second World War   204

26 The Era of Consensus, 1945–59   212

27 The Decline of British Power, 1945–74   220

28 Affluence and Decline, 1960–75   228

29 Thatcher and the End of Consensus Politics, 1975–97   235

Bibliography   245

Index   249

List of Maps

1 Britain and the European Powers in the Late
  Eighteenth Century   16
2 Industrial Development, Pre-1850   30
3 The Railway Network in 1850   75
4 British Territory in Africa c. 1902   131
5 Britain and the European Powers in 1871   158
6 The British Empire in 1919   196

Preface

This book originated in a proposal made to me by Professor Emile Gentile of the University of Rome and Gianluca Mori of La Nuova Italia Scientifica in 1992 for a volume on modern British history designed for Italian students. I hesitated for a time, but was encouraged by the cogent arguments put by Dr Eugenio Biagini, then a Sir James Knott Fellow at Newcastle University, to go ahead. In writing it I attempted to put myself in the position of my audience, which perhaps one ought to do more often, and to try to avoid making too many assumptions about the knowledge my readers would already possess. Among other things this seemed to point to fairly short and well-focused chapters that would combine a thematic treatment with chronological development. It was a surprise to me when Jonathan Reeve of Macmillan raised the possibility of an English version, or rather the original version. His enthusiasm overcame my initial reservations, and I am grateful to him for pushing ahead with the project so energetically. Since I completed the first draft a general election and a new government appear to have rounded off the whole topic with one of those neat turning-points which litter the pages of history books. It is too early to say for certain whether this conclusion is soundly based or not.

MARTIN PUGH

I

British Society and Economy in the Eighteenth Century

In the early eighteenth century Britain was little more than a middle-ranking European power. Her population in 1700 has been estimated at 9 million compared with 19 million for France and 17.5 million for Russia, for example. Britain's army, some 75,000 men, was dwarfed by the 350,000 French troops and the 222,000 Russians. However, during the 1740s and 1750s a fundamental change began to occur in British society. Her population, which had been fairly stable since 1700, began to rise and continued to do so throughout the late eighteenth century and the nineteenth century at what was, historically, a very high rate. In the process both the economy and the politics of the British Isles were transformed.

THE DEMOGRAPHIC REVOLUTION

The cause of the original rise in population remains rather obscure. However, it is accepted that good harvests during the mid-eighteenth century helped to reduce death rates in England and that the spread of potato cultivation in Ireland boosted the population there. As the area under cultivation expanded, birth rates increased, largely because people felt encouraged to marry at an earlier age. In this way the country began to escape from the traditional demographic cycle in which higher birth rates were effectively cancelled out by higher death rates.

Between 1740 and 1790 these changes raised the population of England and Wales from around 6 million to 8.3 million. From the

1780s onwards the annual increase exceeded 1 per cent. Consequently, by 1801, when the first civil census was conducted, the population of the whole country stood at 15.8 million, which included 8.48 million in England, 5.2 million in Ireland, 1.6 million in Scotland and 0.54 million in Wales. This uneven distribution reflected the predominance of poor, mountainous terrain in much of Scotland and Wales; migration southwards and eastwards was a well-established pattern. The only significant concentration of people was in London, which had 775,000 people by 1800; the next largest towns were pre-industrial commercial centres such as Edinburgh (85,000), Bristol (55,000) and Norwich (39,000). The importance of agriculture at this stage is reflected in the relative status of southern England, which held 39 per cent of the people, and northern England, which held only 26 per cent; industrial growth in the nineteenth century was to stimulate a move to the north.

SOCIAL STRUCTURE AND SOCIAL MOBILITY

Historians lack the accurate records of occupational groups which would allow a satisfactory description of the divisions within eighteenth-century society. In the pre-industrial era the British did not speak about precise social classes, but referred to a multitude of 'ranks' and 'orders'. However, we gain some insights from contemporary attempts to analyse the composition of society. For example, in 1695 Gregory King produced an estimate of population and wealth for England and Wales. He distinguished twenty-six ranks based on occupation and employment, which he divided into three: the 'better sort' amounting to 1.2 per cent, the 'middle sort' amounting to 30.2 per cent, and the 'lower sort' amounting to 68.6 per cent. In 1815 another exercise, by Patrick Colquhoun, which included Scotland and Ireland, arrived at a similar picture.

In Colquhoun's analysis some 203,000 people, including their family members, formed what in the nineteenth century was to be called the 'upper' or 'landed' class comprising 1.2 per cent of the total. At the top stood the royal family and about 220 peers (dukes, marquises, earls, viscounts and barons), followed by 4400 who enjoyed the title of baronet, knight or esquire, and around 16,000 landed gentry. In the eighteenth century it was recognised that a peer should possess several thousand acres of land and an annual income of £3000, though the richest among them enjoyed ten times as large an income and up to 200,000 acres.

The 'middle classes', to use nineteenth-century terminology, comprised 4.9 million people or 28.8 per cent in Colquhoun's analysis. In this group the rural elements still loomed large. He estimated 1.2 million freeholders (that is, men who owned the land which they farmed), and 1.3 million farmers (that is, tenants who rented the land they cultivated). Colquhoun also placed in the middle group 600,000 shopkeepers, 450,000 manufacturers and master craftsmen, 115,000 clergymen, 40,000 merchants and bankers, and 40,000 lawyers and higher civil servants. The income of many of the wealthiest lawyers, bankers, merchants and bishops of the Church of England exceeded that of most of the landed gentry, but if they had not acquired land they usually enjoyed a lower social status.

The third section of society in Colquhoun's estimate comprised 12,000,000 people or 69.9 per cent. The largest group, 4.5 million artisans or skilled craftsmen, probably represents an exaggeration on his part. They were followed by 3.5 million agricultural labourers, miners, and seamen, 1.3 million domestic servants and 1.9 million variously classed as paupers, vagrants, lunatics and prisoners.

Those who suffered from poverty were dealt with by means of the 'poor law' system, which dated back to 1597. Essentially this meant that each local parish raised a poor rate, with which it could pay either 'outdoor relief' in cash or in kind, or 'indoor relief' to those who entered the 'poor house' or 'workhouse'. A more liberal law of 1782 allowed the overseers who administered this system to supplement men's wages if necessary and to require only the infirm, not the able-bodied poor, to live in the workhouse.

For many members of society there was little possibility of achieving a higher or a lower social status. At the bottom of society, agricultural labourers could rarely escape their lot except by emigrating to the colonies. At the opposite end, the peerage was a very stable, if not quite closed, caste, for few new peerages were created during the eighteenth century. However, social mobility was certainly possible. The most common method involved obtaining an apprenticeship to a skilled craft, trade or profession, which usually meant finding the fee required by an established master craftsman. Once trained a man might set himself up in business, become an employer and move into one of the expanding towns. The more successful farmers often moved up the social scale by accumulating more land, abandoning manual labour and eventually marrying their daughters into professional or gentry families. Marriage, indeed, provided a crucial vehicle at several social levels; for example, younger sons of peers did not inherit their father's estates and were therefore obliged to build careers in the church, the law, the army or politics. In the process they frequently married into the middle classes. For the most adventurous young men in almost any class, it proved tempting to seek one's fortune in the Empire. Some of the most conspicuously successful of these were employees of the East India Company, such as Robert Clive. In Bengal they could acquire a large fortune very quickly and, if they retained their health, might return to England, buy land, set themselves up as country gentlemen and even became members of parliament.

AGRICULTURE

During the eighteenth century most of the farms of England were 'mixed', that is to say, they cultivated arable crops and reared live-stock. However, variations in climate, soil and markets produced some regional specialisation. The counties of eastern and southern England, for example, grew more wheat and barley because summers were warmer and rainfall lighter. Further north and west, lower temperatures and heavy rainfall made permanent pasture and cattle and sheep production more typical. In the mild, wet climate of Ireland the potato flourished. As a result of poor communications the cattle farmers of the north and west could not sell their surplus milk in the local markets and they therefore turned to cheese-making instead. When their cattle and sheep were ready for slaughter the animals were simply driven for hundreds of miles south to the great London markets, or, on a smaller scale, sold in local market towns.

It has been estimated that in 1700 the agricultural sector employed 45–50 per cent of the labour force, but that by 1800 this had fallen to around 35 per cent, compared with 29 per cent for mining and manufacturing. Undoubtedly agriculture was in relative decline by the later eighteenth century so that by 1871 it employed only 15 per cent of the labour force. Traditionally historians believed that workers had been driven off the land by a process known as enclosure, by which the multitude of small cultivated strips of land were amalgamated into larger units under fewer owners. However, it is now clear that the absolute number of men employed *increased* during the eighteenth century partly because enclosure itself created more intensive work such as digging ditches, making drains and planting hedges. But the distinctive feature of British agriculture was certainly the steady decline of the small peasant proprietors and their replacement by a society dominated by large landowners, tenant farmers and many landless labourers. This did not begin in the eighteenth century, but the spread of enclosures in that period accelerated the process. As a result many workers were ready to move into employment in factories when industrialisation began.

THE ORIGINS OF INDUSTRIALISATION

By comparison with most European societies Britain had few workers in agriculture even in the early eighteenth century; as a result, by the 1780s most of the value of her exports was derived from manufactured goods. In that decade the average annual figure for exports and re-exports stood at £14.5 million and that for imports at £13.8 million. However, during the 1790s exports rose steeply to £26.9 million and imports to £21.8 million – an unmistakable sign of a significant rise in economic activity. Of course, the traditional view of Britain's industrial revolution emphasised the 1760s as the 'take-off' stage, largely because of the innovations in cotton textile production. However, the impact of this development now seems too narrow to justify the term 'industrial revolution'. The 1780s seems a more significant turning-point, for it was then that the annual growth of industrial output reached 3–4 per cent compared with the 2 per cent of earlier decades. Even then, only a few sectors of the economy experienced significant increases. For example, iron production rose from 25,000 tons to 70,000 tons in the 1780s; and cotton textiles, as measured by the pounds of raw cotton consumed, rose from 4.8 million in the 1770s to 14.8 million in the 1780s and to 28.6 million in the 1790s. Industrialisation advanced by means of technological improvements in certain leading sectors of the economy: first cotton, then iron and steel, and then, in the 1830s and 1840s, in railways.

But why the whole process began in the first place remains a matter of controversy. Because the first industrial revolution took place in Britain it has been tempting to assume that her economy enjoyed special advantages. It has become clear, however, that the British economy was not very different from that of France, which was at least as sophisticated and enjoyed a larger domestic market. Consequently some historians resort to non-economic explanations. For example, the relative political stability of Britain may have been advantageous. Yet this can be no more than a helpful precondition for industrialisation rather than a cause. Others point to social–ideological influences such as the prominent role of Nonconformists amongst early industrialism, and the moral belief in the virtue of work, associated with Protestantism. However, empirically minded historians are very doubtful about claims that the culture of Britain really favoured entrepreneurialism. After all, there were just as many Anglicans as Nonconformists among the early industrial pioneers; moreover, the spirit of enterprise also manifested itself among the landed aristocracy who were not Nonconformists and often not very religious at all. The industrial innovators were simply exceptional men from all kinds of backgrounds, and so it is unwise to draw general explanations from their experience.

Amongst the economic explanations, much emphasis has been placed upon the formation of capital arising partly out of the profits of commerce. Some historians argue that the crucial take-off into industrialisation occurs when a society saves 10–12 per cent of its income. But in fact there seems to have been little increase in capital during the eighteenth century in Britain. In any case, capital proved to have been only a marginal factor, for the early cotton manufacturers met their limited capital requirements either from personal and family sources or by ploughing back their profits rather than by extensive external borrowing.

Thus, historians have increasingly regarded population increase and the growth of consumer demand for goods as the underlying factor. Extra population produced a labour force for new textile mills; but it also stimulated the price of food items, thereby encouraging landowners and farmers to improve their techniques and to expand the cultivated area. What was once called the 'agricultural revolution' is now regarded as simply a very gradual process of innovation involving crop rotations, the use of fodder crops, better drainage and the selective breeding of superior animals. But this steady process of change meant that when the domestic market expanded in the eighteenth century, agriculture was able to raise its output to satisfy it. In this way population growth could be sustained and manufacturers could reap the benefit in the form of a buoyant demand for their goods.

2

British Politics and the Political System in the Eighteenth Century

As a result of the civil wars between the Stuart Kings and parliament in the seventeenth century the British political elite established what many regarded as an ideal form of government. They wanted a hereditary king, but not the absolute monarchy characteristic of other European countries. They also wished to prevent the succession of the Stuarts and of any Catholic ruler. In 1714 they effectively *appointed* George I, a German Protestant prince from Hanover, as King. Consequently he and his heirs could never credibly claim to rule by divine right. In practice their power, though great, was limited by law. The British called this a mixed or limited monarchy; later generations have usually referred to it as 'constitutional monarchy'. By way of justification for this system, the political philosopher John Locke developed a theory of popular sovereignty. He argued that men joined together to place themselves under a government in order to protect their life, liberty and property. In short, the regime was based on a contract between property owners and the monarchy; it was liberal but not democratic.

THE BALANCED CONSTITUTION

King George III, who had reigned since 1760, fully upheld this system. Under the Bill of Rights (1689) he could not suspend parliament nor could he raise taxes without parliament's approval or maintain a standing army in peacetime. In effect, the King had to summon parliament every year so that essential revenue could be raised legally. In return, parliament granted the royal family an annual payment known as the 'civil list'.

However, none of this made the King a subservient figure. He appointed peers to sit in the House of Lords and could dissolve the House of Commons so as to force a general election on them. Indeed, the Septennial Act of 1716 restricted the life of parliament to seven years without a fresh election; and when a new king ascended the throne an election was always held. Above all, the King enjoyed the right to choose his chief minister, subject only to the qualification that his choice must be capable of commanding a majority in the House of Commons in order to enact the business of government.

Traditionally the Privy Council, a body of advisers to the Crown, had formed an intermediary linking the King and parliament. But with thirty members the Privy Council grew too large and unwieldy for day-to-day policy-making. In practice, therefore, business came to be transacted in a smaller body, known as the cabinet, comprising a lord treasurer, two secretaries of state, a Lord President and a Lord Chancellor. During the eighteenth century the cabinet usually met weekly without the King. The first lord of the Treasury became known as the Prime Minister and he usually sat in the House of Commons, though he could be a member of the House of Lords. In this period most ministers sat in the Lords.

Britain thus enjoyed a tripartite system of government in which power was shared between the King, the Lords and the Commons, representing respectively the monarchical, the aristocratic and the popular elements. British constitutional theorists argued that if any one of the three dominated, as was the case elsewhere in Europe, the system would degenerate: monarchy into tyranny, aristocracy into oligarchy, and democracy into anarchy. In Britain, by contrast, each of the three checked the potential abuse of power by the others. It was a balanced constitution.

In addition, the central government largely abstained from interference in local administration at least until the 1830s. Local affairs were handled at two levels – the parish and the county. The chief county officials were the Lord Lieutenant and the Justices of the Peace, unpaid but prestigious roles. Appointed by the King to maintain law and order, the Lord Lieutenant was invariably a major landowner and peer. The JPs, who were chosen by the Lord Chancellor from among the gentry, enjoyed a wide range of powers as magistrates. At the most local or parish level the overseers looked after the poor, and the vestries set a local tax based on property values. In some areas vestry meetings were open to all local inhabitants, but more typically their work was confined to a handful of property owners and clergymen.

In practice, the central government at Westminster involved far less participation by the people than a formal description of the system suggests. The House of Lords, for example, comprised only about 200 peers in the eighteenth century, and the King might strengthen his own influence there by creating new titles. In the Commons, the 558 MPs were drawn largely from the younger sons of peers or the landed gentry. Until 1911 they were unpaid members, who regarded their work as a duty and as a part-time occupation, not as a profession or career. In order to maintain its influence in parliament the Crown distributed official posts and pensions freely among politicians, and at elections it used government funds in order to ensure the return of a group of loyal supporters. One check on royal and governmental influence was the requirement that any MP who accepted an office of profit under the Crown must resign his seat and seek re-election. But of the 509 who did so between 1715 and 1761 no fewer than 501 were successful.

In any case the popular constituency from which MPs emerged was a narrow one. In the early eighteenth century only 250,000 to 300,000 men (or 5.5 per cent of the population) enjoyed the vote. Moreover, the proportion actually decreased over time so that by 1832 it represented only 2.6 per cent of the population. In the 52 counties of England and Wales, about 180,000 men qualified to vote by possession of freehold land worth £2. But in the borough seats there existed a complicated range of qualifications going back hundreds of years and largely based on residence, payment of rates and ownership of property. Thus, although there were a few comparatively democratic constituencies, like Yorkshire with 10,000 voters, in many boroughs two MPs were returned by a mere handful of voters. In this situation the representation became vulnerable to patronage and bribery; for example, 111 members were, in effect, nominated by 55 peers. In addition, some of the more corrupt borough corporations offered seats in parliament to any candidate willing to pay their debts or finance new buildings for the town. As a result the late eighteenth century saw a number of attempts to purge the system of corruption; critics wanted to shift representation from small boroughs to the larger centres of population, to eliminate the royal placemen, and to repeal the Septennial Act so as to have more frequent elections.

RELIGIOUS DIVISIONS

Throughout this period, politics was closely bound up with religion. Religious affiliation determined who could participate in government and it generated many of the controversies of British politics right up to 1900. The official or 'Established' religion was Anglicanism, or the Church of England. According to estimates made in 1800, the Church's active membership represented 46 per cent of the population, which is probably an over-estimate because many people found it convenient to be nominally Anglican. Roman Catholics numbered 10 per cent and the Dissenters or Nonconformists comprised 43 per cent. The latter included Presbyterians, Congregationalists, Baptists, Quakers and Methodists. Most of these Dissenting sects dated from the seventeenth century, but the Methodists were the product of early eighteenth-century revivalism. Their support lay in the North of England, the Midlands and the Southwest – areas much neglected by the Church of England. They took their strength from evangelicalism – a creed which placed less emphasis on theology and more on the need for a Christian to be active in the practice of his faith; hence evangelicals characteristically organised missionary work, charities, moral crusades and Sunday Schools. Between 1780 and 1810, Methodism tripled its membership, and, in combination with the other Nonconformist churches, began to represent a serious threat to the Established Church, especially in urban and middle-class England and Wales.

However, Anglicanism enjoyed the advantages of huge accumulated wealth, the support of almost all the political elite, and a good deal of discriminatory legislation. As a result of the struggle with the Stuart Kings, parliament had passed the Act of Settlement in 1701, which decreed that the King must be an Anglican; and in order to block the Catholic claimants to the throne the King was not permitted to marry a Catholic. Of more practical importance were the Corporation Acts of 1661, which affected Dissenters, and the Test Act of 1673, which affected Catholics. In effect, this legislation excluded Dissenters and Catholics from all national and local offices unless they were prepared to take communion in the Anglican Church. These acts were not repealed until 1828. In addition, Dissenters suffered all kinds of legal disabilities including an obligation to pay a tax, known as a tithe, for the benefit of the Anglican Church, restrictions on their meeting places (which were lifted in 1812), and compulsory burial according to Anglican rites.

It was to take a long time – in effect the entire nineteenth century – before the Nonconformist Churches resolved their grievances by gaining the political influence to which they felt their numbers and wealth entitled them. Meanwhile their growing membership represented a challenge to Anglicanism. Many evangelicals within the Church of England, such as William Wilberforce, felt anxious to arrest the apparent moral laxity especially amongst the higher clergymen. Many clerics did not reside in their parishes and bishoprics. In the north and in the towns clergymen were often so poorly paid that they gathered several parishes together in order to attain a satisfactory living, but neglected their flock in the process. As Wilberforce pointed out, this laxity was a threat not just to the Church but to the State because it called into question the privileged status of the Anglican Church.

SCOTLAND, WALES AND IRELAND

Although England contained over half the population of the British Isles and returned no fewer than 489 of the 558 MPs, she was only one of four territories ruled by George III. Wales, with 24 MPs, had been assimilated to government from London for 600 years; and although over half the Welsh people spoke their own language, they did not aspire to separate political status. Welsh people moved freely across the border taking advantage of the economic opportunities offered by England.

Scotland was more complicated. Historically it had maintained a separate throne until the beginning of the seventeenth century when the Stuart King James VI became King James I of England. As a result of the civil wars and the revolution settlement, the English had effectively repudiated the Scottish King in favour of the Hanoverians. Inevitably, therefore, Scotland formed a base of support for attempts to recover the throne for the Stuarts. The most recent and dramatic of these occurred in 1745 when Prince Charles Edward Stuart landed in the west of Scotland and marched his army hundreds of miles south into England before suffering a crushing defeat at the Battle of Culloden in 1746.

However, the key point about the rebellion is that few urban and lowland Scots had supported it. By and large they now accepted the 1707 Act of Union between England and Scotland. This left the Scots represented at Westminster by 45 MPs though with only 4500 voters. Essentially it was the economic attraction of access to the English market, employment south of the border and opportunities in the British Empire that kept Scotsmen largely content with the Union. Even the martial instincts of the Scottish Highlanders had been turned to advantage by recruiting them into the Highland regiments of the British army.

If Scotland represented a problem largely solved, the same could scarcely be said of Ireland. She suffered from two fundamental problems – economic and religious – complicated by the system of government. Although the majority of Irishmen were Catholics they were obliged to contribute tithes to help maintain the Anglican Church as the Established Church in their country. About 80 per cent of the land was owned by an Anglo-Irish gentry and aristocracy, some of whom were absentees. Beneath them there existed a large and growing population of tenant farmers and labourers scratching a precarious living on small plots, often by growing potatoes. Their natural resentment when evicted for non-payment of rent was exacerbated by the feeling that the owners represented an alien church and an English government. As a result, violence was always present in the Irish countryside, offering the raw material for a mass nationalist movement.

Ireland's government was controlled from London through a Lord Lieutenant and a Chief Secretary, both of whom were Protestants. But in 1782, legislative powers had been devolved to an Irish parliament in Dublin. However, this compromise failed to make government more acceptable to the people. In fact it provoked opposition. Since only Protestants were allowed to vote, the Irish parliament scarcely commanded popular support. Henry Grattan, its leader, represented the moderate Protestant gentry, but supported the enfranchisement of Catholics. His position became less secure during the 1770s when Ireland suffered from the loss of markets as a result of the war with the colonists of North America.

She also felt some sympathy for the rebellion against British rule, and was even more encouraged in 1789 when revolution broke out in France. This situation was to lead to the abolition of the Dublin parliament at the turn of the century.

BRITAIN'S EXTERNAL INTERESTS

Eighteenth-century governments devoted very little time to legislation or to domestic affairs generally. Their energies were concentrated much more on international diplomacy, the colonies and foreign trade. Indeed, it is hardly an exaggeration to say that the promotion of overseas trade became Britain's chief interest. All four of the wars she fought between 1739 and 1783 were primarily undertaken for commercial ends. In the process, Britain had acquired a substantial empire, notably in India, Canada, the West Indies and at Cape Colony in South Africa. In 1788 the Australian territory of New South Wales was officially added to this list and a whole new continent began to fall under British control.

Yet expansionism was not without its drawbacks, not least because the home government rarely enjoyed effective control over the settlers and merchants who roamed the world claiming territory in Britain's name. For example, the Indian Empire was run by the directors and shareholders of the East India Company, whose agents in Bengal exploited their territory without regard to British interests. The result, by the late eighteenth century, was a series of costly campaigns and mounting debts. Thus, from 1784 onwards the London government imposed certain controls over the Company which paved the way for its eventual demise. A minister known as the President of the Board of Control became ultimately answerable to parliament for Indian affairs, and every twenty years the charter of the East India Company was to be renewed, and effectively rewritten, by parliament. By the turn of the century the anomalous situation created by a large empire ruled by a company had been widely recognised, though it was not until 1858 that the state finally took over.

A far more dramatic complication had occurred in the North American colonies, where London's attempts to impose taxation on British settlers provoked a full-scale war for independence in the late 1770s. This war left Britain militarily humiliated and diplomatically isolated, for the French and Spanish had taken the opportunity to aid the rebels. However, the loss of the American colonies did not impair Britain's trade. The United States continued to rely on the West Indies for many of its imports and by 1800 she bought over a quarter of all Britain's exports.

As long as such lucrative trade could be safeguarded Britain's interest in the affairs of mainland Europe remained limited. She had a standing interest in keeping the Low Countries out of the control of a major military power because of the vulnerability of the British Isles to invasion. She also feared Russian expansion through the Black Sea into the eastern Mediterranean, which would have threatened trade routes to India and the Far East. Britain's traditional strategy for dealing with a threat involved forming alliances with the lesser continental powers against the strongest. In the past, France had most frequently appeared to be the dominant power in Europe. But the commercial treaty signed between the two countries in 1786 seemed to indicate friendly relations. It opened the French market to British manufactures at reduced rates and conferred similar concessions upon French wines in Britain. As long as such conditions prevailed, the British saw little need to be involved in Europe; military interventionism was an expedient to be adopted only in case of real emergency.

THE WHIGS AND KING GEORGE III

Although eighteenth-century politicians wore the labels 'Whig' and 'Tory' the differences between them were by no means clear. Early in the century, party allegiance had been strong in the sense that the Whigs stood as the champions of the Hanoverian succession and, as a result, generally held office, whereas the Tories posed as a 'country' party and criticised the court and central government. To some extent, social characteristics also divided the two, for the Tories were strong among the country gentlemen, while the Whigs combined some very large titled landowners with business and professional support. However, these distinctions were far from absolute; most politicians enjoyed connections with the land in this period, and party loyalty was often a matter of family tradition rather than political principle. Moreover, as the century wore on

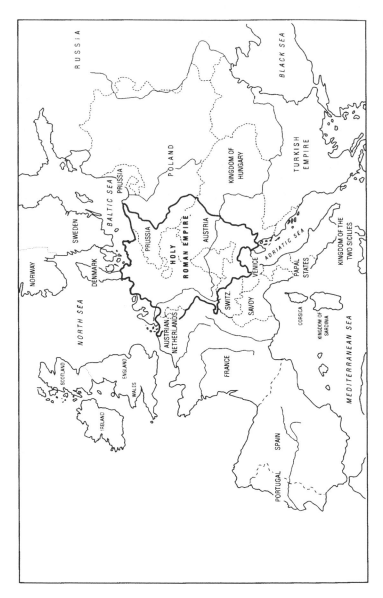

Map 1 Britain and the European Powers in the Late Eighteenth Century

the party lines became less, not more, clear. This is evident from the reduction in the number of contested elections. As political controversies subsided, the elites increasingly merged into a single ruling class, divided largely by personal struggles for office and influence.

The reign of George III from 1760 to 1820 saw a resurgence of political controversy. In this period some of the Whigs accused the King of going beyond his proper constitutional role; they claimed that the disastrous war with the American colonists from 1775 to 1782 was the result of his 'personal rule'. In 1780 this argument led parliament to adopt the famous resolution proposed by John Dunning to the effect that 'the influence of the crown has increased, is increasing and ought to be diminished'.

However, much of the contemporary attack on George III merely reflected frustration amongst disappointed Whigs. To some extent the King did take a more active part in government than his two predecessors, but his choice of chief minister was perfectly constitutional, if sometimes unwise. The King's real difficulty lay in the confused and fragmented condition of the parties. The greater the difficulties of the chief ministers in maintaining their parliamentary majority the more the King felt obliged to intervene. Not until the general election of 1784 did a really capable minister emerge, in the person of William Pitt the Younger. Since Pitt was barely 24 years old at the time, contemporaries scarcely expected his government to last. One wit called it:

> A sight to make surrounding nations stare,
> A kingdom trusted to a schoolboy's care.

Certainly Pitt's administration was never as strong as it appeared. Nominally the election gave him 253 supporters against 123 confirmed Opposition members. But this did not allow Pitt control over legislation. In 1785, for example, his parliamentary reform bill suffered a defeat in the Commons. Significantly, Pitt reacted to this in the manner typical of an eighteenth-century prime minister: he simply carried on governing as though nothing had happened. Since he had no really cohesive party behind him, he was obliged to govern by perpetually patching up a parliamentary majority from week to week. Thus Pitt dominated politics up to 1806 largely by his own skill and because the King appreciated that he represented the best alternative to the detested Whigs. He was essentially the last of the eighteenth-century prime ministers, not a forerunner of Victorian political leaders. Although Pitt acted as the focus for the emerging Tory Party after 1793, this was largely the result of the reaction against the revolution in France rather than because he aspired to build a coherent political party.

3

The Impact of the French Revolution, 1789–1815

During the 1780s British society and the political system began to undergo a process of fundamental change initiated by two forces: the industrial revolution on the one hand and the political ideas of the Enlightenment on the other. By the mid-nineteenth century this had turned Britain into a predominantly urban society and a major world power; and by the early twentieth century it had transformed the old aristocratic system into a democracy.

Yet none of this was apparent in the 1780s. As the political situation in France deteriorated, the British continued to be largely absorbed in their domestic concerns, unaware that they stood on the edge of traumatic events. Politics was very much dominated by the repercussions of Britain's defeat in the war with the colonists in North America. This war had cost £100 million and left the government with annual debt charges of £9 million; as a result, in 1783 expenditure exceeded revenue by over £10 million. Thus when William Pitt took office in 1784 he became primarily concerned with improving the efficiency of government and strengthening its finances. As it turned out, his work proved an essential contribution to sustaining the European war in which Britain was soon to be engulfed. Aware that much revenue was lost through smuggling, he made the illegal trade less attractive by reducing the duties levied on goods; this boosted the government's income from legitimate trade. He also found new sources of revenue, such as a tax on windows, and began the process of eliminating official posts which involved no real function. Finally, he reduced the burden of debt charges by means of a 'Sinking Fund', which involved using any surplus revenue to pay off the original debt. Pitt's innovations created an annual surplus of income over expenditure for the government which, among other things, enabled him to pay for an additional 33 battleships for the Royal Navy, a most timely step, as it turned out.

REVOLUTIONARY WAR AND THE BLOCKADE

When revolution broke out in France in 1789 the British politicians believed that it was unlikely to have significant implications for them. Indeed, in so far as the revolution kept the French absorbed in domestic affairs it seemed to be advantageous for Britain. It is striking that as late as 1793 Pitt was actually reducing the expenditure on the army.

Why, then, did Britain enter the war with France in 1793? No doubt the revolutionaries' offer of fraternal assistance to other peoples anxious to throw off their own monarchies was provocative. However, to see the war chiefly in ideological terms would be simplistic. The conflict soon became a traditional struggle over territory, trade and colonies, between a sea power and a continental power, rather than a fight between monarchism and republicanism. The immediate reason for British participation lay in the defeat of Austria, which put Belgian and Dutch territory under French influence, thereby exposing Britain to possible attack.

Pitt has suffered much criticism for his record as a war minister. Yet he had little option but to build up an anti-French coalition by offering subsidies to other powers. He could not risk putting too many British troops onto the Continent because the army was badly led, undermanned and, as yet, inferior to the French forces. His chief contribution lay in mobilising Britain's resources to sustain a prolonged war effort. Thus he imposed heavy taxes on luxuries such as servants and carriages. In 1799 he introduced the income tax, which generated one-fifth of all government revenue by the end of the war.

These expedients enabled Pitt to spend a total of £66 million on subsidies to foreign powers during the wars, mostly during the last years of the conflict. Initially Prussia and Hanover seemed the most promising allies since they shared Britain's interest in curbing the French influence in the Low Countries. But the coalition rapidly collapsed and by 1795 even Austria was prepared to abandon her Belgian territory. By 1797 she felt obliged to seek peace following her shattering defeats in Italy. As a result, the French enjoyed military supremacy over a huge area of Europe.

The second and more successful aspect of Pitt's strategy was naval and colonial. In this sphere the British confidently expected gains to offset their setbacks on the land. A series of victories followed in which Britain defeated the navies of France, Spain, the Dutch and the Danes. As a result she was able to seize valuable territories in the West Indies, Ceylon and the Cape of Good Hope. However, this simply produced deadlock, with the French victorious on land and the British in command of the seas. Thus, after Pitt resigned from office in 1801 his successor, Addington, made peace at Amiens in 1802. This was unpopular because most of the colonial gains were surrendered. However, Addington understood that the country had grown dangerously weary of war and required a brief relaxation of tension. He regarded the peace as merely a ceasefire and surprised the French by resuming war in May 1803.

When Pitt returned to office from 1804 to 1806, for the last time, he adopted exactly the same strategy as before. By 1806 the West Indies and the Cape of Good Hope had been recaptured. Another coalition, comprising Britain, Austria and Prussia, was assembled only to be destroyed by Napoleon at the Battle of Austerlitz in 1805. 'Roll up that map of Europe,' Pitt exclaimed, 'it will not be needed these ten years.' Napoleon's domination on the Continent encouraged him to prepare an invasion of the British Isles, to which end some 80,000 troops were gathered at Boulogne to be transported across the Channel if the British fleet could be diverted from the southern coast. However, Admiral Nelson blockaded French ports and comprehensively defeated the French fleet at Trafalgar in October 1805.

As a result Napoleon abandoned the invasion in favour of a blockade – known as the Continental System – which was designed to strangle the British economy by closing all French-controlled ports to her trade. In fact this policy could never be effectively implemented, for Britain imposed a counter-blockade which proved to be far more damaging to France, whose customs revenues fell by 80 per cent. Napoleon never succeeded in sealing off Europe from British trade; for even at the worst, Portugal and the Baltic remained open to British exports. In addition, her trade with South America and the West Indies flourished, and by 1810 Russia had decided to re-open her trade with the British.

However, if the navy prevented a British defeat, only a painstaking and costly reconstruction of the army could ensure eventual victory. By 1815 the army had grown to an unprecedented size – some 260,000 men. The extra troops were used effectively against Napoleon's rule in Spain and Portugal after 1808, where they were sent in order to support a nationalist revolt against the French. Britain also granted subsidies to keep the Spanish and Portuguese forces in the field, and used the navy to maintain supplies. The final factor was the military skill of Arthur Wellesley, later the Duke of Wellington, who, despite unfavourable odds, led his men to victory over the best French generals. The Peninsular War drained French troops and thereby hampered Napoleon's control over Central and Eastern Europe. After 1813, when Wellesley entered France itself, a new coalition was assembled with Russia and Prussia. It was kept in being from 1813 to 1815 partly by means of subsidies and partly by the diplomatic skill of the Foreign Secretary, Lord Castlereagh, until Napoleon had finally been defeated. There was always some danger that one of the allies would withdraw and make a separate peace, but the Battle of Waterloo in June 1815 resulted in the permanent exile of the French Emperor to St Helena. Peace had returned after twenty-two years.

RADICALISM AND REPRESSION

During the 1770s and 1780s a very respectable movement for parliamentary reform had emerged in Britain under the leadership of middle-class radicals such as John Cartwright and Christopher Wyvill; their demands included manhood suffrage, annual parliaments, lower taxation and less government patronage. But the outbreak of revolution in 1789 gave a tremendous stimulus to this modest movement. Large numbers of skilled workers now began to be mobilised on a scale not seen since the seventeenth century. Support for reform permeated all levels of society. Thomas Hardy, a shoemaker, established the London Corresponding Society for manual workers; middle-class Nonconformists founded the Society for Constitutional Information, which sought the repeal of the Test and Corporation Acts; and some of the upper-class Whig politicians launched the Society of the Friends of the People.

There followed a prolific phase of propaganda in the form of pamphlets, letters and newspapers by the parliamentary reformers. By far the most influential publication was *The Rights of Man* by Tom Paine, which appeared in two stages in 1791 and 1792. In this, Paine defended the French Revolution against critics such as Edmund Burke; he advocated universal male suffrage, the abolition of hereditary wealth and power, reductions in expenditure on military defence, and a redistribution of state spending to finance free education, old age pensions and family allowances. In the short term, Paine popularised the abstract cause of reform for a working-class audience, as is indicated by the sale of 200,000 copies of his book. In the longer run, *The Rights of Man* helped to set the agenda for radicals throughout the nineteenth and much of the twentieth century.

It was not long, however, before a reaction developed. This manifested itself in the form of 'Church and King' parties in the country. Self-styled patriots took to breaking up the meetings of radicals and Nonconformists, rioting and setting fire to their houses. In 1792 the government intervened with the King's Proclamation Against Seditious Writings. By this time the aristocracy had become alarmed, partly by the external threat posed by the revolution and partly by the sale of Paine's book amongst workingmen. Yet the authorities reacted as though they faced an organised revolutionary movement rather than a demand for constitutional reform. Nothing really subversive existed. Even the London Corresponding Society recruited a membership of only 5000 at its peak in 1795. However, the government took alarm at the large number of sympathisers who attended public meetings organised by the small radical societies; this was especially the case during 1793–5 when food shortages, inflation and unemployment brought men out onto the streets in unusual numbers.

As a result, from 1793 onwards the government began to prosecute reformers either for circulating radical literature or for holding 'National Conventions' on the French model. Pitt himself now abandoned his reforming views for the fashionable reactionary stance; he condemned *The Rights of Man* as 'that monstrous doctrine'. Government repression soon had the effect of deterring the middle-class radicals from expressing their views publicly; and even workingmen such Hardy abandoned propaganda, while Paine fled the country. However, the authorities derived little comfort from this because general discontent was greatly stimulated by economic distress throughout the country. Harvest failures in 1795, 1797–8 and 1801–2 drove the price of wheat up to 70 per cent above its 1789 level. As a result, any radical who risked holding a meeting to demand parliamentary reform attracted mass support. The government responded to this with more severe measures, including an Act to prohibit meetings of over fifty people and a Treasonable Practices Act designed to facilitate the prosecution of anyone who spoke or wrote in criticism of the constitution. As the Whig politician Charles James Fox observed, this placed even the most mild and respectable advocates of parliamentary reform at risk of being punished by transportation to Australia. By 1797 the meetings of the London Corresponding Society were being dispersed by troops and the remaining leaders had been arrested and imprisoned.

There is little doubt that Pitt's repression of the reform movement was a serious over-reaction. Moreover, it proved to be counter-productive in the sense that it forced the radicals underground. As a result, some of them made contact with Irish agitators who really did hope for a French invasion to topple the aristocratic government of Britain. The best that can be said to explain Pitt's response is that the politicians gave way to panic at a time when the forces of law and order seemed inadequate, mutinies were breaking out in the navy, and the fear of an invasion had gripped their imagination.

THE UNION WITH IRELAND

Inevitably the French Revolution inspired many Irishmen to seek redress of their grievances from the London government. In 1791 Wolfe Tone founded the Belfast Society of United Irishmen, which demanded reform of the Dublin parliament and the abolition of discrimination against Catholics. But as the United Irishmen spread across the country the movement became increasingly republican and nationalist in character, and in the process it adopted intimidation and even terrorism in the rural areas. As a result, in 1795 the Protestants formed a counter movement, the Orange Society, which was ostensibly a celebration of the victories of the Dutch Protestant King, William of Orange, in the 1690s.

These developments put the London government in a dilemma. As expressed by the Duke of Rutland, the English view was: 'Ireland is too great to be unconnected with us, and too near us to be dependent on a foreign state, and too little to be independent.' In the event, Pitt attempted a mixture of conciliation and coercion. For example, in 1792 and 1793 he introduced Catholic Relief Acts designed both to free Catholics from restrictions on marriage, education and the professions, and to admit them to the local and parliamentary franchise on the same terms as Protestants. Yet he also found himself driven towards repression of the United Irishmen by the fear that a French invasion might coincide with a republican rebellion. Indeed, a force of 14,000 French troops was sent to Ireland in 1796; but the Irish revolt did not break out until 1798 and, in the absence of effective outside assistance, it was easily suppressed.

However, these events convinced Pitt that the time had come to terminate the experiment with an Irish parliament. By representing wealthy, Protestant landowners it had merely symbolised the divisions within the country. Thus he entrusted Lord Cornwallis (Lord Lieutenant) and Viscount Castlereagh (Chief Secretary for Ireland) with the task of persuading the Dublin parliament to vote itself out of existence. Naturally the Protestants felt afraid of abandoning the status quo, but Cornwallis argued that the economy of Ulster (the north-eastern province in which Protestants were concentrated) would prosper from closer connections with England as the Scots had done. Eventually the Act of Union was passed in 1800. Under its terms, Ireland would continue to be governed through the Chief Secretary and the Lord Lieutenant. But it would also send 100 MPs to Westminster and 32 peers to the House of Lords. The Irish were to contribute 12 per cent of the United Kingdom's annual budget and Ireland's manufacturers were to enjoy special protection for twenty years.

Although these were generous terms, the Union left the underlying Irish grievances untouched. Pitt himself wished to consolidate the Union by granting Catholics a parliamentary vote, but this was opposed by several cabinet ministers and was killed off by the King himself in 1801. As a result Pitt resigned. Subsequently the Protestant community in Ulster did prosper and thus looked increasingly to the Union with England as a guarantee of their privileged position. But between 1801 and 1841 the sharp rise in the rural population led to evictions of agricultural tenants, anti-landlordism and the spread of secret societies ready to use violence. Here lay the seed-bed of modern Irish nationalism. In retrospect the Act of Union was an historic mistake, for it merely generated controversy for British governments throughout the next two centuries.

THE EMERGENCE OF A TORY PARTY

The ideological issues raised by the French Revolution served as a catalyst to British domestic politics by forcing a drastic realignment amongst the politicians. The first indication of this came with the disintegration of the Whigs, who had hitherto dominated politics. Their leader, Fox, initially welcomed the revolution on the assumption that the French were creating a constitutional monarchy as Britain had done in the seventeenth century. However, this analysis suffered from the attacks of another Whig, Edmund Burke, in a famous book, *Reflections on the Revolution in France* (1790). In this, Burke condemned the revolutionaries as levellers who would pervert the natural order of things and soon descend into bloodshed.

By 1791 events in France seemed to many politicians to vindicate Burke's warnings. Soon the more conservative figures began to discern revolutionary potential behind even the most mild proposal for reform of the British parliament. In this way the Whigs began to pull in opposite directions, leaving Fox as leader of a mere minority. The Whigs were condemned to languish in opposition for a generation. Fox himself was no great radical, and his followers were distinctly aristocratic, but they did believe in checking arbitrary and royal power by means of an elected parliament. The more progressive or liberal Whigs were given a lead by Charles Grey, who introduced a motion for parliamentary reform in 1793. In the circumstances he inevitably suffered a crushing defeat by 282 votes to 41; and when he tried again in 1797 he lost by 256 to 91. However, these votes signified the gradual development of a more coherent party based on the defence of individual liberties and representative government. In this lay the origins of the nineteenth-century Liberal Party.

In the short term, however, Pitt gained most advantage from the Whig splits. From 1793 onwards the more conservative Whigs began to join his government, a trend accelerated by the declaration of war on France. Thus a new coalition government emerged in which six of the thirteen cabinet posts were given to Whigs, notably the Duke of Portland, Earl Fitzwilliam and Lord Spencer. However, this failed to produce stable government; the period between 1801 and 1812 saw five weak ministries. The causes of this instability lay in personal rivalries, in Pitt's aloofness and his death in 1806, and in the strains created by the war effort.

None the less, at the election of 1807 most of the candidates who supported the King's government chose to describe themselves by the term 'Tory'. This indicated the emergence of a more coherent party on the right. In effect, the supporters of Pitt and the conservative Whigs had joined with the existing Tories to defend property and aristocracy out of a fear of real threats from abroad and imaginary threats at home. In addition Tories defended the Established Church against attacks by Nonconformists and Catholics; 'No Popery' was to be a characteristic Tory cry at elections for decades to come. The aura of patriotism bestowed by the war with France completed the foundation of what was to become the nineteenth-century Tory Party. Indeed, in this period a whole generation of Tory politicians – Liverpool, Castlereagh, Canning and Peel – emerged who were to dominate government until the 1840s. In the short term, the new alignment took the form of Lord Liverpool's government, which held office from 1812 until 1827. This proved to be the first stable Tory ministry of the new century; its position was underpinned by success in war and repression of the reform movement in the country.

4

The Industrial Revolution and the British People

The term 'Industrial Revolution' was first used in 1884 by Arnold Toynbee to describe the changes in British society in the period between 1760 and 1832. He regarded the process as a sudden and fundamental change in which the medieval restrictions on production and enterprise were swept away. Although there has been much disagreement as to whether the industrial revolution was as dramatic as Toynbee believed, there is little doubt about the essential features implied by the use of this phrase. It involved radical innovation in certain industries, which led to significant increases in output and to the economies of mass production. In round terms the annual increase in industrial production rose from 1 per cent in 1760 to 3 to 4 per cent by 1850. In the process, industry overtook agriculture as the chief source of income and employment; by 1851 for example, it employed 3.25 million people, and agriculture only 2 million.

COTTON AND IRON

Many favourable preconditions for economic growth have been identified in British society by the mid-eighteenth century: political stability, Protestantism, an expanding population, agricultural innovation, commercial expansion, scientific inventions and capital accumulation. While the significance of several of these is doubtful, it is clear that in so far as there was a distinct take-off into rapid growth, it was associated with one or two sectors of the economy.

Initially the cotton textile industry seems to have led the way. Cotton was the first to respond to the stimulus of a mass market, to apply new technology on an extensive scale, to increase its output significantly, and to develop a factory system of production in place of the traditional domestic system.

Cotton advanced by means of a series of innovations affecting first spinning and then weaving. This began in 1765 with Hargreaves' famous 'spinning jenny', which enabled each spinner to operate eight spindles. Since the machine was cheap to instal, some 20,000 had come into operation by 1788. Arkwright's water frame followed closely on the heels of the spinning jenny in 1769. Its advantage was that it could be harnessed to non-human sources of power – horses, water and steam – and when its patent lapsed in 1785 it spread rapidly. The process was completed by Crompton's 'mule' (1779), which managed to combine the fine quality product of the spinning jenny with the strength of the thread from a water frame. Together these three innovations raised efficiency by about three times. This put pressure on the weaving side of production, which was met by Cartwright's loom of 1785. Operated by steam power, this loom spread slowly at first because it was expensive to instal. But it enabled one man and a boy to operate four looms. As a result the number of looms rose from 2400 in 1813 to 250,000 by 1830.

It is some indication of the importance of cotton textiles that as early as 1815 the industry was generating 40 per cent of the value of all British exports, a position that was retained until the twentieth century. By 1800, cotton had achieved annual growth rates of 6 or 7 per cent, and already seven mills were employing over one thousand workers each. The key to success was threefold: a reduction in the unit cost of production due to innovation, a fall in the price of raw cotton, and the availability of a large market. As a result, the owners generated high profits, which enabled them to invest in new machinery, larger buildings and power supplies.

Important as it was, however, cotton's effects on the rest of the economy were limited. Improved efficiency in the iron industry, by contrast, offered benefits to many other sectors because it could reduce the costs of their equipment as well as their products. Traditionally Britain had struggled to satisfy her own requirements and had imported high-quality iron from Sweden. By comparison with cotton it was difficult to expand output because of the heavy costs and the complications involved in smelting and refining the ore.

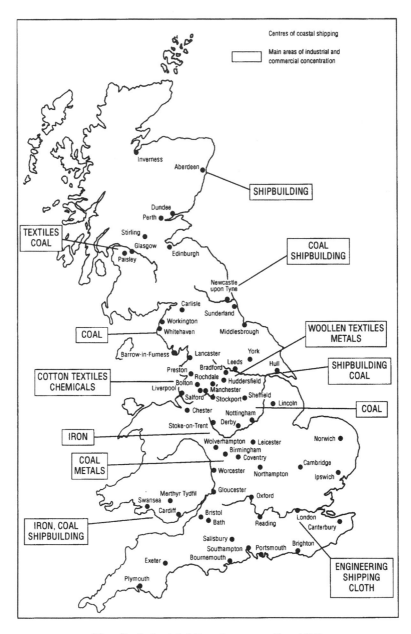

Centres of coastal shipping

Main areas of industrial and
commercial concentration

SHIPBUILDING

TEXTILES
COAL

COAL
SHIPBUILDING

Inverness

Aberdeen

Dundee
Perth

Stirling
Glasgow
Paisley

Edinburgh

Newcastle
upon Tyne

Carlisle
Sunderland

Workington
Whitehaven

COAL

Middlesbrough

WOOLLEN TEXTILES
METALS

Barrow-in-Furness

Lancaster

York

SHIPBUILDING
COAL

Preston
Bradford
Rochdale
Bolton
Liverpool
Salford
Stockport

Leeds
Huddersfield
Manchester
Sheffield

Hull

COTTON TEXTILES
CHEMICALS

Chester

Nottingham

Lincoln

COAL

Stoke-on-Trent

Derby

IRON

Wolverhampton
Birmingham
Coventry

Leicester

Norwich

COAL
METALS

Worcester

Northampton

Cambridge

Ipswich

Merthyr Tydfil
Swansea
Cardiff

Gloucester

Bristol
Bath

Oxford

Reading

London

Canterbury

IRON, COAL
SHIPBUILDING

Salisbury
Southampton
Bournemouth

Portsmouth

Brighton

Exeter

ENGINEERING
SHIPPING
CLOTH

Plymouth

Map 2   Industrial Development, Pre-1850

During the eighteenth century the ironmasters struggled to use water power and only gradually exploited local coal supplies in the smelting process. However, the demand for armaments created by the Seven Years War (1756–63) raised prices and thus gave them a strong incentive to become more efficient. A series of improvements during the 1770s and 1780s enabled them to use coke to remove the impurities in iron ore and thus to achieve a higher-quality product. By the 1780s it had become possible to combine English coal and local iron ore to establish integrated iron and steel works on the coalfields of the Midlands, the North, Wales and Scotland. Again, the period of prolonged warfare after 1793 stimulated innovation and expansion.

Innovations continued through much of the nineteenth century. Thus, whereas it had taken seven tons of coal to produce one ton of iron around 1800, by the 1850s only one and a half tons of coal were required. As a result, British prices undercut those of Sweden, previously the most efficient manufacturer of high-quality iron, and she exported 1000 tons every year by the 1850s. Cheap iron supplies led to the wider installation of new machinery in industry, iron bridges, iron ships, and iron pipes for sewage systems. But above all, iron and steel made possible a railway system – the third leading sector of the industrial revolution – from the 1830s onwards.

TRANSPORT AND COMMUNICATIONS

Although investment in new roads took place throughout the eighteenth century the pattern of improvement was very haphazard. In any case even the best roads were an expensive means for transporting heavy and bulky raw materials; poor communications therefore kept manufacturers' costs high and limited the size of the market. For this reason Britain had traditionally made extensive use of the sea and the main rivers for transporting commodities such as coal. From the 1750s onwards the advantages of water were maximised by the construction of canals linking the chief ports and industrial centres. By the 1790s, when £6 million was spent, canal investment had become very fashionable. In some cases the enthusiasm was justified. For example, the Trent–Mersey Canal, which linked the Midlands with the north-west of England, yielded a 75 per cent return on investment. However, the average was around 6 per cent by the 1820s and many of the later canals were never profitable. Canals offered an economical method for moving bulky items because they used little labour and fuel; whereas a wagon might carry eight tons weight, a barge could take fifty tons. This cut transport costs by three-quarters and helped to remove certain bottlenecks in production, notably the use of coal. It became possible to locate industries in more convenient places and to integrate the factors of production.

However, canals suffered from severe limitations. They were slow, they could only reach a limited part of the country, and they had little impact on passenger transport. By the 1840s they had been completely overtaken by the railways. The railway-building phase was inaugurated in 1825 with the construction of the Stockton to Darlington Railway, which carried passengers and freight and was operated by steam. There followed the Liverpool to Manchester line in 1830, Birmingham to Lancashire in 1837, London to Birmingham in 1838, and the Great Western Railway from London to Bristol in 1841. The network spread slowly because of the cost, geographical obstacles and political objections. By 1838 only 500 miles of track had been laid. But after the spectacular boom during 1845–7 Britain had 4600 miles of railway lines. By the middle of the century the basic system of trunk lines had been established, though branch lines continued to be built for several more decades. By 1886, 16,400 miles of railways were in operation.

The railways had four major effects on the British economy. First, they created fresh sources of employment; about 250,000 men built the lines in the 1840s, and by 1880, 174,000 were employed to operate the system. Secondly, they hugely expanded the movement of passengers – 600 million rail journeys were made every year by the 1880s. This made the labour force more mobile and stimulated the development of suburbs and seaside resorts. Thirdly, they not only reduced the costs of heavy goods, but also expanded the market for perishable goods, which could be conveyed quickly to consumers. Fourthly, the railway expansion stimulated the demand for the products of other industries, notably iron and coal, and thereby maintained the level of demand during periods of slump.

The significance of railways for capital formation is more problematical. By 1847, 12 per cent of all national income went into railway capital; in fact it became a favourite form of investment for the middle classes. By the 1840s railways were attracting more capital than any other industry in Britain. However, much of this investment was devoted to buying off opponents of railway building and to buying out the canals, one-third of which were taken over between 1845 and 1847 alone. Above all, capital was wasted on duplicating services, for far too many companies set up in competition on the same routes. Many failed because no one had yet fully grasped that transport was naturally a monopoly service that could be most efficiently provided by a single operator.

WORKING-CLASS STANDARDS OF LIVING

The impact of industrialisation on the living standards of working people has long been a highly controversial subject. The traditional view, based on subjective contemporary accounts of hardship and agitations, was very pessimistic. However, during the twentieth century economic historians introduced statistical evidence to demonstrate improvements in living standards. In recent decades, Marxist historians have countered by showing the unreliability of the statistical evidence, and the debate has fragmented as scholars have produced contradictory local studies. In spite of this, there is wide agreement about the broad chronological pattern of change from the later eighteenth century to the mid-nineteenth.

There are, in fact, four major problems in assessing living standards in this period. The first is that generalisation is made difficult by regional variations and especially by the fact that some workers, notably skilled ones, prospered, while others suffered at the same time. Secondly, there is no consistent pattern over time, rather, several fluctuations in living standards; consequently both optimists and pessimists have sometimes been selective in their use of dates for analysis so as to strengthen their case. Thirdly, much of the evidence is either unavailable or unreliable. Among other things, we need to know about national income and consumption per head of population, death rates, and movements in real wages, that is, money wages in relation to prices. The calculation of real wages has proved to be particularly complicated. Finally, even if the statistical evidence were to be satisfactory it is not clear that it would be adequate. Some historians, especially the pessimists, place the emphasis on the intangible aspects of industrialisation and urbanisation such as the destruction of the rural lifestyle in favour of a working life dominated by the clock. However, optimists rightly point out that for ordinary people life in pre-industrial communities was far from idyllic. Features often associated with industrial towns such as overcrowding, ill-health, child labour and long working hours were just as prevalent in earlier periods.

Amongst the main criteria, the sustained rise in population appears to give the best indication of rising living standards. However, on inspection it becomes clear that the pattern was more erratic in that death rates fell from the 1760s to the 1790s, then remained largely unchanged to 1820, when they rose for about twenty years before falling again in the 1840s. This suggests that after several decades of uncontrolled urban growth, living conditions deteriorated. We know that urban land prices increased by 50 per cent between 1780 and 1810, which resulted in more densely packed housing; as costs were rising faster than rents, builders tried to maintain their profit margins by finding cheaper materials or by building to lower standards. The building industry came under great pressure both because of the rise in population and because of a fall in the age of marriage. As it was customary in Britain for newly married couples to leave their parents and establish a separate household, there was a growing demand for houses. Although the building industry did not benefit from improved technology it managed to increase the supply of housing sufficiently to avoid putting a check on the formation of new households. However, the deterioration in housing standards and the lack of water supplies and drainage resulted in the spread of diseases such as typhoid and cholera in closely packed towns.

On the other hand, national income increased faster than population; between 1801 and 1851 it rose from £232 million to £523 million while population doubled. But the distribution of income complicates the picture. Some was absorbed by investment rather than consumption. Taxation, which rose sharply between 1793 and 1815, was regressive in that it fell heavily on consumer goods and thus on the incomes of the poor. Also, the interest paid on government loans went largely to the middle classes. Thus, up to the 1850s the benefits of industrialisation seem to have accrued disproportionately to the middle classes.

This does not mean that the working classes did not gain. The long-term fall in prices clearly made their wages go further. Some evidence for this may be found in the increasing membership of friendly societies, which offered insurance in return for small weekly contributions, and the growth of small deposits in Savings Banks, which doubled between 1829 and 1850. This indicates that at least some working-class families enjoyed an income surplus to their immediate requirements.

Contemporaries certainly believed that the workers were consuming more food from the 1770s onwards, and sales of tea, sugar and tobacco seem to bear this out. However, there were food shortages during the war, and after 1800 agriculture could no longer increase wheat production to keep pace with population. To some extent this was compensated for by a marked rise in potato consumption by workers especially in the north of England.

This brings us to the central question of real wages. For several groups of workers money wages rose from the 1760s to the 1790s, especially where industrial growth attracted men away from traditional occupations. Other groups such as handloom weavers, who were undermined by technological innovation, suffered shrinking incomes. Their case is a reminder that over time the industrial revolution helped manual workers by creating new skilled employment in iron and steel, shipbuilding and the railways. By moving from low-paid to higher or more regularly paid jobs the men often raised their real wages even though money rates remained unchanged. It is estimated that skilled wages rose about 50 per cent between 1790 and 1850. We have better information for skilled workers, which, unfortunately, introduces a bias into the discussion in favour of the optimistic view.

From a chronological perspective it seems that on the whole living standards improved in the later eighteenth century up to the early 1790s. Then during the period down to 1815, dominated by war, many of the gains were lost through rising prices. The years between 1815 and 1840 remain controversial because the evidence is so mixed. Patches of high unemployment and the decline of some traditional industries caused hardship, but many workers benefited from higher wages and falling prices. From 1842 to the 1860s the general growth of the economy spread improvement widely among the working population. In the long term the process of industrialisation raised working-class living standards, though the period of transition produced great suffering.

REVOLUTION OR CONTINUITY?

Despite the historically high rate of economic growth between 1750 and 1850 historians have become doubtful about using the term 'industrial revolution'. This is partly because the search for causes and preconditions has pushed the explanatory framework back a long way. Indeed, the breakdown of feudal restrictions in favour of enterprise and capitalist practices can be traced back through the seventeenth and sixteenth centuries. This begins to make revolution look more like evolution.

Conversely, studies of the supposedly mature industrial society of the later nineteenth century reveal striking continuities with the pre-industrial economy. Small-scale workshops remained very typical of British industry; agriculture survived as the major single employer until the mid-nineteenth century; domestic servants outnumbered coal miners and continued to grow in number until 1900; and many of the skills and techniques used by workers remained much as they had been for several centuries. Above all, the apparent decline in manufacturing efficiency after the 1870s has forced many historians to ask whether the values and aspirations of entrepreneurialism ever became really dominant in British society. Seen in the long term, Britain's record seems much more successful in international finance and trade than in manufacturing; her characteristic entre-preneurs were the 'gentleman-capitalists' rather than the provincial manufacturers.

These doubts have been underlined by revision of the evidence for the growth of national income between 1700 and 1860, which suggests a more gradual improvement. However, this does not entirely discredit the idea of a significant leap forward in the period between 1831 and 1861 when national income grew four times as fast as between 1700 and 1750, and five times as fast per head of population.

The revisionist view of industrialisation is at its strongest over the productivity of the labour force. Traditionally great emphasis was placed on the accumulation of capital and its application to industry. But in fact it was as late as 1851 before domestic capital formation reached 12 per cent. Put another way, the amount of capital available for each employee increased by only one-third between 1760 and 1861. This is scarcely evidence of the sudden, concentrated take-off traditionally believed to have been the hallmark of Britain's industrial revolution. It suggests that the gains in production were not simply or primarily the result of new technology or improved organisation, but were a reflection of additional inputs of labour, land and investment. Up to 1850 the gains in productivity seem to have been concentrated in textiles and the iron industry, they were not characteristic of the economy as a whole. In short, the industrial revolution appears to have been a more narrowly based phenomenon than once thought; Britain's difficulties in the period after 1870 were partly the result of the inability of the rest of the economy to emulate the leading sectors in raising efficiency.

5

Reaction and Radicalism, 1815–27

The Treaty of Vienna, which finally brought the era of revolutionary wars to an end, was largely satisfactory from Britain's point of view. Although some of France's colonies were restored to her, Britain retained Tobago, St Lucia and Mauritius as well as Malta, Heligoland and the Cape of Good Hope, all useful extensions to her Empire. In Europe the best Britain could achieve was to confine France to her former boundaries and encircle her with strong opponents; thus the Treaty re-established the Netherlands on the north-east side, extended Prussian territory to the River Rhine, and left Austria in control of Savoy and Piedmont in the south-west. With the exception of Russia, now the strongest military power in Europe, Britain had no major opponent in the world.

However, when peace suddenly returned in the summer of 1815 it took the British politicians by surprise. For although Lord Liverpool's government, which had been in power since 1812, enjoyed the prestige arising out of victory in the war, it was scarcely prepared to handle the social problems that peace brought with it. It soon emerged that although the revolution had been defeated on the battlefield its legacy in the form of a domestic radical movement would be more tenacious. Indeed, the chaotic economic conditions prevailing between 1815 and 1820 gave it fresh momentum.

THE SUPPRESSION OF THE REFORM MOVEMENT

The year 1816 proved to be a thoroughly depressing one in Britain. Few of the 300,000 soldiers, recently demobilised, found employment and most were thus forced to seek poor relief; this drove up the local rates paid by householders. In addition the end of the war destroyed much of the market for Britain's capital goods industries, especially iron, coal and shipbuilding. On top of the trade depression and rising unemployment, 1816 also brought a poor harvest; soon the price of wheat had risen to £5 per quarter.

In this situation many people became angered by the actions of Liverpool's government, which seemed designed to benefit a few of its more prosperous supporters. For example, the income tax was abandoned in 1816. An even more controversial expedient was the introduction of the Corn Law in 1815. The origins of this lay in the expansion of the cultivated area during wartime, which had been intended to feed the population during the blockade. However, much of the extra cultivation on less fertile land was quite uneconomic in normal conditions. Thus, when peace returned, farmers and landowners demanded protection against imports of wheat which threatened to undercut their prices and drive them out of business. The government responded to this by simply banning the importation of corn until the domestic price reached £4 per quarter.

Both workingmen and manufacturers reacted with anger to the Corn Law, for it seemed to be class legislation at its worst. In general, Liverpool's government was committed to the free market and to reducing state intervention; to introduce a special form of restriction was to use parliament to protect a sectional interest at the expense of the majority who were obliged to pay high food prices. Thus the Corn Law rapidly became a symbol of the corrupt nature of parliament in the eyes of many reformers. The Corn Law made it somewhat easier for middle-class reformers to join with workingmen in a general attack on the political system after 1815. This was evident in the upsurge of newspapers and journals in the postwar years. Working-class papers included Thomas Wooler's *Black Dwarf* (1817), Richard Carlile's *Republican* (1819) and William Cobbett's *Political Register* (1816). The latter sold up to 50,000 copies at one penny each. Its attacks on government extravagance in providing pensions and sinecures for its wealthy supporters aroused radical opinion throughout the Midlands, the North and in Scotland. But demands for parliamentary reform and repeal of the Corn Law were also backed by provincial newspapers catering for a more middle-class readership, notably the *Leeds Mercury*, the *Sheffield Independent* and the *Manchester Guardian*.

However, while the case for reform was effectively articulated in print and on the platform, the organisation behind it was not yet co-ordinated adequately. In particular the leaders had by no means decided how far to rely upon persuasion and how far to try to mobilise a physical attack on the system. From 1816 onwards workingmen began to join 'Hampden Clubs', especially in Lancashire and York-shire, to demand manhood suffrage. During 1819, Political Union societies sprang up, often with the support of Methodist ministers, and presented thousands of petitions to parliament. But public meetings began to lead to violence almost spontaneously. For example, in December 1816 a huge gathering at the Spa Fields in London, addressed by Henry 'Orator' Hunt, got out of control when part of the crowd looted a gunsmith's shop and marched on the Tower of London, which they saw as a symbol of repressive govern-ment. The most famous incident occurred at a rally of 60,000 people at St Peter's Fields, Manchester, in August 1819. There the local magistrates panicked unnecessarily and called out the volunteer cavalry to arrest Orator Hunt and forcibly disperse the crowd. However, they had to be rescued by professional troops, who killed eleven people and injured hundreds more. Radicals named this the 'Peterloo Massacre' in ironic reference to the Battle of Waterloo.

In this situation Liverpool and his ministers reacted with severity; their experience of the French Revolution had convinced them that concessions to popular pressure inevitably led to a complete break-down of order. Therefore they suspended the Habeas Corpus Act in 1816, which allowed the authorities to make arrests without bringing people to trial. In fact, by 1819 only 44 men had been arrested and most of them were released. In 1819, however, the government passed the notorious 'Six Acts', which prohibited meetings without the permission of a magistrate, and imposed a tax on newspapers in order to kill off the circulation of cheap, radical journals. Although highly illiberal, this legislation was less of a deterrent than it appears simply because it was not effectively implemented.

THE RISE OF LAISSEZ-FAIRE

While the battle over parliamentary reform was being fought on public platforms, a much less dramatic but ultimately more cru-cial struggle was being waged over economic and constitutional ideology. The chief partisans in this were intellectuals and academics including Adam Smith, the author of the famous *Inquiry into the Nature and Causes of the Wealth of Nations* (1776), and Jeremy Bentham, one of the founders of Utilitarianism. Traditionally such figures have been seen as part of a broad trend of opinion towards a laissez-faire approach; in many ways they did indeed advocate the lifting of restrictions on individual enterprise so as to allow the free play of market forces. However, this is to simplify their views. Bentham in particular pointed the way towards a considerable extension of the role of the state during the nineteenth century.

Smith had attacked the traditional mercantilist assumption that national prosperity required that governments should protect British producers by means of tariffs on imports, bounties for exporters, and granting monopoly rights over trade. In his view these measures simply reduced world trade and depressed standards of living in all countries. On the other hand, freedom of trade and the ending of controls brought the benefits of competition; each country would tend to specialise in what it could produce most efficiently, consumers would enjoy access to the cheapest goods, and producers would be able to use low-priced raw materials. In arguing thus, Adam Smith did not convert the English to free trade, rather he gave expression to current thinking; Pitt, for example, had admired his work and Liverpool took important steps towards liberalising trade after 1815.

However, the political-economists were by no means uncritical champions of private enterprise. They believed that the state had a role to play in regulating capitalism. David Ricardo, for example, argued that landlords should not simply be permitted to appropriate the rent generated by their property; in his view the value of their land was invariably the result of the enterprise and labour of others and rent should therefore be taxed for the benefit of the community as a whole. Smith and Bentham also recognised that certain functions would never be performed effectively if left to individuals; thus the state must take responsibility for such matters as education and communications.

Bentham made a particularly important contribution to the debate over political reform in the sense that he developed a distinctively English approach to the question. He followed neither Burke's negativism nor the revolutionary doctrines of the French. He declined to base his analysis on natural rights or abstract ideas, which the English Conservatives ridiculed. Instead Bentham examined British institutions by asking whether they worked efficiently. His empirical approach suggested that parliamentary reform might be undertaken without necessarily endangering the political system. For the Benthamites, parliament and the electoral system were only two examples of institutions in need of reconstruction; they also wished to overhaul the poor law and the prisons as well as abolishing patronage and opening public posts to men of ability by means of competitive examinations.

The Benthamites made a tangible impact on several aspects of British public life. For example, in 1814 parliament abolished the Elizabethan Statute of Artificers, which had controlled the labour market by regulation of wages and a seven-year apprenticeship system. In effect, abolition created free trade in labour, leaving the market to determine wage levels. Benthamites also believed that the poor law system subsidised wages and encouraged idleness. In the 1830s they were instrumental in its replacement by a new and stricter poor law. But the poor law required a degree of centralisation which was typical of their thinking. In 1835 they devised a system for the inspection of prisons by professionals, which added further to the bureaucracy in central government. Naturally this provoked a good deal of criticism throughout the nineteenth century. For example, in 1822 Peel failed to establish a national police force, which was seen as a threat to local government. He managed to set up a Metropolitan Police Force in 1828 on the grounds that London was a special case, but he intended this as a first step towards the national police force that Benthamites desired.

Benthamite doctrines were perhaps at their most influential in the administration of the Indian Empire, which served, in effect, as a huge laboratory in which ideas might be tested. On becoming Governor-General of India in 1827 Lord William Bentinck reputedly told Bentham: 'You will be the Governor-General, not me.' In fact Utilitarians became influential at all levels in the Indian government. For example, James Mill, who wrote *The History of British India* (1817), worked for the East India Company in London from 1819 to 1836 as chief examiner of correspondence. Moreover, many young district officers absorbed Utilitarian doctrines, such as Ricardo's ideas about land taxation as part of their training; they proceeded to apply them in the Indian countryside, sometimes with very damaging results.

Meanwhile, at home, the reformers focused on the monopoly status enjoyed by the East India Company. They argued that this enabled the Company to withhold supplies of commodities such as tea with a view to creating a shortage and thus forcing up the price paid by consumers. Consequently, when parliament renewed the Company's charter in 1813 it deliberately opened up the Indian trade to merchants outside the Company. In combination with a gradual increase in the supply of tea and reductions in duties charged on imports, this lowered the price at home – a good illustration of Benthamite claims about promoting the interests of the whole community by the elimination of the privileges of a few. On the other hand the vested interests were so strongly entrenched that many of the reformers' goals took years to achieve. Free trade in corn was delayed until 1846; the East India Company survived until swept away by the mutiny of 1857; and landed wealth was never effectively taxed – at least in the opinion of nineteenth-century radicals.

LIVERPOOL AND LIBERAL TORYISM

Derided by Benjamin Disraeli as the 'Arch Mediocrity', Lord Liverpool has enjoyed a reputation as a blind reactionary at worst and, at best, as a cautious prime minister surrounded by more able men. Yet the very survival of his government from 1812 to 1827 – the longest of the nineteenth century – suggests some skill on his part. At the least, Liverpool succeeded in consolidating the Tory Party that had emerged as an ad hoc coalition during the chaos of wartime. He survived for so long largely by conciliating certain vested interests and offering judicious reforms to the rising business interests. Above all, by trying to maintain law and order in a very disturbed period, by giving way over the income tax, and by maintaining protection for farmers, Liverpool reassured the small electorate that their interests were safe in his hands; he won general elections in 1818, 1820 and 1826. During these years the Whig Opposition hesitated to join forces with the popular reform movement because they feared being dragged into supporting the cry for one-man-one-vote. Liverpool also enjoyed the support of George III, who still hated the Whigs; but his death in 1820 undermined the government's position.

Traditionally historians have claimed that the Liverpool era fell into two halves, a repressive phase up to 1822 followed by a period of 'Liberal Toryism'. This is only really valid in the sense that as circumstances changed the government grew less authoritarian. Certainly the recovery of trade after 1820 eased the general discontent in the country and parliament became a little more relaxed in its attitude towards the working classes. This was shown by the willingness to repeal the Combination Acts, which, since 1799, had effectively made trade unions illegal organisations. The campaign led by Francis Place and by the radical MP Joseph Hume won for workers the right to bargain over wages and conditions collectively. However, as the immediate result was a rash of strikes, parliament passed a new Combination Act in 1825 which made violence, intimidation and picketing in support of a strike punishable by three months in prison; even the right to strike peacefully was left in doubt by the legislation.

The other change that lends some credence to the idea of a more liberal approach is the rise of some younger and more reformist ministers into high office in the later years of the ministry; Canning as Foreign Secretary, Peel as Home Secretary, Robinson as Chancellor of the Exchequer and Huskisson as President of the Board of Trade. However, none of these appointments modified the government's stern opposition towards parliamentary reform. Even when parliament voted to withdraw representation from a particularly corrupt rural town in 1821, Liverpool refused to grant the two seats to one of the large industrial boroughs; he clearly hesitated to come to terms with the industrial revolution and the middle class that it had generated; and in this lay the eventual undoing of the Tory government.

On the other hand his economic policies did reflect a more liberal line of thought. Liverpool had always favoured free trade; but after 1815 it was difficult to advance very rapidly towards this goal because the state, having lost the income tax, was very dependent upon indirect taxes for its revenue. The wars had increased Britain's national debt from £200 million to £900 million, leaving the government with an annual charge of £30 million in interest payments. Although state expenditure was reduced by 50 per cent in the first three years of peace, spending still exceeded revenue. The government found itself taking out new loans at high rates in order to pay off old debts at lower rates. In this situation it was decided to restore a stable currency by resuming the cash payments which Pitt had abandoned in 1797. Both farmers and economists welcomed the decision to fix the currency in terms of gold in place of the paper notes issued by the state. Thus, from 1821 Britain was effectively on the Gold Standard; this checked speculation and inflation and paved the way for a resumption of industrial expansion. For the remainder of the century the Gold Standard policy became a cornerstone of British finance.

The return of economic growth made it feasible for Liverpool to begin to liberalise trade. Between 1824 and 1825 Robinson and Huskisson reduced the duties charged on a wide range of raw materials and consumer goods; they also signed a number of Trade Reciprocity Acts with foreign governments, designed to maximise the cuts in tariffs. In spite of this, some goods still paid a maximum tariff of 30 per cent, so there was a long way yet to go before free trade had been attained. But meanwhile the reductions stimulated trade so much that the revenue derived from customs rose by 64 per cent between 1821 and 1827, an increase nearly twice as great as that engineered by Pitt.

Despite these achievements the Liverpool regime stubbornly left many issues unresolved. In particular, the Corn Law looked increasingly anachronistic in the context of other reductions in tariffs; but the fear of hostile reactions by MPs representing agricultural interests deterred the government from tackling this question. Liverpool also adhered rigidly to his opposition to parliamentary reform. In 1822 Lord John Russell introduced a bill to redistribute seats for the benefit of industrial towns and counties. Although defeated, this initiative was a sign that at last the Whigs were ready to align themselves with broader opinion in the country. Finally, Liverpool failed to cope with the resurgence of the Irish problem after 1823 when a new Catholic Association was formed by Daniel O'Connell to campaign for political rights for Catholics. When O'Connell got himself elected to parliament at a famous by-election in County Clare in 1828 the Tories were humiliated and forced to back down.

As these issues accumulated the government steadily lost authority in the country. Liverpool himself suffered a stroke and was forced to resign as prime minister in 1827. But the speed with which the Tory Party then collapsed was an indication that his negative approach was ultimately self-defeating.

6

The Era of Reform, 1828–41

By the 1820s the process of industrialisation and urbanisation had rendered Britain's medieval system of political representation dangerously anachronistic. The 'balanced' constitution now excluded not only most workingmen but many middle-class people from the rights of citizenship. In England and Wales only about one adult man in every ten could vote. Moreover, the long-standing over-representation of the south of England now seemed unjustifiable; for example, the industrial county of Lancashire contained four times as many people as Cornwall in the far south-west, but elected only 14 MPs to Cornwall's 42.

In spite of this the opponents of reform successfully resisted pressure for radical change for some decades. They used three kinds of argument. First, if the electorate were to be extended so as to enfranchise poor men it would merely tend to increase the scope for bribery, corruption and influence. Secondly, the political system was intended to represent not individuals but local communities; an employer or landlord might vote on behalf of his workers as a husband might vote on behalf of his wife. Thirdly, the system did give approximate representation to the agricultural–industrial, rural–urban elements in society. The danger of reform lay in allowing any one interest to predominate; farmers in particular stood to lose if the urban majority chose to abolish protection of agriculture. No doubt much of this argument amounted to a mere rationalisation of vested interests by a privileged minority. None the less, in a period dominated by fear of revolution the case for maintaining the status quo always commanded strong support in parliament.

THE GREAT REFORM ACT OF 1832

It was not until the late 1820s that support for the status quo decisively crumbled at Westminster. One crucial underlying cause was the deterioration in the economic situation. A poor harvest in 1829 led to high bread prices, while an industrial slump brought wage cuts and increased unemployment. This attracted mass support to new radical organisations such as Thomas Attwood's Political Union in Birmingham, and the National Union of the Working Classes led by William Lovett and Henry Hetherington. The distinctive feature about these groups was their ability to draw middle-class men, especially shopkeepers and small businessmen, into alliance with workingmen. Determination to achieve the higher status of voters led many middle-class men to risk joining the agitation. But this development threatened to leave the landed class isolated in its resistance to reform. As Lord Holland told Lord Grey in 1830: 'If the great mass of the middle class are bent upon that method of enforcing their views, there is not in the nature of society any real force that can prevent them.'

The second factor lay in the collapse of political resistance to reform following Liverpool's resignation in 1827. At this point the Tory party began to fragment, especially when the elderly Duke of Wellington became Prime Minister in January 1828. Though a military hero, he proved wholly incompetent at maintaining his party's unity. Indeed, he triggered the collapse by offering a measure of conciliation in 1828 when he repealed the Test and Corporation Acts. This removal of the political disqualifications suffered by Nonconformists immediately antagonised many Anglican Tories. The effect was compounded, rather unluckily for Wellington, by events in Ireland. Daniel O'Connell won a famous by-election in County Clare, but, as a Catholic, was not eligible to sit in parliament. Since Wellington feared a violent reaction in Ireland if he excluded O'Connell, he decided to pass the Catholic Emancipation Act in 1829. However, many Tories bitterly resented this as they believed it would lead inevitably to the disestablishment of the Church in Ireland. Indeed, it is almost impossible to exaggerate the significance of Catholic Emancipation at this crucial stage, for it entirely destroyed the credibility of Wellington in the eyes of his own party. Moreover, it convinced many Tories that the parliamentary system was not worth defending any longer; they argued, with some justification, that if the ordinary English people had been able to make their views felt, Catholic Emancipation would probably not have been carried.

The results of these controversies became apparent when, owing to the death of George IV, a general election took place in 1830. Wellington's supporters were badly beaten wherever contests occurred; but the Prime Minister remained out of touch with opinion. In November 1830, when the agitation for reform was at its height, he declared that the political system 'possessed the full and entire confidence of the country'. Within two weeks of this tactless statement Wellington had been defeated in parliament and the new King, William IV, appointed Earl Grey to form a Whig government.

The new government replaced one set of aristocrats with another. But though Grey was no radical he recognised the necessity for reform; indeed, he accepted that minor adjustments to the old system would no longer suffice to quell the agitation. Consequently his first reform bill in March 1831 went further than the radicals had expected. It proposed to enfranchise male householders who occupied property worth £10 a year in rent; and it abolished 168 seats in very small boroughs while redistributing 43 seats to large industrial towns.

As this bill passed its second reading in the Commons by only one vote, Grey persuaded the King to agree to a fresh election. This certainly delivered a mandate for reform. Grey's bill was still rejected by the House of Lords, however. Their action provoked a violent response in the country in the form of attacks on the houses of peers and also of bishops, most of whom had voted against reform. For several months during late 1831 and early 1832 Britain appeared to be close to a popular revolution. If another bill had failed and the Tories had returned to office there would have been armed resistance to the government. However, in this crisis the readiness of middle-class people to collaborate with the radicals proved crucial. They made threats to withdraw funds from the banks and to refuse to pay property taxes. As a result, by June 1832 the King had agreed reluctantly to create enough new peers to get the reform bill through the upper house. In the event, this proved unnecessary, for the anti-reformers backed down and the crisis was suddenly over.

THE SIGNIFICANCE OF REFORM

In spite of the immense controversy aroused in 1832 it has seemed to many historians that the changes introduced by the 'Great' Reform Act were remarkably slight. Essentially the number of voters was doubled to 717,000, but this was equivalent to only one in five adult males. By creating a new vote for £10 householders, parliament had effectively enfranchised the middle classes. But in the North, where house prices were low, fewer people would qualify; on the other hand, in time, inflation boosted the electorate. Workingmen remained largely excluded. In the counties an additional vote was created for £50 tenants; but as such men were highly vulnerable to the pressure of their landlords, the effect seems to have been to increase aristocratic influence. As the ballot remained a public affair there was still much scope for corruption and intimidation at elections throughout the mid-Victorian period.

In the long term a more significant innovation was the formal registration of voters. Unfortunately the Act failed to create a bureaucracy to compile the register, and as a result the party agents filled the gap. Each year they advanced the names of their own known supporters and made objections to those of their opponents. Disputes were settled in court before a new register of voters could be published. This stimulated the development of elaborate party organisations but it also left the system open to manipulation by those who had money to spend.

In some ways the redistribution of constituencies proved to be the more radical aspect of reform. Eventually 56 small boroughs lost both their MPs and another 30 lost one MP; 22 new double-member constituencies and 20 single-member constituencies were created, which gave representation to many industrial towns for the first time. This in itself reduced the scope for patronage and corruption, which had always been concentrated in the medieval market towns. In addition several industrialised counties gained extra seats, including Yorkshire, which sent six MPs to Westminster instead of two.

In some ways, however, the detailed changes made in 1832 were of less significance than the underlying political implications. Grey had never concealed his intention of avoiding really radical reforms such as the secret ballot, annual parliaments or universal suffrage. He sincerely believed that some bold, but judicious modifications offered the best way of preserving the influence of the aristocracy. He understood that the enfranchisement of the middle classes would not destroy aristocratic government, but consolidate it by giving the political system greater legitimacy. The soundness of his judgement was demonstrated later in the 1830s and 1840s when the government successfully withstood the Chartist agitations. By then most of the middle class had become detached from its alliance with the working men; once enfranchised, it wanted to defend the status quo.

However, while reform gave the middle class formal recognition it did not allow them extra power, at least in the short term. The social composition of the post-1832 parliaments proved to be very similar to those of the earlier period. Most MPs continued to be drawn from landed and titled families in spite of the reduction in the number of small patronage boroughs. In short, 1832 failed to bring about a bourgeois revolution. On the other hand, those Whigs who claimed that the Great Reform Act represented a final solution of the reform question were over-optimistic. Indeed, no further reform took place until 1867, but once the old system had been altered there could be no fundamental objection to further change.

SOCIAL REFORM AND THE DECLINE OF THE WHIGS

In their great victory in 1832 the Whigs had won 483 seats to only 175 for the Tories. This kept them in power until 1841, at first under Grey and from 1834 under Lord Melbourne. However, their majority was steadily reduced at successive elections largely as a result of the antagonism aroused by the social and humanitarian reform enacted in these years.

For example, 1833 brought a trio of major innovations for which evangelicals and Nonconformists had long campaigned. Slavery was abolished throughout the British Empire, though complete emancipation was delayed for seven years for existing slaves working on the land. Former slave-owners received £20 million in compensation.

Another long-standing cause tackled by the Whigs was education. For the first time an annual government grant of £20,000 was to be made to voluntary societies offering elementary education. This had immense long-term implications in extending the role of the state. Unfortunately the method adopted in 1833 – subsidies to religious organisations – created huge political complications for future governments up to 1914. The third great reform of 1833 was Graham's Factory Act, which limited the hours of children employed in cotton textile mills. Like the education measure, this was only a timid first step and satisfied few people (see p. 56), but it also proved to be significant. By creating an official inspectorate the Act effectively guaranteed that evidence about working conditions in mills and factories would be regularly brought to light; this inevitably generated further legislation and a steady expansion of state regulation of private industry.

By far the most controversial Whig measure was the new poor law introduced in 1834. This reflected a growing belief that the old system of, in effect, paying subsidies to make up for low agricultural wages had become too expensive for ratepayers and had the effect of turning workingmen into paupers. Benthamite reformers wanted a uniform policy administered more strictly. Thus parishes were to be grouped into larger poor law unions, which would build new workhouses and hospitals for the needy. Above all, the system was intended to deter applicants, on the assumption that poverty was largely the result of individual failings rather than economic conditions. To this end, the poor law guardians were instructed to refuse to grant outdoor relief and instead to require applicants to enter the workhouse, where conditions were intended to be worse than the worst available outside. Although this measure passed with little opposition in parliament, it proved to be immensely unpopular in the country, so much so that it was never fully enforced in many areas.

In 1835 the Whigs introduced a Municipal Corporations Act, which created elected councils in a number of the larger towns and cities. This was a long-overdue attack on the corruption in the boroughs and it paved the way for the extension of elected local authorities to all parts of the country later in the Victorian era. In the mid-Victorian period the new municipal councils offered an excellent opportunity to radical politicians such as small shopkeepers, businessmen and Nonconformists who were still unlikely to become MPs, but who could now play an influential role in governing their own communities.

Finally the Whig government under Melbourne became engulfed in religious controversy especially in Ireland. During 1831–2 a 'tithe war' had broken out involving the destruction of crops, burning of farm buildings and maiming of animals in the Irish countryside. Troops sent out to recover tithes from the farmers proved to be ineffective and provocative. Therefore the government tried a mixture of coercion – the banning of public meetings and the use of courts martial in place of civil courts – and conciliation. But as conciliation of Irish Catholics involved attempting to purge the Church of Ireland of some of its worst abuses, it only had the effect of antagonising Protestants and Tories in England. They chose to regard the Whigs' efforts as a step towards disestablishing the Anglican Church in Ireland altogether, and portrayed them as the puppets of Catholics and radicals. Their charges proved all the more damaging because Melbourne's government was also attempting to satisfy some of the grievances of the English Nonconformists. For example, in 1836 they allowed Nonconformists to be married outside Anglican Churches, even by a civil ceremony if they wished; they also reduced the payment of tithes and passed a law enabling London University – which unlike the older universities admitted non-Anglicans – to award degrees.

Although much had been achieved by the Whigs, their popularity steadily diminished. From 484 MPs in 1832 they fell to 385 after the 1835 election and to 345 at the 1837 election. Like many reforming governments they suffered by disappointing their radical supporters while driving the vested interests into the hands of the Tories. This culminated in the remarkable general election of 1841. Queen Victoria had granted Melbourne a dissolution of parliament in the belief that he would be re-elected. But the emphatic rejection of the Queen's favoured prime minister was unprecedented: 1841 signified that royal support was no longer a guarantee of success, for in the country, politics was increasingly a matter of party loyalty.

The evolution of the party system in this period owed much to Sir Robert Peel. In 1834 he issued a famous document, the 'Tamworth Manifesto', in which he lay down the principles on which a future government would operate. It was during this decade that his party increasingly called itself 'Conservative' rather than Tory. For Peel, this change in terminology symbolised his readiness to accept the

Reform Act and abandon the reactionary politics associated with Wellington. Peel's personal reputation for competence in administration and his business background helped to reassure middle-class voters who had supported Grey in 1832 but lost confidence in Melbourne. As a result the Conservatives won 367 seats compared with 291 for the Whigs in 1841. However, the chief reasons for their success lay in the bitter Protestant backlash against the Irish and the Nonconformists, and also in the agriculturists' fears about losing tariff protection. Peel had barely begun to refashion his reactionary party into a more progressive, middle-class and urban one; within a few years the task was to prove to be beyond his powers.

7

The Condition of England Question, 1832–48

In a famous pamphlet entitled *Chartism* in 1839 Thomas Carlyle summed up the current state of British society thus:

> A feeling very generally exists that the condition and disposition of the working classes is a rather ominous matter at present; that something ought to be said, something ought to be done, in regard to it.

The problem to which Carlyle referred arose from both economic and political causes. The reactions to a major economic depression between 1837 and 1842 were inflamed by the consequences of the 1832 Reform Act. Working-class men who had campaigned for the vote but had been deliberately excluded from the Reform Act now felt betrayed. Since most of them rented their houses at between £4 and £8 per year they seemed most unlikely to qualify for the new £10 householder franchise. This almost inevitably meant that when moved by social grievances they would resort to extra-parliamentary methods of protest. Workingmen, especially in the North, were antagonised by the new poor law introduced by the Whigs in 1834. Richard Oastler said of this innovation that it 'lays the axe to the root of the social compact; it must break up society and make England a wilderness'. Such reactions remind us that workers enjoyed some sympathy amongst the higher social classes from those who believed that the drift towards centralised administration and the spread of a factory system were destroying the traditional sense of duty and respect that bound the different social classes together; social cohesion was giving way to impersonal relationships based on money. One of the most famous expressions of this view came from a young radical Tory, Benjamin Disraeli. In *Coningsby* (1844) and *Sybil* (1845) he attacked the emergence of two separate nations, the rich and the poor, and belaboured the Conservative leader, Peel, for abandoning the traditional Tory belief in deference and duty in order to pander to the selfish, laissez-faire attitudes of the bourgeoisie.

ANTI-INDUSTRIALISM

It is scarcely surprising that many Victorians reacted with dismay to the new society generated by the industrial revolution. Smoky towns expanding into the countryside and densely packed streets of unhealthy houses rife with crime, drink and disease appeared to make social revolution inevitable. It would be a mistake, however, to overlook the social evils of rural England, which generated as much conflict and hardship as industrial society. Bread riots, the burning of hay ricks and the destruction of agricultural machinery were endemic features of the countryside. The 1830s began with riots throughout the southern counties of England and it was Dorset in the south-west that provided the most famous example of persecuted workers – the Tolpuddle Martyrs of 1834. Six agricultural labourers in the village of Tolpuddle had attempted to form a trade union but thereby infringed the law against secret oaths. The magistrates determined to make an example of them and sentenced the men to seven years' transportation to Australia. However, in 1836 the government cancelled their sentences and brought them home. Though exceptional in some ways, the Tolpuddle Martyrs symbolised the dilemma of isolated groups of labourers who wished to organise in order to defend their living standards. In the aftermath of the Reform Act the national organisations of workingmen found it difficult to mobilise support or to give assistance to workers in remote areas of the country.

The new issue that gave these problems a focus was the reduction of working hours. This controversy was launched in a famous letter on 'Yorkshire Slavery' by Richard Oastler in the *Leeds Mercury*, in which he referred to 'thousands of little children ... sacrificed at the shrine of avarice, without even the solace of the negro slave'.

In addition to Oastler, the chief leaders of the campaign for a ten-hour working day were Michael Sadler and the Reverend George Bull, all from Yorkshire. Also supportive were several factory owners including John Fielden and John Hornsby of Lancashire, and in parliament Lord Ashley (later Shaftesbury). All these men were Tories and they represented a Tory–Radical alliance characteristic of this period. Moved partly by humanitarian concern for women and children subject to long working hours in dangerous and often inhumane conditions, they also felt outraged by both the ruthlessness and the aggressive Nonconformity of many of the industrial entrepreneurs.

Under pressure from Sadler, who introduced a Ten Hours Bill in parliament in 1832, the government appointed a parliamentary select committee to investigate working hours. However, the Whigs' sympathies remained largely with the employers. Thus their 1833 Factory Act was a concession designed to remove the controversy from the issue; it prohibited factory work by children under nine years, made some schooling compulsory, and instituted the inspection of factories. But the Whigs regarded this as an exceptional measure; in general they believed that the state should avoid interference in working conditions. Inevitably the radicals felt let down once again, but much of the momentum behind Ashley's campaign was diverted into the protest over the new poor law. On the other hand, inspection of factories brought many abuses to light and revealed the ineffectiveness of the 1833 Act, thereby paving the way for further legislation in 1844 (see p. 65) and in 1847 when John Fielden at last passed a Ten Hours Act.

THE NEW POOR LAW

Much the most emotive single issue of the 1830s was the reform of the poor law system. This was not surprising because those who framed the legislation of 1834 intended to introduce a radical change. In particular they wished to end the control exercised by local squires, whom they blamed for demoralising the poor by their generous payments based on the current price of bread. Instead, those who received poor relief were to be required to enter a 'workhouse' rather than receive help outside, and to endure conditions sufficiently bad to deter men from applying in the first place. This reflected a fundamental belief that the poor tended to be idle and irresponsible, and thus in need of a stimulus to live industrious lives. Once set free, it was assumed, the surplus labour would be absorbed by the expanding economy.

Unfortunately, the new system had been designed to deal with the southern agricultural counties, which suffered from low wages and seasonal unemployment. When applied to the North and the Midlands during 1836 the poor law encountered massive resistance from all concerned, for the industrial districts experienced sharp fluctuations between labour shortages and high wages during the booms, followed by mass unemployment during the slumps. In these areas the workers naturally saw the new poor law as a means of forcing them to accept lower wages and longer hours. The depression of 1837–42 had the effect of thoroughly undermining the new system throughout the North, for the workhouse test was irrelevant when thousands of men were being thrown out of work. Attempts by the poor law commissioners to establish a new administration provoked boycotts and rioting that could only be suppressed with the aid of troops in some areas.

However, the protests collapsed fairly quickly, partly because discontent was diverted into Chartism from 1839 onwards. Also, the new poor law was never applied as the legislators had intended. In the South, the poor law guardians, who often felt sympathetic towards the agricultural labourers, resorted to illicit ways of paying extra poor relief. In the North, the elected guardians frequently ignored their instructions and continued to offer outdoor relief as before. By 1844, 84 per cent of those who were granted relief received it outside the workhouse. In many areas the guardians were very slow to build new workhouses, often because of the expense involved or because none of the guardians wanted to incur the unpopularity of imposing the workhouse test. They evidently managed to escape their responsibilities for some time because the poor law commissioners who were supposed to enforce the new policy had been shaken by the popular hostility; the low political standing of the Poor Law Department at Westminster meant that the commissioners themselves were allowed to be flexible in their dealings with the local guardians. As a result there was little attempt to enforce a uniform national policy for some years.

On the other hand it would be a mistake to assume that the Victorian poor law made no impact. For one thing, expenditure on

relief fell by 30 per cent per head of population between 1832 and
1844. Workhouses gradually appeared throughout the country; by
1870 four out of five of the 647 poor law unions had built one. The
working classes regarded them with fear and loathing. Conditions
inside the workhouse were both severe and humiliating; uniforms
were worn by inmates; husbands and wives were split up, and
consumption of tobacco and alcohol was often prohibited. Elderly
people lived in dread of spending their last years in the workhouse
and suffering the indignity of being buried as paupers. During the
1850s 4 to 5 per cent of the population received poor relief, but by
the 1890s surveys began to reveal that thousands of people in great
distress from poverty still refused to enter the workhouse.

TRADE UNIONISM

In view of Britain's early industrialisation it has often been assumed
that the working class organised themselves into trade unions in the
early nineteenth century. On the contrary, a large and effective
union movement proved to be very slow to emerge, and it was not
until the First World War that it became typical for a workingman
to be a member. We can begin to understand why this was so by
considering the attempts made during the 1830s to organise trade
unions. Of these the best known was Robert Owen's Grand
National Consolidated Trade Union, founded in 1834. Similarly
ambitious unions were the National Association for the Protection
of Labour (1829–31), and the Grand General Union of Cotton
Spinners (1829–30). The GNCTU's objectives reflected Owen's
utopian brand of socialism, that is to say, it advocated a complete
reorganisation of society on co-operative principles so as to win for
the workers 'the fruits of their own industry'. This was both too
sophisticated and too vague to attract many workingmen. Those
who joined looked for more immediate and tangible benefits. In an
initial burst of enthusiasm many of the new members came out on
strike spontaneously, thereby placing their leaders in a dilemma
that was to be faced throughout the nineteenth century. On the one
hand, the leadership felt obliged to support their members, but on
the other hand, they simply lacked the resources to do so for any
length of time. Thus within six months the GNCTU had been
undermined because its funds ran out; members soon lost heart and

the whole enterprise began to collapse as it appeared that the union could do little to defend the men.

This experience demonstrated that attempts to recruit workers in different trades or even men with different skills in the same industry were too ambitious to be attainable. In fact, for most unskilled workers effective bargaining with employers was impossible because their labour simply lacked scarcity value; with a large surplus labour force available to them the employers could invariably recruit enough men to break a strike, and they often responded to a strike threat by simply locking out the workers until hunger drove them back on the owners' terms. Only in times of rapid economic growth when employers were eager to increase output were they susceptible to pressure for better wages or conditions.

By the 1840s it had become clear that only skilled workers who could not easily be replaced or undermined by new technology could realistically expect to sustain a trade union organisation. Viable unions did establish themselves amongst building workers, spinners and potters. In 1842 another important union emerged in the form of the Miners' Association of Great Britain, which had recruited 70,000 members within two years. Significantly, it opposed violence and avoided any association with Chartism. This is a reminder of the extent to which the British working class remained divided. The Chartist movement was regarded as an alternative for those really poor and desperate workers who could not defend themselves by means of trade unionism.

CHARTISM

In numerical terms, Chartism was much the most significant working-class movement in this period; between 1837 and 1848 it mobilised hundreds of thousands of men and women in a bitter and sometimes violent protest. It reached its height after 1838 when bread prices rose and Britain suffered the worst depression of the century. Support for Chartism appears to have fluctuated according to the condition of the economy, and for this reason it was regarded by contemporaries as essentially a 'knife and fork question'. However, academic study has revealed that the strength and character of Chartism varied by region and social conditions. Its heartland lay in Yorkshire, Lancashire, the East Midlands and western Scotland.

But it won less support from factory operatives than from workers in the older, pre-industrial trades. The movement was also weaker in large towns like Leeds or Manchester where the more varied economy made it easier for men to find employment. Conversely, it often reached its peak in smaller industrial towns and villages where the workers were dependent upon a single industry for their livelihood. This accounts for Chartist activity in declining textile towns in the south-west of England which had been undermined by the more efficient producers in the North.

However, it would be an over-simplification to portray Chartism as no more than a spontaneous response to material hardship. Though it lacked an ideological base, it none the less developed a precise political programme. The movement grew out of the London Workingmen's Association, founded in 1836 by William Lovett and Henry Hetherington, the editor of the *Poor Man's Guardian*, and took its name from the 'People's Charter' which was drawn up in 1838 by a radical London tailor, Francis Place. The Charter listed six aims: universal suffrage, abolition of the property qualification for MPs, annual parliaments, the secret ballot, equalised constituencies and the payment of MPs. These proposals were by no means new, but they constituted a coherent and readily understood programme.

Traditionally Chartism has been seen as being divided between a 'moral force' wing led by such men as William Lovett, Francis Place and Henry Vincent, and a 'physical force' wing associated with Feargus O'Connor, John Frost and Bronterre O'Brien. Although differences in style and tactics undoubtedly existed, there remained much common ground between these leaders. The characteristic method adopted by Chartists was the presentation of petitions to parliament – an obvious example of moral force. In 1839 the petition bore 1.3 million signatures, that of 1842, 3.3 million and that of 1848 allegedly 5.7 million, though the real number is thought to have been far lower – it was discovered that such unlikely names as 'Queen Victoria' and the 'Duke of Wellington' appeared on the lists. Huge rallies were held in support of these petitions. When the National Convention met in London in 1839, it planned a general strike following parliament's rejection of its demands.

Another moral force tactic involved participation in elections. Although they were excluded from the electorate, workingmen held meetings of their own to nominate and elect candidates prior to the official election in order to underline their claim. Feargus O'Connor was the only Chartist to win a seat himself, as the MP for Nottingham in 1847. But Chartists also exerted pressure by means of 'exclusive dealing', which meant withholding custom from shopkeepers, who were voters, unless they supported pro-Chartist candidates. This was a tactic often practised by female Chartists.

However, the ruling elite did not appear unduly influenced by all this. Parliament refused even to consider the 1839 petition, by a vote of 235 to 46; and it rejected the 1842 petition by 287 to 49 votes. As a result most scholars have regarded Chartism as a failure, at least in the short term, and have concentrated on finding explanations for its weakness. Yet this is an over-simplification, for Chartism was really two movements, one a long-term attempt at persuading the political class of the need to broaden the system by incorporating workingmen, and the other a mass movement designed to achieve immediate concessions. In the latter sense Chartism can appropriately be viewed as a failure. Even the most extreme leaders such as O'Connor were scarcely revolutionaries. Although they used inflammatory language at their meetings this only gave an impression of revolutionary fervour; there was neither organisation nor ideology behind it. The most violent incident occurred in November 1839 when John Frost led 3000 colliers and ironworkers in a march in South Wales. The authorities regarded this as an armed rising and called out troops, who killed twenty-four Chartists in the process of dispersing the crowds. Frost was sentenced to death but reprieved and transported to Australia for seventeen years. Elsewhere there was much talk of revolution and some occasional attempts to arm the men. Around five hundred Chartists were arrested between June 1839 and June 1840, and most of the leaders spent some time in prison. However, none of this sporadic violence amounted to an attempt at revolution.

The years of violence coincided with fresh economic hardship rather than with organised revolt. The anti-climax came in April 1848 when the Chartists held a mass rally at Kennington Common in London with the intention of marching to parliament to present a petition. Another refusal by the politicians was to be met with violence. But the government recruited 100,000 volunteers to repel the threat and banned the procession. In the event, fewer than expected attended the rally, only to be advised by O'Connor to disperse peacefully while he presented the petition himself. As a result the movement petered out at this point with the authorities able to claim a victory for the forces of law and order.

The events of 1848 demonstrated the wisdom of the politicians in attaching the middle classes to the political system in 1832. This meant that although moral-force Chartism was strong amongst skilled workers in London, Birmingham, Scotland and Tyneside, it never attained the parliamentary strength required to force the ruling elite to take its claims seriously. This is not to say that there was a complete split between workingmen and the middle class. Nonconformists provided one definite link; many Methodist ministers regarded Chartism as an expression of Christian teaching and allowed their chapels to be used for Chartist meetings. There was also some common ground with the middle-class radicals of the Anti-Corn Law League (see pp. 65–7). Richard Cobden recognised the desirability of an alliance when he commented on the need for 'something in our rear to frighten the aristocracy'. Many Chartists, however, felt suspicious of the League as an organisation of employers, and argued that cheap bread would simply be used as an excuse for reducing wages. Occasionally Chartists even went so far as to break up League meetings. Consequently a joint campaign never materialised. This was unfortunate because the case for incorporating workingmen into the political system would have gained great force from more middle-class backing in parliament. The parliamentary sympathisers were undermined by the use of violent language by some Chartist leaders in the country.

However, the collapse of Chartism as a mass agitation in 1848 should not obscure the long-term achievements of the movement. Its arguments for reform entered the political debate and some of the leaders, such as Ernest Jones, were still active in the 1860s when the Reform League agitated successfully for the vote. In fact the first item in the Charter to be won was the abolition of property qualifications for MPs in 1858. Some workers received the vote in 1867 and the secret ballot was achieved in 1872. These examples remind us that in spite of the demise of Chartism as an organisation, its ideas had become practical politics in the mid-Victorian period. But the radicals changed their tactics. Gradually an alliance emerged of workingmen, Nonconformists, former Anti-Corn Law League activists and parliamentary radicals. Their chief political vehicle was to be the Victorian Liberal Party.

8

The Triumph of Free Trade

The most effective challenge to the new system created by the 1832 Reform Act came not from the working classes but from the middle-class radicals of the Anti-Corn Law League. Established in 1838 in the city which, more than any other, symbolised the industrial revolution – Manchester – the League accused the landed class of using its political power to preserve its privileges at the expense of both the workers and British industry. The crucial step towards the resolution of this issue came with the emergence of Sir Robert Peel as Prime Minister following the Conservatives' victory at the 1841 general election. For Peel was more in tune with the aspirations of industrial England than were Lord Melbourne and the aristocratic Whig leaders. He had already made some progress towards modernising the Conservative Party. Under his leadership Conservatives accepted the reforms of 1832 as permanent; but it remained unclear in 1841 whether they would go further by recognising the need to remedy the economic grievances of the manufacturers.

PEELITE CONSERVATISM

Peel entered upon office at a time of deepening economic depression, rising unemployment, higher food prices and falling profits. Essentially the problem lay in the fact that industrialisation had begun to generate more goods than the domestic market could absorb, while foreign markets were not yet large enough, or sufficiently willing, to take the surplus. However, by comparison with previous prime ministers Peel was more resolute about responding to these problems, and held firm ideas about the role of the government in relieving social and economic distress. His weakness lay largely in his party, which continued to be dominated by narrow-minded country gentlemen. Unfortunately Peel himself was too aloof and arrogant to cultivate the country squires and carry them with him; indeed, he could scarcely conceal the contempt he felt for them. He warned fellow Conservatives at the outset that he would not be restrained by 'considerations of mere political support', which was interpreted as meaning that he would sacrifice the agricultural interest if necessary. In this way he soon exposed himself to attack by ambitious young Tories such as Benjamin Disraeli who accused Peel of catching the Whigs bathing and running off with their clothes.

In spite of this, Peel's government succeeded in imposing its will on parliament for some years. Under the Whigs, national finances had been in deficit for three years running. Peel decided to tackle this boldly by re-introducing the income tax, previously regarded as a temporary expedient. This was bound to be unpopular, but Peel calculated that if income tax were set at a high enough level it would allow the government to reduce taxes on consumption, thereby reducing the cost of living and stimulating the demand for goods. This thinking led him to review the whole system of tariffs charged on imports. During 1842–3 the duties were cut on no fewer than six hundred types of imported goods. Moreover, the controversial Corn Laws were modified by means of a sliding scale, so that the duty fell as the British domestic price of wheat rose. This represented a drastic cut in the level of duty set in 1828, though it still gave farmers some protection.

As a result of their innovations, by 1844 Peel and his ministers believed that they had solved the economic problem. Income tax was yielding more than expected and the government enjoyed a surplus of 4 million pounds revenue over expenditure. This enabled them to reduce duties still further in 1845; for example, the duty on sugar was cut by 50 per cent. However, in the House of Commons large numbers of Conservative backbenchers had begun to rebel against their government. As the price of wheat fell in 1842 and 1843, angry English farmers held protest meetings to set up Agricultural Protection Societies, especially in the southern and eastern counties where cereal crops were cultivated. Inevitably the MPs began to reflect this anger. They complained that income tax had become a permanent form of taxation and that it was being used as a means of achieving wider social and economic objectives. In effect, by using income tax to allow it to lower consumption taxes, the government was giving precedence to the interests of industry and the towns over agriculture. In this way a deep gulf opened up between Peel's cabinet and their followers.

The claim that Peel had become the champion of the manufacturers lay behind a major revolt over Sir James Graham's Factory Act in 1844. This was designed to exclude all children under nine years from work in factories and to restrict working hours for children to six and a half in order to allow time for them to receive some education. However, Graham's bill left unchanged the existing law limiting the working day for women and for those under eighteen years to twelve hours. For this reason another Conservative, Lord Ashley, proposed to reduce maximum working hours to ten for women and children, which would in effect have given men a ten-hour day too. For the Peelites, however, this was going too far in interfering with the rights of owners to run their businesses profitably; as prosperity had just begun to return to manufacturing it seemed unwise to risk any new setback. In spite of this, nearly one-third of Conservative MPs voted for Ashley's proposal. In fact, since the 1830s a number of Tory radicals had shown active sympathy with the workingmen's Ten Hour Movement. By the 1840s they felt provoked on the one hand by the attacks of the Anti-Corn Law League, and on the other, by the apparent betrayal of agriculture by Peel. Although the Prime Minister forced most of his MPs to support the government over the factory legislation by threatening to resign, he could scarcely hope to run his party in this way for long.

THE ANTI-CORN LAW LEAGUE

Ever since their introduction in 1815 the Corn Laws had attracted bitter criticism. However, it was not until 1838, when the Anti-Corn Law League was founded, that they became the target of an organised campaign. The League's early strength lay in the industrial towns of Lancashire and Yorkshire. Its leaders, Richard Cobden and John Bright, focused on the Corn Laws partly for tactical reasons, for they saw the issue as a means of advancing the general cause of middle-class radicalism. By contrast with the Chartists they concentrated on a single, easily articulated objective; and they confidently expected that success on this narrow front would open the way to further attacks on the privileges of the landed class.

The League's case against the Corn Laws involved four main lines of argument. First, they believed the legislation was a selfish policy designed to advantage a minority of the population at the expense of the majority who were obliged to pay higher prices for food. Secondly, the Corn Laws hampered the development of the economy. Abolition would lower the cost of living and thus reduce the pressure on employers to increase wages and make their products more competitive. Thirdly, the League claimed that the laws were largely ineffective in giving protection to English farmers. And fourthly, they argued that the spread of free trade across the world would enable each country to reap the benefits of economic growth; as a result they would become so dependent on one another for their prosperity that they would be less likely to go to war. This moral line of argument helps to explain why many Nonconformists rallied to the cause and why free trade remained central to popular Liberalism throughout the nineteenth century even when the Corn Laws had long disappeared.

From 1841 onwards the Anti-Corn Law League began to concentrate on direct electoral pressure on the politicians. For example, it ran candidates against the Whigs who failed to support repeal, with a view to splitting their vote. In fact the Whig leaders were by now drifting towards a modification of the Corn Laws, but the League hoped to accelerate this leisurely process. At the 1841 election the repealers scored some direct victories in northern towns, notably Stockport where Cobden was elected. However, as the committed repealers still represented only a minority within the Whig–Liberal ranks in parliament, the League accepted that it would have to fight a lengthy campaign. Its funds were boosted by the economic recovery that began in 1843, so much so that they reached a total of £250,000 for the year 1846. This enabled the League to run an effective modern campaign using large quantities of propaganda and employing lecturers to visit both urban and rural districts. It also tried to exploit the electoral system by creating extra votes for its supporters, which could be done by purchasing property which would entitle the owner to a place on the electoral register.

In spite of these efforts, however, it is by no means clear that the Anti-Corn Law League was primarily responsible for repeal.

Its leaders, who had been preparing for a general election in 1848, were undoubtedly surprised by the turn of events in 1845–6. Though they enjoyed widespread sympathy in parliament they were unlikely to be able to achieve any sweeping conversion in the Whig–Liberal ranks. On the other hand, like many articulate pressure groups they gradually won the argument, and thereby influenced the position taken by the Whig leaders. Lord John Russell began the 1840s committed to lowering the duty on corn and by 1845 he had come out in favour of complete abolition. In short, repeal increasingly seemed inevitable; the only question was which prime minister would risk the controversy that repeal was bound to provoke. Cobden shrewdly judged that Peel was more likely to do so than Russell, despite the party complications, because he was a far more decisive politician.

IRELAND: RELIGION AND THE FAMINE

In the end the problems of Ireland precipitated the economic and political crisis that destroyed both the Corn Laws and the career of Peel. During Melbourne's premiership the campaign for repeal of the Union with England had been suspended, but it was revived when the Conservatives returned to office. During 1842 and 1843 huge outdoor rallies took place throughout the west and south of Ireland. However, many Conservatives argued that O'Connell and his movement should simply be crushed; indeed, by 1843 some 34,000 troops had been stationed in Ireland, meetings had been prohibited and O'Connell arrested.

In spite of this, Peel evidently wished to reduce nationalist fervour by conciliating Irish Catholic opinion. He felt reluctant about maintaining the Anglican Church Establishment and also began to look for ways of helping the poor tenant farmers at the expense of the Protestant landlords. But in this way he played into the hands of Conservative rebels such as Disraeli. At this time religion had become a highly sensitive issue in England. This was partly the result of the launching of the 'Oxford Movement' by the Reverend John Henry Newman in 1833, which provoked an anti-Catholic backlash. Newman's followers, known as Tractarians, argued that there was essentially harmony between the doctrines of the Church of England and those of the Catholic Church, and also that the Anglican Church stood to lose more than it gained by maintaining its formal links with the British state. In 1845 Newman himself became one of the most prominent converts to Catholicism.

However, these developments only made Protestant Conservatives more antagonistic towards Peel's attempts to conciliate Irish Catholics. Though he declined to interfere with the Church Establishment, he recognised the grievances of the Catholic majority, which was denied a fair share of resources for education and the training of clergymen. Thus, in 1845 the government proposed to triple the grant paid to the Catholic seminary at Maynooth, a college established in 1795 and already financed by the state. But in the excited state of Protestant opinion this could not but be controversial. The young W. E. Gladstone immediately resigned from the government over the Maynooth grant and Peel admitted that the issue might well be fatal to his survival. His critics eagerly reminded their colleagues that in 1829 Peel had betrayed the Protestant cause by supporting Catholic Emancipation; in this way the charge of treachery against the prime minister was firmly established. Meanwhile thousands of petitions rained down upon parliament from Anglicans and Nonconformists protesting against the Maynooth grant. Nonconformists simply believed that Church and State should be kept separate, and in 1844 they set up the Church Liberation Society to campaign for complete disestablishment. The Anglicans argued that since Catholics owed their primary allegiance to the Vatican, they were potentially disloyal to the British state and ought not to be given any support; they feared that the small grant to Maynooth might lead to greater endowments for Catholics.

On top of this controversy, Ireland had a further blow to deal to Peel. During 1845 a mysterious disease began to devastate the potato crop, and by October it was clear that a major disaster was inevitable. Half of the crop had been ruined already and much of the remainder was rotting in store. Since the potato had become the staple food item for Irish peasants, many of them now faced starvation. In the event, approximately 1 million died in a population of 8 million, while another million people emigrated; by the 1860s Ireland's population had fallen to around 5 million as families fled to Liverpool, Glasgow and London, and, subsequently, to the United States of America. It was there that the Irish exiles, newly prosperous and more assertive, began to organise nationalist movements such as the Fenian Brotherhood which, by the later 1860s, were ready to instigate a violent campaign against the Union with England.

THE REPEAL OF THE CORN LAWS

The Irish famine certainly appears to have been the immediate cause of the abolition of the Corn Laws in 1846. The Anti-Corn Law League was quick to urge that the only obvious solution to the crisis lay in opening British ports to the free entry of corn. Peel also felt convinced that the famine meant the end of the Corn Laws. He could hardly suspend them temporarily without admitting the League's charge that they kept grain prices artificially high. Nor could he expect taxpayers to pay for costly food to feed the Irish while maintaining protectionism for England. By January 1846 his cabinet had agreed, with only two resignations, to propose to parliament a bill to repeal the Corn Laws.

However, the fact that Peel and his leading ministers, Lord Aberdeen, Sir James Graham and Sidney Herbert, agreed so easily was an indication that they were already convinced of the need for change; the famine simply provided an opportunity to extend the work of Peel's earlier free trade budgets. By 1846 the Corn Laws stood out as the great anomaly in Britain's trading policy.

The third element in the explanation for repeal lies in party politics. Peel had hoped to give his party a little longer to adjust to the need for repeal before fighting the next general election on the issue, thereby depriving the Whigs and Liberals of the popularity that would arise from a policy of 'cheap bread'. In short, another judicious retreat by Conservatives was necessary if they were to outmanoeuvre their opponents. The competitive element was only too clear when the Whig leader, Russell, publicly advocated repeal in December 1845. He, too, was alive to the danger of a split between the landed and the middle classes, and to the electoral implications. Above all, he wished to avoid the impression of being driven into repealing the Corn Laws under pressure from the League, which would be seen as a triumph for middle-class radicals.

Eventually Peel proposed to parliament that the duty on corn should be reduced to a very low level for three years and then abandoned altogether. He had always believed that the duties had been ineffective in giving farmers protection, and, in any case, the best response to foreign competition lay in investment to improve efficiency. However, the agricultural interests disputed these views by pointing out that in the 1840s wheat prices had been on average only half as high as they had been during the Napoleonic wars; moreover, many landowners lacked the capital needed to invest in long-term improvements. Ultimately, the argument was over whether Britain should commit herself irrevocably to becoming an urban, industrial country. The continued growth in the population showed that in the long run Britain would not be able to feed all her people adequately; social and political stability thus dictated that Britain must gain access to the cheapest food supplies available.

In the debates over repeal, as many as 241 of the Conservative MPs voted against the government, which represented 86 per cent of those who sat for county constituencies. Against this the Peelite Conservatives numbered between 112 and 117, so repeal could only be carried by the votes of the Whigs and Liberals. As soon as repeal had been passed the Whigs withdrew their support from Peel and he was then defeated on an Irish bill when 74 Conservatives, determined to have their revenge, rebelled against him. Peel resigned office in June 1846 leaving his party split and demoralised. A new era of Liberal dominance was about to begin.

9

Mid-Victorian Britain: Progress and Prosperity

Defined on one side by the repeal of the Corn Laws (1846) and the collapse of Chartism (1848), and on the other by the Second Reform Act (1867) and the 'Great Depression' of 1873, the mid-Victorian period was an era of unusual economic growth and social stability. While other European states experienced outbreaks of revolution the British people appeared to accept their political system as legitimate and to take satisfaction in their economic achievements.

Yet in some ways this version of events seems implausible, for Britain continued to suffer the enormous strains arising out of uncontrolled industrialisation and urbanisation. British society held the seeds of a revolutionary working-class movement; and yet, contrary to the expectations of Friedrich Engels and Karl Marx, the English revolution failed to materialise. Why was this? Naturally enough contemporary Victorians had their own explanations. The Whig view, as expressed by T. B. Macaulay, the famous historian, held that Britain had already undergone her revolution in the seventeenth century, and achieved an open, liberal, representative system of government. Other mid-Victorians convinced themselves that there was something distinctive in the English national character, perhaps influenced by the climate, that fostered a practical, non-ideological, industrious temperament. A more sophisticated version of this view was articulated by Walter Bagehot in his book *The English Constitution* (1867), in which he argued that the key lay in the *deferential* attitude of the British; on the whole, people accepted the social hierarchy and consented to be governed by their superiors. From a different perspective the Radical Richard Cobden

71

made a similar diagnosis when he complained: 'we are a servile, aristocracy-loving, lord-ridden people'.

However, modern historians have been less convinced by these ideas. Some have simply explained the relative stability in terms of *contingencies*, notably the skill of the ruling class in making timely concessions, as in 1832 and 1846, so as to deflate a threat of revolution. Those who take a more sociological approach to history stress the nature of class relations in Britain. In particular it can be argued that the middle class played a crucial role in maintaining social and political stability by its moral influence on the behaviour of both the workers and the aristocracy; moreover, the middle class was the engine that generated the prosperity of mid-Victorian Britain and thus made possible the complacency and equilibrium of that era. All classes could participate in economic success, but none really dominated. At times the middle and working classes collaborated to push the aristocracy into reform; but when threatened by Chartism the middle class threw its weight behind the traditional elite to defend order and property; at other points landed men joined forces with workingmen to campaign against middle-class interests over factory legislation or the poor law. Although the middle class had been incorporated into the political system, large sections of the bourgeoisie, especially Nonconformists, continued to develop a political alliance with radical workers which was to remain a feature of British politics up to 1914. In this respect Britain differed from many European societies where Liberalism became increasingly conservative. Organised workers in Britain usually espoused radical Liberalism and adopted parliamentary methods; consequently, despite the residence of Marx in London for thirty-five years, revolutionary doctrines occupied only a marginal place in radical politics, and Marx himself remained largely unknown to British workers.

THE MID-VICTORIAN BOOM

The Great Exhibition at the Crystal Palace in London in May 1851 symbolised mid-Victorian economic success. Six million visitors, including Queen Victoria, toured the 14,000 exhibits of machinery, raw materials, manufactured goods and fine arts. The Crystal

Palace itself – virtually a cathedral built of glass and metal 520 metres long and 125 wide – was a manifestation of the industrial age. But behind the patriotic propaganda lay solid achievement and progress. Britain's national income rose from £523 million in 1851 to £916 million in 1871; per capita income stood at £32 in Britain in 1860 by comparison with £21 in France and £13 in Germany; the economy expanded at a rate of around 3 per cent per year on average, which compared favourably with both the preceding decades and the post-1873 period. Textiles, steel, engineering, railways and shipbuilding led the way, but even agriculture enjoyed prosperity in spite of all the warnings of the protectionists. The chief explanation for agricultural success lay in the rising population, which absorbed wheat supplies, kept prices up and thus allowed British farmers to sell in the domestic market. Not until large-scale imports from North America began in the 1870s were the full effects of repealing the Corn Laws to be felt.

However, it is easy to present an unduly optimistic picture. In fact the mid-Victorian economy suffered a succession of slumps, caused by overproduction of goods, which led to falling profits and bankruptcies in 1852, 1857–8, 1862–3 and 1867–9. The early 1860s saw severe hardship in Lancashire when the civil war in America interrupted supplies of raw cotton, which forced many workers into temporary unemployment. By contrast, the years 1853–4, 1864–6 and 1871–5 produced economic booms and rapidly rising money wages, especially for skilled workers who were able to bargain effectively with employers. In the absence of comprehensive statistics about unemployment we have to rely on the information collected by some unions among skilled workers; this shows a range from as low as 2 per cent in the boom years to nearly 12 per cent in 1867.

The other important qualification to make about the boom period is that Britain's balance of trade was less impressive than her manufacturing strength might suggest. Throughout this period Britain's visible imports usually exceeded her exports by about £100 million each year. For example, in 1860–4 imports were £235 million and domestic exports only £138 million. However, the gap was more than covered by re-exports plus income from foreign investments, insurance and shipping. Between 1850 and 1875 Britain's overseas investments rose from £225 million to £1000 million, much of the increase being in the form of railway construction in the United States, South America and India. Thus the strength of the overall

balance of payments lay essentially in *finance* rather than in manufacturing; in an era of free trade this was not a major flaw, but later
in the century it was to become so.

THE RAILWAY AGE

In spite of the emigration of no fewer than 3.7 million people, largely
to America and the British colonies, between 1850 and 1870,
Britain's population grew from 21 million to 26 million. The immediate cause for this lay in the rising birth rate, which ranged from
33.9 births per thousand population to 35.3 during this period.
Increasingly this expanding population concentrated in the towns;
indeed the census of 1851 showed 54 per cent of the British people
living in urban communities for the first time. Above all it was the
spread of railways which accelerated this urbanisation process. With
some 6000 miles of railways in 1850, Britain's network had grown to
13,000 miles by 1871, and the number of passengers carried rose
from 67 million to 322 million. As branch lines were extended, rural
England and even remote parts of Wales and Scotland emerged
from their historic isolation, and young men and women moved to
the towns in search of work in factories or in domestic service.
Parliament promoted this trend in 1844 when it required every
railway line to offer third-class carriages, in which passengers could
travel for only one penny per mile; and during the 1860s cheap fares
for workingmen were widely introduced. As a result, some manual
workers began to move out of the overcrowded districts in central
London to live in suburbs to the north and south-east of the city.
Since the middle classes had already begun to quit the town centres
for the healthier, semi-rural suburbs, a distinctive pattern of settlement now developed. Whole districts became dominated by a single
social class, a trend which eventually contributed to the polarisation
of political representation between capital and labour.

Railways also made an impact upon the leisure activities of the
British people. For example, they enabled middle-class families to
travel long distances to seaside resorts such as Brighton on the south
coast, and later led working-class people to patronise their own
resorts such as Blackpool on the Lancashire coast. Thus there soon
arose a ring of new towns whose existence was solely to serve as

Map 3   The Railway Network in 1850

holiday centres and which depended largely upon railway communications. Railways also improved communications in other ways,
for example, by carrying the post. Founded in 1861, the Post Office
delivered an average of 32 letters a year per head of population by
1871. Telegraphic communications also helped the development of
the national and provincial press in Britain. Many medium-sized
towns supported several newspapers of their own. The local press
helped to foster the civic pride that became so characteristic of mid-
Victorian cities.

It was a point of honour for each town to enjoy its own elected
council and Mayor under the 1835 Municipal Corporations Act; and
middle-class radicals such as Cobden and Bright regarded municipal elections as a step towards the attack on aristocratic power in
national government. Municipal pride expressed itself in fine new
railway stations, public libraries and gardens, even if these were
often financed by individuals. But above all the towns aspired to
build town halls, such as the one at Leeds in Yorkshire, which cost
no less than £122,000 in 1858. Such projects often represented an
attempt to achieve the status of a regional capital, or to prove that
the provinces could equal London in wealth and style. Yet the habit
of copying the styles of classical Rome and Greece, and making
merchants' warehouses resemble Italianate palaces, suggested an
underlying insecurity; aware of their reputation for vulgar material-
ism, the urban bourgeoisie visibly aspired to clothe their smoky
cities in a veneer of culture.

THE TRIUMPH OF THE BOURGEOISIE?

The census suggests that the middle classes comprised about 4 million
people, or roughly one in six, in this period. However, definitions
cannot be precise. In terms of annual income, most middle-class men
earned between £150 and £1000. But the most prosperous bankers
and merchants far exceeded this and were, indeed, richer than many
aristocrats; conversely, many clerks and schoolteachers received
under £100 but still regarded themselves as middle class. Much
insecurity blighted the lives of the Victorian middle classes. Inadequate incomes put the appropriate lifestyle out of reach; business
failure forced some families down the social scale; and male deaths
left thousands of widows struggling against genteel poverty.

The outward manifestations of middle-class status were obvious, however. One attended church or chapel regularly, joined a professional association (such as the British Medical Association, formed in 1856), kept one's wife as a leisured woman, and above all employed at least one servant. Between 1850 and 1871 the number of domestic servants rose from 848,000 to 1,300,000, an indication of growing middle-class prosperity.

It was the professionals and businessmen who imparted a sense of complacency and self-righteousness to Victorian society; for they were convinced that the credit for Britain's success lay largely with them. They felt that they represented the general good, by contrast with those below and above them who formed essentially selfish and sectional interests. This has encouraged some historians to argue that middle-class values and ideas dominated Victorian society. Indeed, the missionary tone of mid-Victorian writing is almost impossible to miss. The most famous example is the work of Samuel Smiles who published *Self Help* (1859), *Character* (1871), *Thrift* (1875) and *Duty* (1880). On the one hand, working men seemed increasingly to reflect middle-class behaviour by joining Friendly Societies and putting money into Post Office Savings accounts. On the other hand, the aristocracy may also have been influenced because in the mid-Victorian period their sons were increasingly educated at public schools alongside the sons of middle-class men in an atmosphere of middle-class piety and self-improvement.

However, many of these claims are exaggerations or misrepresentations. For example, studies of working-class organisations show a capacity for independence and even rejection of middle-class practice and influence. The steady decline in religious attendance by workers is one symptom of this. Nor did the temperance movement have much effect in reducing the attractions of alcoholic drink in any level of society. On the contrary, consumption of alcohol rose, to reach a peak by 1876. The fact is that much of the evidence about middle-class respectability consists of *prescriptive* literature, which is often misleading as a guide to behaviour. This is especially true of the fashionable emphasis on marriage and motherhood as the only possible role for women. Woman was seen as domestic, decorative and retiring, a support for her husband and a civilising influence upon her children. In practice this ideal was frequently not attained because women greatly outnumbered men in the population. Consequently many never married while others became widows early in life and were thus obliged to enter the supposedly male sphere of employment to support themselves. By the later 1850s the dilemmas faced by single women had generated the first organised women's movement. This took the form of a series of pressure groups campaigning for divorce law reform, married women's right to their own property, improved education and the parliamentary vote.

RELIGION: REVIVAL AND DECLINE

In many ways, mid-Victorian Britain appears a deeply Christian society. Certainly visitors from the Continent were impressed by the sight of the gloomy English Sunday when most public activities apart from Christian worship were supposed to close down. Sabbatarians even made some progress towards stopping the consumption of alcoholic drink on Sundays by limiting the opening hours for public houses in 1854 and banning sales entirely in Scotland.

However, laws were only the outward props to a declining religion. The religious census of 1851 revealed that only two out of every five people attended a place of Christian worship on Sundays; this ranged from 44 per cent in rural areas to as low as 25 per cent in London and the eight largest cities. Over the decades the Church of England had failed to follow the working population into the urban districts. As a result, between 1840 and 1876 the Church was obliged to spend huge sums of money on the construction of 1750 new churches in an attempt to recover its following.

Yet the Anglicans' dilemma was complicated by the challenge of other denominations. The 1851 census showed that among church attenders the Church of England attracted 19.7 per cent of the population, the Nonconformist churches 19.4 per cent, and the Roman Catholics 1.4 per cent. In view of their rapid growth the Nonconformists seemed likely to overtake the Anglicans during the second half of the century, though in the event, their membership was reaching a peak. In any case the Nonconformists were scarcely more successful in recruiting the working classes. Wesleyans, Methodists, Congregationalists, Baptists and Unitarians were strongly entrenched in the middle class and, indeed, attracted those who aspired to rise in the social scale; this made them a formidable threat politically and a significant economic pressure group.

The revival of Catholicism also proved a serious distraction for Anglicans. Extensive Irish immigration was the most visible sign of this revival; and it resulted in a major increase in Catholic churches and priests in England. Moreover, a number of prominent Anglicans became converts to the Catholic Church, notably John Henry Newman in 1845 and Henry Manning in 1850, both of whom subsequently became the first English cardinals since the sixteenth century. The fear that a Catholic offensive was underway was strengthened in 1850 when the Pope appointed thirteen new English bishops. Such initiatives attracted fierce criticism from politicians and fuelled anti-Catholic riots, especially in areas such as Lancashire where Irish immigrants were concentrated.

At a more fundamental level, mid-Victorian Christians faced the challenge presented by the publication of Charles Darwin's book *The Origin of Species* in 1859, in which he argued that evolution occurred by a process of natural selection rather than divine intervention. Although such thinking gained acceptance among a minority of educated people, it did not create much alarm. The debate on Darwinism remained largely confined to an elite and made little impact on society in general. However, clerics feared that the debate might accelerate the drift away from the Church if it gained wider currency.

More immediately worrying was the *political* implication of religious allegiance. For example, Conservative Anglicans believed that the radicalism among workingmen was strengthened by their contact with Primitive Methodism. Others feared the newly formed Christian Socialist movement, led by F. D. Maurice, which was an imaginative attempt to take Christianity to the poor. It proved difficult to do this without in the process associating Christianity with the attack upon laissez-faire policies and with the demands of the Chartists. More threatening was the challenge posed by middle-class Nonconformists to the Anglican political elite. In 1844 Edward Miall focused Nonconformist grievances by forming the Church Liberation Society, whose object was to disestablish the Anglican Church. Though a distant goal, disestablishment began to look attainable as the Nonconformists threatened to overtake Anglicans in church attendance and establish themselves within the Liberal Party. As a result, the politics of the last quarter of the century were to be dominated by religious controversies.

WORKING-CLASS RESPECTABILITY

By comparison with the 1820s and 1830s the period between the Great Exhibition and the Second Reform Act appears one of rising living standards for working people. However, the improvement was concentrated in the boom years when skilled men managed to bargain effectively with employers. Inflation reduced their gains, but by the mid-1870s the average worker is estimated to have improved his real wages by around 25 per cent since 1850. Yet the investigations conducted by Henry Mayhew in London during the 1850s revealed that about one in three families lived in poverty. The average figures for wages still concealed huge variations within manual occupations, and wage rates are a misleading type of evidence at a time when many men worked only on an irregular basis. The highest-paid workers, such as watch-makers, engine drivers, tool-makers, printers and iron workers, received 25–35 shillings a week; the middle range, including tailors, textile workers, boot and shoe makers, coal miners and postmen, earned around 20 shillings; and the worst paid, such as agricultural and general labourers, had only 12–15 shillings.

However, the key lay in the changing distribution of men between these occupations. The process of industrialisation stimulated better-paid jobs in iron, shipbuilding and printing, and created new and regularly-paid occupations such as the railways, to which men steadily moved. In this way, even when money wage rates remained unchanged, living standards could rise.

Mid-Victorian observers like Marx and Engels were surprised by the growing prosperity of some workers and by their tendency to emulate aspects of the behaviour of the middle class. Some men achieved social mobility by joining the ranks of clerks, salesmen, draughtsmen and schoolteachers. Other manual workers aspired to become small businessmen by employing labour, or setting up as shopkeepers. Self-help strategies approved of by the middle class included the use of Friendly Societies, which provided cash benefits in return for small weekly subscriptions, and savings accounts in the Post Office, which attracted over a million subscribers between 1861 and 1871. By the 1860s leading politicians such as Gladstone were much impressed by such evidence of thrift and responsibility among workingmen. This helps to explain their willingness to extend the vote and to allow trade unions to acquire legal status.

However, union membership was untypical for workingmen. Only around half a million men, mostly skilled artisans, could afford the fees. The relatively high wages of engineers and carpenters allowed them to make regular subscriptions in return for benefits, including insurance against death, injury and ill-health. This enabled the unions to register under the Friendly Societies Act of 1855, until a legal decision in 1867 disallowed their claim and deprived them of legal status. Though trade unionists represented only a sectional interest, rather than a class one, at this time, it is misleading to describe them as a 'labour aristocracy'. Their self-help strategies were in fact very widely adopted within the working-class community, and aspirations to respectable status seem to have been commonly held; respectability was not achieved simply or even primarily by level of income, but rather by the manner in which family income was spent by wives and mothers. Moreover, skilled workers were not deferential; rather, pride in their achievements led them to seek admission to the political system as voters in 1867 as the middle class had done in 1832.

THE SURVIVAL OF ARISTOCRATIC POWER

The idea that the crises of 1832 and 1846 marked the triumph of the bourgeoisie over the aristocracy is largely a myth. In fact the landed aristocracy retained its wealth, status and power largely intact, at least until the 1880s. This may seem remarkable in view of the small size of the landed class: around 400 peers and 3000 country gentlemen. Yet despite attacks on aristocratic privilege by such radicals as Cobden and Bright, there was, as yet, no general will to abolish the hereditary basis of the House of Lords or to tax landed wealth. It has often been assumed that the upper class in Britain was acceptable because it remained open to entry from below. Yet in fact it was a closed elite in this period. Only three or four new titles were created each year, and these went either to families who already had them or to the landed gentry. The only significant social mobility occurred in marriages between middle-class women and the younger sons of peers, who were usually obliged to seek careers in the law, banking, the army, politics or the Church.

Why did the aristocracy retain its position? Partly because of its huge wealth in agricultural land, mineral royalties, investments in banking and railways, and not least its urban landholdings, whose value was rising fast as towns expanded. Wealth had obvious implications for the political role of the peerage because fighting elections continued to be expensive and no salaries were paid except to ministers. The sons of landed aristocrats enjoyed the advantage of being able to enter the House of Commons at an early stage in life using their family's wealth and local influence. Even after 1832 the electorate was still so small in most constituencies that personal connections determined the outcome both in counties and in the traditional boroughs. This form of influence was not necessarily coercive, for tenant farmers and landowners often shared a common interest in economic questions such as protectionism, and in the defence of the Church. By contrast, businessmen who aspired to a parliamentary career invariably waited until they could pass on the management of their firm to a son. As a result they did not become MPs, until much later in life and were unlikely to be strong candidates for ministerial posts. Consequently, the social composition of parliament showed no significant change during the thirty years following the Great Reform Act. Up to the 1860s a majority of MPs were either landowners or gentlemen of leisure. In the 1841–7 House of Commons, for example, no fewer than 172 sons and 27 grandsons of peers held seats. All cabinets, regardless of party, continued to be dominated by peers; and men such as Gladstone and Peel, who did come from commercial backgrounds, were exceptional at this level. To the frustration of the radicals, the English system still seemed to reflect the deferential attitudes of pre-industrial society.

10

Pax Britannica

The period between the defeat of Napoleon in 1815 and the 1860s represented a golden era for Britain in foreign and imperial affairs. She enjoyed the benefits of expanding trade and was not seriously threatened by hostile powers except at the peripheries of her possessions. Preservation of the status quo seemed to be pre-eminently Britain's object. Although imperial expansion involved numerous minor expeditions and one war with Russia in the 1850s, the British regarded themselves as essentially at peace throughout this period.

In fact, however, even in this happy era Britain suffered from inadequate resources. At either end of Europe stood two superior military powers, France and Russia; and in order to meet their aggression British governments continued to look to the inter-mediate powers – Austria, Prussia and Turkey – with whom Brit-ain's interests were not so obviously in conflict. In the Vienna Settlement of 1815 Britain had obtained certain safeguards designed to limit the French. But France's defeat only left Russia as the most formidable single land power; and British statesmen soon became obsessed with the territorial expansion of the Tsars throughout Asia. Britain's dilemma lay in the inability to bring her naval strength to bear upon what was essentially a land power.

After 1815 Britain rapidly reduced her armed forces, partly for financial reasons and also because a large army was regarded as politically undesirable. As a result, by the mid-Victorian period Britain spent only 2–3 per cent of her gross national product on the armed forces. In the process Wellington's victorious army was dismantled and limited to around 140,000 professional soldiers; these were split into four parts – one retained at home, one in Ireland, one in India and the fourth scattered around the other colonies. By mid-century the army had become seriously deficient in terms of organisation, supply and training; officers obtained their commissions by purchase not by merit, and by the time of the Crimean War in the 1850s many of the senior officers were too elderly to be of much use on active service.

Similarly, the Royal Navy suffered from elderly admirals, untrained crews and obsolescent ships. Whereas in 1813 Britain had ninety ships-of-the-line, by 1817 she had only thirteen in active service, which was dangerously inadequate in view of her vast imperial interests. In spite of some improvements during the 1850s, the British could count themselves fortunate not to have been attacked by a major naval power in this period. Their ships were adequate for use in brief skirmishes with African and Asian territories but little more.

NATIONALISM AND LIBERALISM

After 1815, foreign policy was dominated by Lord Castlereagh and his successor Canning. They sought to contain conflicts in Europe by means of the 'Concert of Europe', that is, periodical consultation between the great powers – Britain, Russia, Austria and Prussia, in addition to France once the Bourbon monarchy had been restored in 1818. Yet in time this system ceased to be viable, largely because Britain did not share the interests of the Continental autocracies in suppressing the series of revolts that occurred in Germany, Spain, Portugal, Italy and Greece. Castlereagh and Canning refused to support requests by Austria and Russia for intervention, often resorting to the claim that it would be difficult to persuade the British public that it was in Britain's interests to do so.

Clearly the pressures of nationalism and liberalism greatly complicated the British strategy. Ideally governments hoped to be able to use Austria, Prussia and Turkey as a counter-weight to France and Russia. In practice, however, this was complicated by the rivalry between Austria and Russia in the German states, and by Britain's reluctance to guarantee the territorial integrity of either Austria or Turkey. Consequently the Congress system gradually collapsed, especially after 1822 when Canning succeeded Castlereagh and Britain's detachment from the eastern autocracies became more marked. The revolt of the Greeks against Turkish rule in 1823 posed an awkward dilemma for the British. Canning felt reluctant to encourage the break-up of Turkey, which could be exploited by the Russians; but on the other hand the views of the British ruling class – thoroughly educated in the culture of classical Greece – dictated a sympathetic policy towards the revolt. In the event, collaboration between Britain and Russia succeeded in forcing the Turks to concede self-government to a Greek state, but only after a major naval battle at Navarino in October 1827.

Similar problems arose from the revolutions that occurred in France, Belgium, Poland, Germany and the Papal States in 1830. Much the most serious for Britain was the attempt by the Belgians to break away from the Netherlands, a state which had been intended by the authors of the Vienna Settlement to prevent French domination of territory from which an invasion of Britain might be launched. Fortunately for Britain, the new French ruler, Louis Philippe, believed that France should avoid antagonising Britain. As a result, the issue was resolved by the creation of a Belgian state, independent of France. By the Treaty of London (1831) all five great powers gave guarantees of the territorial integrity of Belgium.

This proved to be the greatest success for British foreign policy in this period. It was an early sign of the skills of Lord Palmerston, who dominated foreign policy, either as Foreign Secretary or as Prime Minister, during 1830–41, 1846–51, 1855–8 and 1859–65. Unfortunately, Palmerston had a habit of alienating the French, who were, in fact, anxious to maintain British friendship. For example, in 1834 the two countries became entangled in disputes over the civil war in Spain. Palmerston also excluded France from his eastern policy when he signed the Quadruple Alliance with the three eastern powers in 1840, leading to the Straits Convention of 1841, which prohibited passage of the Dardanelles to foreign warships in time of peace. This brought Anglo-French relations to a low point. However, changes in government led to the replacement of Palmerston by the more conciliatory Lord Aberdeen, so that relations improved during the 1840s.

THE EASTERN QUESTION AND THE CRIMEAN WAR

The deficiencies of British foreign policy and the weaknesses of her armed forces were graphically exposed by the Eastern Question.

By common agreement her national interest dictated a pro-Turkish strategy as the best means of excluding Russia from the eastern Mediterranean and safeguarding communications with India. However, since several parts of the sprawling Turkish Empire were in revolt or semi-independent, it was not clear how far Turkish authority should or could be maintained. Moreover, moral considerations also entered into the debate, for many politicians sympathised with the claims of Christian peoples to self-determination from Turkey.

To make things worse there was genuine misunderstanding between Britain and Russia about the Turkish Empire. After discussions with Peel and Aberdeen the Tsar believed that the two powers had reached agreement about a joint partition of Turkey when she finally collapsed. The British, however, seemed to think that this would not occur for a long time and was thus hypothetical, while the Tsar wished to accelerate the process. By 1853 he had begun to demand the imposition of a Russian protectorate over Turkey's Christian subjects, and to this end occupied the provinces of Moldavia and Wallachia. Meanwhile a French fleet was sent to the Aegean and the British Mediterranean Fleet to the Dardanelles. Unfortunately these actions only encouraged the Turks to risk war with Russia. By January 1854, British battleships had entered the Black Sea in support of Turkey, negotiations had broken down and war was declared. This, in fact, proved to be unnecessary as the Russians had already withdrawn from the occupied provinces. But the British and French forces, not knowing what to do, landed on the Crimean peninsula with a view to attacking the Russian naval base at Sebastopol. After several costly battles, peace was made in March 1856. Britain's only obvious gain from the war was a commitment given by the Russians not to maintain warships in the Black Sea. However, this proved to be a temporary advantage, for the promise was renounced in 1870 during the Franco-Prussian War.

This highlights the weakness of Britain's position in spite of her victory. She was too weak to fight Russia by herself in 1854. The 60,000 troops put into the field by Britain were only half as many as the French forces who carried the main burden. In addition, Austria had remained neutral, thus helping to keep Russia isolated. Only in this situation had it been possible for Britain to risk war. Such conditions would not arise again; hence Russia's ability to renounce the Black Sea clauses in 1870 and get away with it.

Nor was Russia's defeat any more than marginal. It failed to deter the Tsar from his expansionist strategy; he simply shifted the emphasis away from Turkey for a time to Central Asia. During the 1860s and 1870s the Russians occupied all the territory to the east of the Caspian Sea, which brought them up to the borders of Afghanistan. This development greatly agitated the British in India, but they were powerless to stop it. Thus the question of Turkey and Britain's communications with the East remained unresolved despite all the blood and money expended on the war in the Crimea.

INDIA AND MID-VICTORIAN IMPERIALISM

The mid-Victorian era was once regarded as an era of anti-imperialism in Britain. This is true only in the sense that most governments resented the costs involved in campaigns to extend British territory. Critics of empire such as Richard Cobden argued that formal political control was both wrong and unnecessary; free trade represented the only advantageous aspect of expansionism. However, the Cobdenites never represented more than an articulate minority. All governments, however reluctantly, intervened with military force to compel Asian and African peoples to engage in trade and to defend British interests. The empire usually expanded when British settlers and traders, who could not be controlled from London, got into difficulties with the local inhabitants and had to be backed up by troops or gunboats. This invariably resulted in informal settlements being turned into official British territories. Thus, the 1840s and 1850s saw Britain taking over New Zealand, Hong Kong, Burma, Sind and the Punjab.

The complications involved in commerce are well illustrated by relations with China and India. The East India Company had long ago discovered that one of the few commodities for which there was a ready demand in China was opium, which it transported from its Indian territories. However, the Chinese authorities pronounced the trade illegal and this led to an 'Opium War' in 1839 when the British representatives resorted to force to support their merchants. This conflict resulted in the cession to Britain of the island of Hong Kong in 1844 and the opening of four 'Treaty Ports' on the Chinese mainland to British trade. Hong Kong proved attractive to British merchants and soon developed into a prosperous colony. This pattern of expansion – through local initiatives rather than through any central strategy – was typical of the British approach to Empire.

In India, imperialism certainly generated its own momentum. Up to the 1850s a succession of Governor-Generals ignored both the home government and the East India Company and engaged in campaigns which led to the seizure of huge territories from the Indian princes. Although the Governor-Generals were frequently recalled by way of punishment, the new territory was invariably retained. Moreover, Palmerston supported the Governor-Generals' expansionism out of fear about a possible threat to India across the north-west frontier. This led Lord Auckland to launch the first invasion of Afghanistan, in 1839, in order to prevent the country falling under Russian influence. Though initially successful, the invading force became trapped in hostile territory and was forced to retreat to British India, suffering horrendous casualties on the way. This disaster led subsequently to more realistic attempts to strengthen the frontier by occupying Sind in 1843 and the Punjab in 1849.

However, the reckless territorial expansion at the expense of the Indian princes, combined with heavy taxation of the land, and social reforms which aroused the fears of many Hindus about their religion, provoked a major internal revolt, known to the British as the 'Indian Mutiny', in 1857. For a time the British completely lost control of the north Indian plain from Delhi to Bihar. Scarcely 40,000 British troops were stationed in the whole of India in 1857, in addition to 240,000 Indian sepoys on whose loyalty the government had relied. In fact most sepoys did remain loyal, and, as a result, the British managed to restore control during 1858. But if rebellion had spread beyond the northern plain the entire Empire might have been lost.

The mutiny was unquestionably a great shock. Its immediate casualty was the East India Company, which was blamed for the revolt. It had long been regarded as an anachronism by free traders, and parliament had abolished its trading monopoly by stages in 1813 and 1833. Its role in India was now taken over by the Crown in the form of a Viceroy in Calcutta and a Secretary of State in London. After 1857 the British began to conciliate the princes and landowners and avoided offending Hindus and Muslims by not imposing western reforms on them. But British control continued to rest on precarious foundations. The number of British troops was increased, but only to 65,000, while the number of Indian soldiers fell to 140,000, a modest army for so large an empire. Moreover, all the troops were paid for out of the Indian revenues even when the soldiers were used to fight campaigns in other parts of the Empire. This underlines the point that the British were never prepared to pay for the costs of their huge and growing imperial territories.

PALMERSTONIAN DIPLOMACY

Throughout this period Palmerston used imperial and foreign issues to strengthen his domestic position, outmanoeuvring his opponents and exploiting popular patriotism by his bold defence of British interests. However, his real achievements in foreign policy were few, especially in Europe where he scarcely understood the changes that were taking place. The revolutions of 1848 and the emergence of new states in Italy and Germany left him an increasingly ineffectual by-stander. After 1848 Palmerston alienated Austria by supporting the Hungarian revolution, despite his recognition that Britain needed Austrian co-operation. Similarly, he antagonised the French and spurned the desire of the Emperor, Louis Napoleon, for co-operation over the Italian Question. Once the Crimean War was over Britain returned to a state of virtual diplomatic isolation.

Her vulnerability was partly obscured by interventionist actions against weak opponents using naval power. For example, in 1850 Palmerston blockaded the Greek coast in the 'Don Pacifico' incident where he claimed compensation for damage suffered by a so-called British national. In 1857 British ships bombarded Chinese forts along the Canton River over the seizure of a merchant ship which, according to Palmerston, was English. After a second expedition in 1860 the Chinese agreed to open more ports to trade, to regulate the opium trade and to allow foreign diplomats into Peking.

But these were cheap and peripheral triumphs. On European issues Palmerston never showed the same resolution. For example, over Italian unification he was trapped between his public support for self-determination and the evident need to maintain Austria as a great power. In the event, France took the initiative by engaging in a war with Austria in 1859 in which Britain watched from the sidelines. Italy's unification went ahead without substantial help from Britain; Austria was weakened, and meanwhile France grew stronger territorially and politically.

The outbreak of civil war in the United States of America further undermined Britain's position during the 1860s. Although the government proclaimed itself neutral, the Northern states regarded this as an unfriendly attitude. Moreover, several warships, built in Britain, were allowed to fall into the hands of the South and caused considerable damage to Northern shipping. As a result, the American government claimed reparations from Britain, which Palmerston simply refused to pay. This created a serious rift in Anglo-American relations, which Gladstone had eventually to repair, expensively, in 1871.

In Europe, Britain's inability to act was repeatedly exposed during the 1860s. Palmerston sympathised with the Polish revolt against Russia in 1863, but could do nothing in the face of Prussian and Russian solidarity; the Continental powers knew quite well he could not afford to risk war. An even more embarrassing situation developed in 1863–4 when the two Duchies of Schleswig and Holstein, that had traditionally been associated with Denmark, were absorbed into the new German Confederation. Palmerston foolishly encouraged the Danes to resist Prussian military might by warning that if the German Confederation resorted to force 'it would not be Denmark alone with which they will have to contend'. But the war went ahead, Bismarck won an easy victory, and Palmerston stood by isolated and impotent. Thus by 1865, when his career ended, his policy was in pieces. The Concert of Europe had collapsed, France had recovered, Prussia had emerged as a formidable military power, and Russia's expansion in Asia was undermining Britain's position. Indeed, the country now stood on the brink of a perilous phase in which she lacked allies, but was threatened by the large conscript armies and the naval rebuilding programmes of the Continental powers.

11

Mid-Victorian Politics, 1846–65

The mid-Victorian era can easily be seen as an interlude of unstable ministries between the more dramatic reform crises of 1832 and 1867. Yet it was also a major formative phase in which important and lasting alignments emerged. The slowness of this evolution may be attributed partly to the unrepresentative nature of the electoral system, partly to the fragmentation of the parties, and partly to clashes of personality.

Unquestionably the split in the Tory Party over the Corn Laws in 1846 set the pattern for the mid-Victorian era. In losing his party's leadership Peel managed to take with him one-third of Conservative MPs including most of the ministers. The 1847 elections returned 336 Whigs and Liberals, 201 protectionist Tories and 117 supporters of Peel. For several years the 'Peelites' occupied an independent position but usually supported Liberal governments in order to keep the protectionists out of office. But Peel's death in 1850 left his followers free to rebuild their careers; among them the most important figure was W. E. Gladstone who eventually joined the Liberal Party.

All this left the Conservatives handicapped by lack of experienced administrators; hence John Stuart Mill's famous description – 'the stupid Party'. In the eyes of the largely middle-class voters they appeared to be dominated by extreme protectionists and ignorant country gentlemen. Not surprisingly, after their victory in 1841 the Conservatives failed to win an election again until 1874. Under Lord Derby and Benjamin Disraeli they were cast as the party of opposition throughout the mid-Victorian era except briefly in 1852, 1858–9 and 1866–7 when the Whig–Liberal government disintegrated.

THE EMERGENCE OF A PARTY SYSTEM

The instability and incoherence of the mid-Victorian House of Commons is underlined by the fact that no fewer than eight administrations held office between 1846 and 1868. Clearly any idea that Britain already enjoyed a strong two-party system is premature. Under Peel's leadership the Tories had begun to develop a national organisation based on the Carlton Club and the national party agent. But this was checked by the split of 1846; and subsequently the national party had little influence with the local constituencies because, as yet, it commanded few resources.

It is worth noting that the term 'Liberal Party' had begun to come into use during the 1830s; and by 1847, 163 MPs described themselves as 'Liberals' rather than Whigs or Radicals. However, the voting behaviour of the MPs reveals an endemic indiscipline. For example, under Lord Melbourne's government in 1835–7 three-quarters of all his 'supporters' actually voted against the government in at least 10 per cent of the divisions and only a fifth consistently backed the Prime Minister. This underlines the diversity of parliamentary Liberalism. Its largest element was the Whigs and moderate Liberals, who represented the traditional social elite; as late as 1859, 54 per cent of Liberal MPs had connections with the peerage, or were sons of baronets and landed gentry, while a further 10 per cent enjoyed private incomes. Only 16 per cent were merchants or manufacturers and 15 per cent lawyers. The radicals, who had comprised as many as 150 MPs in the 1830s, dwindled to half that figure during the 1840s. Characteristically they advocated such reforms as the secret ballot, elementary education, temperance, and taxation of land values. Many radicals were also Nonconformists campaigning to abolish the payment of tithes to the Church, and for disestablishment. The final element in the Liberal alliance was the Irish, a vocal but as yet small minority in the Commons.

During the 1850s and 1860s governments enjoyed surprisingly little control over these groups. This was partly because by the mid-Victorian period central government had lost much of the patronage enjoyed in the eighteenth century. Moreover, Members appreciated that they owed their election more to their own connections and standing than to any central party organisation. Indeed, it was customary for only half of the constituencies to go as far as a ballot at general elections; where the result was obvious, candidates avoided the expense and trouble of a contest. Inevitably this meant that, once elected, many MPs behaved as independents; thus mid-Victorian prime ministers suffered regular defeats in the Commons despite having a large majority. Not only were the Whips unable to keep their majority together, they even failed to persuade Members to attend the House with any regularity; politics for many was no more than a part-time activity, a matter of duty but not a career.

However, by the 1860s this was beginning to change as governments undertook more legislation, lengthened the parliamentary year and insisted on more regular attendance. National party organisation began to emerge, and under Gladstone and Disraeli much clearer lines of party division developed. This gradually killed off the traditional, gentlemanly life of the MP and created a role for the professional politicians who cultivated a popular following and a formal party programme. But as long as only 1.3 million people enjoyed the vote, such a change could only be slow; the expansion of the electorate in 1867 was to accelerate the process.

RUSSELL AND LIBERALISM

From 1846 to 1852 the Liberals held office under Lord John Russell, a Whig of distinctly reformist views. He found himself trapped between his traditionalist, landed parliamentary party and his more radical, urban and Nonconformist followers in the country. By committing themselves to repealing the Corn Laws, Russell's party had, in effect, chosen to give priority to the interests of industry and the towns over land and agriculture. In the long run, free trade was indeed to be a crucial focus for Liberal unity and also to give the party a close association with the success of the British nation. But in the medium term, Liberal governments required more organisation and discipline. Russell largely lacked the skills to build a broadly based political party on the foundations laid in 1846. Though he pleased Liberals by further extensions of free trade, he left the radicals disillusioned by the lack of reform. The Irish were

antagonised by the inadequacy of relief schemes designed to alleviate the famine, and Catholics were alienated by Russell's letter of
November 1850 denouncing the Pope's plan to re-establish the
Catholic hierarchy of bishops in England. After the triumph of
1846, Richard Cobden sought a further extension of the vote,
reform of education, and an attack on the influence and wealth of
the landed class. But in every respect it appeared that Russell's
government was merely attempting to perpetuate the role of the
Whig aristocracy. As a result, by 1851 his effective majority had
disintegrated and he remained in office until 1852 only because
Lord Derby was reluctant to form a minority Tory administration. After Russell's resignation in February 1852 a general election
failed to deliver a clear majority. Consequently the new Conservative government proved unable even to carry its budget and
collapsed within months.

THE ABERDEEN COALITION AND
THE CRIMEAN WAR

The demise of both a Liberal and a Tory government in 1852
accelerated matters by bringing into being a coalition of Whigs,
radicals and Peelites under the ex-Peelite Lord Aberdeen. 'England
does not love coalitions', declared Disraeli; this famous aphorism
was rather misleading. Although Aberdeen's government lasted
for little more than two years, it initiated a new pattern of politics.
As the Peelites and Liberals were already united over the key issue
of free trade and had been co-operating since 1846, the formal
absorption of Peel's followers into the Liberal Party was an entirely
natural development. In particular, the personal distaste felt by
such men as Gladstone for Disraeli blocked any prospect of their
return to the Tories; if they did not join a larger group they would
simply be condemned to a life in opposition.

Russell and the other Whigs resented the concession of six out
of the thirteen cabinet posts to the Peelites, and they regarded the
new coalition as a mere temporary expedient deserving of no
loyalty. This soon became all too clear when a crisis broke over the
Crimean War against Russia in March 1854. The government had
not thought out its policy, nor prepared adequately for the conflict.
As a result, the popularity of the war evaporated when heavy

casualties were reported. The *Times* correspondent W. H. Russell embarrassed the authorities by his despatches describing the insufficiency of medical supplies, tents and clothing for the troops. As a result, Aberdeen had to face a censure motion in parliament in January 1855, which he lost by the remarkable margin of 305 to 148. He resigned at once.

However, this fiasco did not check the emergence of the Victorian Liberal Party; in fact it accelerated its birth. By reducing the prestige of several Peelite ministers the war forced them to accept a more modest role in future Liberal cabinets. Russell's own standing was damaged by his disloyalty in resigning on the day on which the censure motion was announced. He, too, was obliged to accept a lesser place in the next government. Finally, the crisis brought to power Lord Palmerston, who had escaped blame over the war, but enjoyed a popular reputation for his aggressive approach to imperial questions. Consequently Palmerston managed to form a largely Whig–Liberal government which incorporated the key Peelite, Gladstone, who was now finally linked with Liberalism, but omitted Aberdeen and Newcastle. He now enjoyed a strong position if only because there appeared to be no alternative. The Whig aristocrats hoped that a Palmerstonian government would save them from further discredit. The radicals had mixed feelings. Cobden disliked Palmerston's approach to external affairs, but welcomed the collapse of Aberdeen's Crimean policy for it greatly strengthened the pressure for reforms of the civil service and the army. These became part of the agenda of Radicalism until they were implemented by the Gladstone government of 1868–74. In this way the key elements of late-Victorian Liberalism were beginning to crystallise.

PALMERSTON AND THE LIBERAL PARTY

Palmerston dominated two administrations, from 1855 to 1858 and 1859 to 1865, and led the Liberals to victory at the elections of 1857, 1859 and 1865. As a result he has a strong claim to be regarded as the founder of the modern Liberal Party, at least in parliament. Yet up to 1828 he had been a Tory. He moved across to Liberalism initially when he accepted the need for parliamentary reform in 1830, and thus joined Grey's government. Moreover, Palmerston stood for the Canningite tradition in foreign affairs, which held that

Britain should avoid entanglements with reactionary Continental powers and promote 'liberty' abroad. By championing liberty against authoritarian and clerical regimes he put himself in the mainstream of Liberalism, which passionately supported the cause of self-determination for Greeks, Hungarians, Italians and indeed all those subject to the rule of Turkey or Austria. On the other hand, Palmerston was rather selective in his Liberalism. He had little in common with the anti-militarism or the domestic reformism of the Cobdenite radicals. Thus, although he made some efforts to cultivate popular Liberalism by making visits to the provinces, Palmerston's chief contribution to the party lay less in building its programme than in welding it together in parliament. When he suffered a defeat in the House of Commons over the war in China in March 1857 he responded by fighting and winning a general election with a majority of around 85. He achieved this by making an appeal to patriotism, on the one hand, and to the pocket, on the other hand, by reducing income tax. In short, Palmerston appeared to have found the right formula: free trade, low taxation, Empire and patriotism. This reassured the middle-class people who dominated the mid-Victorian electorate, and it left very little room for a distinctive or viable Conservative alternative.

However, one must not exaggerate Palmerston's achievement. In 1858 he suffered another defeat in parliament and stepped aside for another minority Tory government. Significantly the various elements in the Liberal coalition soon reunited, stimulated partly by the Conservatives' attempts to pass a new reform bill and partly by the general election in 1859. This played into Palmerston's hands because it took place at a time when war was breaking out between France and Austria over the question of Italian unification. Palmerston's support for the nationalist cause was well known, whereas the Tories were suspected of pro-Austrian sympathies. Not that Palmerston took any decisive action; it has been well said that the Italian cause did more to promote Liberal unity than the Liberals did to promote Italian unity. None the less, the effect at home was clear. On 6 June the Liberals met at Willis's Tea Rooms to regroup, and went on to vote the Conservatives out office. The attempt by Queen Victoria to impose an alternative prime minister failed. By accepting Palmerston, however reluctantly, she signified the extent to which royal patronage had been eroded by the rise of political parties.

The resulting administration of 1859 to 1865 has been regarded as the first real Liberal government. Disputes did emerge, notably between the Prime Minister and his Chancellor of the Exchequer, Gladstone, who effectively established his radical credentials by attempting to restrain government spending. His budget of 1860 also raised his standing in radical eyes because he abolished the duty on paper, an act which was seen as helping the cheap, radical press; that he achieved this over the opposition of both the peers and the Prime Minister could only enhance Gladstone's reputation and raise expectations for the future.

Meanwhile Palmerston continued to disappoint the radical Liberals by resisting domestic reform. In 1860 he most reluctantly allowed Russell to introduce another parliamentary reform bill, and in 1861 he roundly condemned the demand for financial retrenchment as 'a leap in the dark at the bidding of that political fanatic, Cobden'. Increasingly Palmerston seems out of step with his times. He really had no ambition to create a new Liberal Party, but sought rather to maintain traditional Whig influence by restraining the pressures of radicalism. Thus, during the 1860s radicals and Nonconformists looked increasingly to a further extension of the electorate as the only means of making parliament more responsive to their views and grievances. Gladstone appeared to be the key to this strategy. His visits to provincial towns aroused great popular enthusiasm. In 1864, when receiving a deputation from the London Trades Council, he announced his opinion that many workingmen had shown themselves to be responsible enough to exercise the vote without danger to the state. Though Gladstone was far from supporting universal suffrage, his declaration pushed parliamentary reform to the top of the agenda. When the Liberals won another election under Palmerston's leadership in 1865 it was to Gladstone that most of the radicals now looked to realise their aims. Thus, the sudden death of Palmerston after the election immediately opened up a new and dramatic phase in the evolution of Liberalism as his successors struggled to satisfy their followers by extending the popular vote.

12

The Era of Gladstonian Liberalism, 1865–85

During the 1860s and 1870s British politics polarised around an increasingly radical Liberal Party under Gladstone and a Tory Party which, under Disraeli, began to capture some of the middle-class support once attracted to Palmerston. The main battle lines, on both domestic and foreign policy, drawn in this period were to last through most of the twentieth century when Labour inherited the role of the Liberals.

The immediate trigger for this change was the pressure exerted by small shopkeepers and skilled artisans, still excluded from direct representation in parliament, for the vote – a privilege enjoyed by only one man in five. Since the demise of Chartism, parliamentary reform had ceased to be a central issue; but it continued to unite many middle-class radicals and workingmen. The sharp economic slump of the mid-1860s strengthened their cause by creating wider discontent and bringing larger numbers of people out onto the streets in support of political meetings. On top of this came the sudden death of Palmerston in 1865. As he was succeeded by Lord John Russell as Prime Minister, with Gladstone as Leader of the House, the government was now dominated by two committed parliamentary reformers. Popular expectations were understandably very high.

THE SECOND REFORM ACT

In an effort to appease the radicals without antagonising the Whigs and other anti-reformers, Russell and Gladstone introduced a cautious bill in 1866 which would have added only a few hundred thousand new voters, mostly artisans and shopkeepers who were known to be pro-Liberal. However, this bill perished when some Liberal members voted with the Tories. In this situation Russell and Gladstone resigned office, thus putting a minority Conservative government led by Lord Derby and Disraeli into power. Naturally Gladstone expected this new government to be defeated soon, which would make a fresh election inevitable; he intended to fight that election by asking for a popular mandate on parliamentary reform.

In the event, the election did take place in 1868 following a Conservative defeat, but only *after* a second and successful attempt had been made to pass a reform bill. Derby and Disraeli had three main reasons for attempting what looked impossible. First, another reform bill would keep the Liberals divided and thus maintain the minority Tory government; secondly, a successful bill would help to restore the Tories' reputation as a competent party of government; and thirdly, a Conservative Act would prevent Gladstone re-introducing his bill, which would undoubtedly have damaged the electoral interests of the Tories.

Disraeli's chances were transformed by the realisation that some radical Liberals were willing to support his bill because they appreciated that as a minority leader he was more susceptible to pressure than Gladstone had been; thus Disraeli accepted Radical amendments which made the Second Reform Act far more democratic than either he or, indeed, Gladstone had intended. By giving the vote to householders and lodgers in the borough seats, the bill enfranchised many working men and increased the electorate from 1.3 million in 1866 to 2.45 million in 1869, or around one in three adult males.

Moreover, the Second Reform Act proved to be a significant breakthrough in several different ways. First, and contrary to traditional assumptions, it did little to help the Conservatives *directly*. At the general election of 1868 the new voters gave the Liberals an even bigger majority than usual, and, for a time, Conservatives bitterly condemned Disraeli for his folly in trying to outflank the radicals.

However, in the longer run the reform did help the Conservatives, because the new electorate stimulated the radicals to organise their support and increase the pressure on Liberal parliamentarians for further reforms; this gradually began to alienate some voters, to the benefit of the Tories.

The Act also led to many subsequent changes in the electoral system. For example, when it transpired that many of the new voters were subject to intimidation by employers or bribery by election candidates, Gladstone introduced the secret ballot (1872) and a bill to impose strict limits on expenditure at elections and penalties for corrupt practices (1883). Finally, the reform led to the Third Reform Act in 1885, when the new qualifications were extended to workingmen in the counties, which raised the electorate to 5.7 million. In this way, 1867 greatly accelerated the democratisation of British politics; by the 1890s it had led to the emergence of new parties for labour and to pressure for workingmen to become MPs themselves.

GLADSTONE AND RADICALISM

For two decades after 1867 Gladstone was preoccupied with restraining the expectations of popular Liberalism. This reflected his own underlying Conservatism, but it was also dictated by the need to avoid alienating the Whigs, Anglicans and other propertied interests which still supported the party. At intervals Gladstone attempted to impose discipline on the Liberals by launching major campaigns of his own choosing, usually involving political or moral issues. Under Gladstone the unifying themes of Liberalism were the pursuit of free trade and the development of individual freedom; this latter involved legislation to remove the privileges which prevented individuals gaining the positions to which their abilities entitled them. For example, the army was forced to abandon the practice of selling commissions in the infantry; Oxford and Cambridge Universities were required to open their teaching fellowships to non-Anglicans; and the trade unions received the legal status enjoyed by other organisations.

However, Gladstone's followers, especially the Nonconformists, expected more than this. Indeed, religious controversies dominated much of the political debate of the 1870s and 1880s. This was partly because of Anglican alarm at the resurgence of Catholic influence in Europe generally, and within the Church of England where some 'High Churchmen' were introducing Catholic ritual. The Church also suffered from Nonconformist attacks on the establishment. But although Gladstone responded to this by disestablishing the Church in Ireland, where a majority of the people were Catholics, he declined to go any further for fear of alienating the many English Anglicans who still voted Liberal. He did attempt to satisfy another Nonconformist grievance by means of W. E. Forster's 1870 Elementary Education Act, which set up elected school boards with powers to build new state schools where existing provision was inadequate. However, this proved to be complicated because the Church of England had invested large sums of money in establishing its own schools; Nonconformists greatly resented having to send their children to such schools. Unfortunately the new system provoked both sides, the Nonconformists because it still allowed Anglican schools to be subsidised by state funds, and Anglicans because they claimed the board schools were offering 'godless' education.

Gladstone also managed to antagonise the women's movement which had emerged during the late 1850s and 1860s. It enjoyed support from a number of distinguished Liberals such as John Stuart Mill, and campaigned for the parliamentary and local government vote, greater access to higher education, and reforms in the status of married women to enable them to retain their own income and property. However, Gladstone held to the conventional belief in the 'separate spheres', that is, the view that the two sexes had been designed by God, or by Nature, for different tasks and equipped with different characteristics; women's sphere was the home, marriage and child-rearing, men's was employment, war and politics. Yet to Liberals such as Mill, who had attempted to add a women's enfranchisement amendment to the 1867 reform bill, Gladstone's stubborn opposition to votes for women appeared inconsistent with the much-stated claim that those who paid taxes or rates were morally entitled to be full citizens.

The section of society most contented with Gladstone's policy was the skilled workingmen. They largely credited his influence for winning them the vote in 1867. What seems surprising to later generations is that they supported Gladstone's negative approach to state finance. In fact they had no expectations, at least in the 1860s and 1870s, of the state as a source of welfare. They wanted governments to reduce taxation on consumption, which was largely paid by poorer people, and to maintain free trade, which gave them cheap food. They saw that much of the state's expenditure went for the benefit of the wealthy – the royal family, colonial administration, civil service pensions and so on. Consequently Gladstone's advocacy of financial retrenchment won their enthusiastic support. Towards the end of the century this was to change, but until then hostility towards the state helped to cement the alliance between Liberals and the organised working class.

THE RISE OF NATIONALISM

It was in this period that British politicians had to face the implications of governing a multi-national state comprising England, Wales, Scotland and Ireland. The dominant English invariably took the loyalty of the other countries for granted. Yet there was some reason for this complacency. In Wales, for example, although the people enjoyed their own language and followed the Nonconformist churches, their cultural difference did not generate significant support for political separation. Most of the grievances of the Welsh – over land, religion and education – were common to radicalism in England; as a result, nearly all Welsh constituencies elected Liberal MPs and they operated within the Liberal alliance.

Though lacking a widely spoken language of its own, Scotland enjoyed strong cultural traditions, a different legal system and superior education. However, since the Union with England, the country's industry – especially coal, steel, shipbuilding, textiles and chemicals – had profited from access to the English market; and thousands of Scotsmen moved south to find employment or worked in the Empire as soldiers, traders, doctors, tea planters or administrators. By the 1870s Scotland's grievances were widely seen as best resolved through the Liberal Party, and indeed, several Liberal and Tory prime ministers represented Scottish seats. Thus, with their 72 MPs in parliament and a separate seat in cabinet from 1885 onwards, the Scots, too, were integrated into the British political system. The only qualification to be made to this is that the Irish campaign for a separate parliament eventually stimulated opinion in Scotland. It was not until the 1930s, however, that a Scottish Nationalist Party appeared.

Ireland, on the other hand, cannot be said to have been integrated into the British system. By the 1860s, Irish grievances over rural rents and religion received an important lead from outside by the Fenian Brotherhood, an organisation of Irish emigrants in the United States of America. They resorted to violent methods which provoked repressive measures by the government; hence Gladstone's famous announcement after his election victory in 1868: 'My mission is to pacify Ireland.' He attempted to undermine popular support for terrorism by conciliatory measures including the disestablishment of the Anglican Church in Ireland in 1869 and an Irish Land Act to help tenant farmers in 1870. This failed to work, for at the 1874 election 59 of the Irish constituencies elected members pledged to 'Home Rule' – a restoration of the Irish parliament.

Before long, Ireland had become polarised between the Catholic–Nationalist majority and the minority of Protestant Unionists in the north-east. While the Home Rule MPs obstructed the government's legislation in parliament, a campaign of violence and intimidation was waged in the Irish countryside by Michael Davitt's Land League. It encouraged tenants to withhold rent, attacked landlords and their property, and in 1882 was responsible for the assassination of the Chief Secretary for Ireland. Despite this, Gladstone persisted with conciliation; his 1881 Land Act created tribunals which reduced the rents charged to farmers. But the Home Rule Party continued to gain strength. After the electoral reforms of 1885 they won between 81 and 85 of the 103 Irish seats and, as a result, they held the balance of power in the House of Commons in 1885, 1892 and 1910. By 1885 Gladstone had gone as far as he could go without actually conceding Home Rule.

DISRAELI AND THE CONSERVATIVE REVIVAL

Though heavily defeated in 1868, Disraeli hung on just long enough to win real power for the first time in his long career at the 1874 election, when 356 Tories were elected against 245 Liberals. In retrospect Disraeli has been credited with ending his party's long period in the wilderness and, in effect, with founding the modern Conservative Party; the risky concession of votes to workingmen in 1867 looks like a far-sighted attempt to recover popular Tory traditions.

However, in many ways this is a romanticised version of events. In 1874 the Conservatives largely reaped the benefits of the Liberals' radicalism, which antagonised vested interests. Anglicans feared an extension of disestablishment and saw educational reform as an attack on religious education. Licensing reforms offended both the brewers and the drinking public. Whigs and landowners became alarmed at infringements of private property rights. Above all, the Liberals were damaged by their association with the Irish, especially in areas such as Lancashire where Irish immigrants were resented as competitors for scarce jobs and housing. These negative reactions to innovation crystallised the characteristic Conservative philosophy of the next century; opposition to central government interference, regulation and bureaucracy were its key features.

But what contribution did Disraeli make to the revival of Conservatism? His 1874–80 government certainly enacted a remarkable series of social reforms including housing, public health, food adulteration, education and trade unions. Here was at least some basis for the 'One Nation' school of Conservatism that Disraeli had preached in his youth; the reforms gave some substance to the view that the ruling class must do its duty towards the working classes. However, the reforms had little political significance. They were not Disraeli's own ideas, but rather the result of proposals by civil servants to extend legislation previously passed by Liberal Governments. Above all, the reforms do not appear to have been very popular with workers at the 1880 election; and after Disraeli's death in 1881, Tory governments did their best to avoid such innovations.

On the other hand, Disraeli left a lasting mark in external affairs. In the early 1870s he had begun to attack Gladstone for attempting to break up the Empire by withdrawing troops from some of the colonies. As Prime Minister he allowed British representatives in India and Cape Colony to become embroiled in wars in Afghanistan and Zululand, He also dramatised imperialism by making Queen Victoria the 'Empress of India' in 1876. During the Russo-Turkish war in 1877 he nearly embarked upon a conflict with Russia, but emerged, rather fortunately, from the Congress of Berlin (1878) with a triumph; the Russians disgorged most of their territorial gains and Britain received the island of Cyprus, which Disraeli mistakenly described as the 'key to the Mediterranean'. Since all these policies aroused controversy, Disraeli seized the opportunity to appropriate the appeal of patriotism, once associated with

Palmerston, for the Conservatives. Thereafter his party's favourite tactics were to condemn its Liberal and Labour opponents for disloyalty to Queen, Empire and the national cause.

THE CHALLENGE OF CHAMBERLAIN

In the aftermath of the Liberal defeat in 1874, many provincial radicals and Nonconformists considered forming a new party, but it still seemed wiser to work through the Liberal Party even under Gladstone's leadership. Their most original and dynamic leader was the former Mayor of Birmingham, Joseph Chamberlain, who formed the National Liberal Federation in 1877 as a kind of parliament representing local Liberal activists. In effect, the meetings of the NLF marked the start of modern party conferences, and, by voting for detailed programmes of legislation, they increased the pressure on the parliamentary leaders.

Naturally Gladstone disliked many of the Chamberlainite reforms, and in general regarded its new organisations in the country as a threat to his leadership. The greater the NLF's influence over Liberal candidates, the more the Whigs would be squeezed out and the less would be the need for Gladstone's role as a mediator. But instead of opposing Chamberlain and the NLF outright, he used his considerable influence to try to take over the leadership of provincial radicalism. His opportunity came in the form of a campaign against Disraeli's pro-Turkish policy during 1877–8. This certainly enabled Gladstone to capture the enthusiasm of rank-and-file Liberals by appealing to their moral–religious–racial sentiments. 'The Turks are, upon the whole, the one great anti-human species of humanity', he declared in one of his many speeches on the Eastern Question. The campaign culminated in his own triumphant election for the Scottish seat of Midlothian at the 1880 general election when 353 Liberals were returned against 238 Tories and 61 Home Rulers.

Was this, however, a victory for Gladstone or for Chamberlain? Subsequently the Prime Minister ignored the NLF's domestic agenda and became absorbed in reversing Disraeli's policies in Afghanistan and South Africa. In 1882 he became involved in the occupation of Egypt, while in the House of Commons business was largely disrupted by the Irish members. The only measure they supported was the 1881 Land Act, which provoked some of the Whig aristocrats to leave the party. Thus Gladstone seemed to disappoint all sections of Liberalism. In order to appease the radicals he introduced the Third Reform Act in 1884, increasing the number of voters from 3.1 million to 5.7 million, which represented around six adult males out of every ten.

Yet this reform helped to precipitate a further challenge by Chamberlain who was, by now, thoroughly frustrated by Gladstone's negative approach. He left the government to campaign for his 'Unauthorised Programme'. Using extreme language to attack landowners as idle parasites living off the labour of others, Chamberlain advocated graduated taxation of incomes, smallholdings for landless labourers, elected county councils, free education, and the disestablishment of the Church. Although ostensibly directed at the Tories, this campaign's real target was Gladstone, for Chamberlain hoped that many Whigs would be replaced by radical Liberals elected by the newly enfranchised voters. In November 1885 the Liberals did indeed gain seats as a result of the support of the new county voters, but they also lost urban seats to the Conservatives. This left Gladstone with a majority of 86 which was cancelled by the 86 Irish Home Rule members. Thus, while much of Chamberlain's programme was supported by Liberal MPs, he lacked sufficient strength to be able to displace Gladstone from the leadership. Consequently, by 1886 he was on the verge of leaving the party altogether. The opportunity to do so came with the reappearance of Irish Home Rule.

13

The Age of Conservatism, 1886–1905

The crisis of 1886 marked a decisive turning-point in British domestic history. Until that time, politics continued to be dominated by the combination of Whigs, Liberals and radicals that had emerged in the mid-Victorian reform period; the agenda was peace, retrenchment and reform. But for the next twenty years Britain was usually led by Lord Salisbury, an arch-opponent of reform in 1866, whose party won victories at the elections of 1886, 1895 and 1900. Salisbury had the good fortune to succeed Disraeli at a time when the middle classes, as well as Whig aristocrats, were anxious to join the Conservatives in a common defence of property and other institutions from the perceived threat of radicalism, Irish nationalism and socialism. During the late 1880s and 1890s a broad change in the political climate occurred. Many of the radical movements of the 1860s and 1870s had begun to lose momentum, funds and membership. Nonconformists, for example, had by now satisfied many of their grievances; and the wealthier Methodists, now happily within the political system, felt more inclined to behave as middle-class Anglicans by voting Conservative. In addition, the growing sense of external threats in the form of colonial rivalry, the naval race, and fear of an invasion from the Continent, created a more nationalistic mood which helped the Conservatives by pushing domestic issues off the agenda.

THE HOME RULE CRISIS

Unquestionably the chief formative event of this period was the political crisis which resulted from Gladstone's decision to adopt

Home Rule for Ireland in January 1886. Backed by the Irish MPs, Gladstone hurriedly drafted a bill to establish a parliament in Dublin. This was an intelligent attempt to satisfy Irish aspirations *and* to maintain the Union with England; for the London government would have retained control of defence, foreign policy and communications. However, opponents of Home Rule claimed that it would be a step towards a total separation between the two countries, and would weaken Britain's strategic position.

A revolt by 93 Liberals defeated Gladstone's bill. Led by Lord Hartington and Joseph Chamberlain – an ill-assorted coalition of Whigs and radicals – the rebels withdrew to form the Liberal Unionists. The schism reflected not simply disagreement over Ireland, but their wider intention of forcing Gladstone to relinquish his grip on the Liberal leadership. Most of the rebels were Whigs already alienated by the growing radicalism of the Liberal Party; Home Rule only accelerated their drift towards Conservatism. Chamberlain expected his exclusion to be temporary; he intended to return to his old party once Gladstone had retired. In fact Gladstone refused to retire until 1894, and by that time Chamberlain was becoming absorbed into what was now known as the Conservative and Unionist Party.

Although the split left the Liberals a smaller and less wealthy party, it also made them a more coherent and radical one. The provincial members and National Liberal Federation remained loyal to Gladstone. This meant that future Liberal governments were more representative of the rank and file; and, ironically, if Chamberlain had stayed he would have found the Party far more amenable to his political programme. He, however, insisted with some reason that Home Rule was folly for the voters would never support it.

POPULAR CONSERVATISM

No one was more surprised at the electoral success of late-Victorian Conservatives than their own leaders; after losing every election between 1841 and 1874 they now enjoyed years of power at a time when the electorate had been expanded by the addition of several million working-class voters. Traditionally historians explained this in terms of the Conservatives' ability to adapt their organisation and their policy. However, such a view tends to exaggerate the progressive aspects of Disraeli and his impact on the party. In fact Disraeli had no desire to democratise the party or to develop the central bureaucracy that a social welfare programme required. He wished to join the traditional ruling elite not undermine it.

What the Tory leaders discovered was that in order to compete with the Liberals it was by no means necessary to outflank them with political or social innovations; for, as yet, no great demand for state interventionism had arisen amongst the working-class voters. This suited Conservatives such as Lord Salisbury, who regarded all government as a necessary evil and democracy as a threat to private property. Influenced by the young aristocrat, Lord Randolph Churchill, he realised that much could be gained by simply defending traditional causes: the Union with Ireland, the monarchy, the Empire, the Church of England, religious education and private property. If combined with low taxation and financial retrenchment, this programme could reassure middle-class voters alarmed by Gladstone's apparent drift to the left.

What is less obvious is why some working-class voters should have supported a traditional, landed party so strongly, especially in the East End of London, Lancashire and Birmingham. In areas which attracted immigrants – such as the Jews in London and the Irish in Lancashire and Glasgow – workingmen sometimes reacted to the extra competition for employment and housing and blamed the Liberals for allowing free entry of impoverished people. Others were simply influenced by employers or landlords into backing the Conservatives. Many were caught up, if only temporarily, in the enthusiasm for Empire and monarchy, or hostility towards foreigners, which the Conservatives cultivated assiduously. Finally, Tory anti-interventionism proved popular especially with those who felt themselves to be the targets of Liberal temperance reformers.

Yet the Tory leaders saw that the additional working-class and middle-class voters could threaten their control of the party's policy and organisation. This explains why they maintained an official organisation – the Nations Union of Conservative Associations – firmly under their control, but also endorsed a separate organisation, the Primrose League (1883), as a means of mobilising mass support. With a million members by 1890 the Primrose League was Britain's largest political organisation. This was achieved by offering very low subscriptions and by offering *social* activities in combination with political propaganda: musical entertainments, teas, summer fêtes, excursions by train, and sports. Women, who comprised half the members, played a crucial role in these activities and gave the Conservatives a body of volunteers to run elections and maintain local organisation in between elections when interest in politics lapsed. This was a demonstration of how a traditional parliamentary party could, up to a point, develop into a party of social integration without losing sight of its fundamental goals.

GLADSTONE AND THE NEW 'LIBERALISM'

Despite the handicap of Home Rule, the Liberals managed to win a small majority at the election of 1892 with the support of the 85 Irish members. Gladstone chose to interpret this as a victory for Home Rule, but when his second bill was rejected in the House of Lords by a margin of 400 to 41 votes he faced a real dilemma. Salisbury argued that the role of the peers was to ensure that no government could pass legislation for which it had not obtained a mandate. This suffered from the obvious objection that the Lords never exercised their veto unless a Liberal government was in office. But could the Liberals risk challenging the peers by holding another election specifically on the question of Home Rule? Gladstone wished to do so, but his colleagues insisted that they had been elected on other policies and must therefore proceed to enact their reforms. Herein lay the Liberals' dilemma right up to 1910. They lacked a sufficiently popular issue with which to challenge the peers and curtail their powers.

This issue was symptomatic of the underlying problem facing Liberalism. Its old agenda – free trade, parliamentary reform and Nonconformist grievances – was either substantially accomplished or insufficiently popular in the country. Because the supporters of the traditional causes were now entrenched in the National Liberal Federation and the constituency parties, the Party failed to mobilise enough working-class support or to nominate working-class candidates for parliament; in the 1890s Ramsay MacDonald, Keir Hardie and Arthur Henderson, the future leaders of an independent Labour Party, tried unsuccessfully to become Liberal MPs.

Yet a new agenda *was* being born during the 1890s. Influenced both by the studies of urban poverty and by the poor performance of industry, many middle-class Liberals began to re-think their

political creed. For them the defence of individual liberty by establishing political, legal and religious rights now seemed inadequate;
liberty meant little if material conditions trapped the individual in
poverty. Thus the 'New Liberalism', as it became known, added
a social and economic dimension to the traditional creed. New
Liberals embraced the idea of state intervention in social welfare
and accepted that this meant extending national taxation. This was
not entirely novel, for radicals had been urging the taxation of
landed wealth for the benefit of the community for decades. But by
the 1890s they argued that government should move the burden of
taxation away from indirect taxes on consumption, which were paid
largely by the poor, to direct taxes on income and wealth.

Younger intellectuals such as J. A. Hobson, L. T. Hobhouse and
Herbert Samuel were the characteristic apostles of the New Liberalism. Not until after 1906 did their ideas become influential with a
Liberal government. But an important indication of the new thinking came in Sir William Harcourt's 1894 budget, which included a
scheme for death duties payable on estates of £500 at 1 per cent and
rising to 8 per cent on estates of £1 million. Significantly this was the
issue that finally drove Gladstone into retirement from politics.
Although his departure left a gap in the leadership which no one
filled adequately for several years, his party had now begun to
define the agenda of twentieth-century British politics.

SALISBURY AND THE CONSERVATIVE DILEMMA

The twenty-year dominance of the Conservatives up to 1905 was less
secure than it appears; though they won elections in 1886, 1895 and
1900, the Liberals proved they were capable of staging a comeback
in 1892. The key factor in the Tory success lay in their alliance with
the Liberal Unionists, which brought middle-class votes, especially
in Scotland and the Midlands, and effectively created a defensive
union of property owners. However, since Salisbury constantly
feared a drift back to Gladstone by the more radical Liberal Unionists, he felt obliged to make some concessions to Chamberlain. The
creation of elected county councils in 1888 and the introduction of
free elementary education in 1891 were part of this strategy.

Above all, state intervention seemed impossible to avoid in
Ireland if the Union was to be maintained. Now that 85 of the 103

Irish constituencies returned members committed to Home Rule, the Tories were in a weak position morally. It was not enough for the Chief Secretary, Arthur Balfour, to suppress agitation by force; he sought, just as Gladstone had done previously, to remove the economic grievances of the people. To this end the state bought the estates of many of the Anglo-Irish landlords and resold them as small farms to tenants. In this way a society of small proprietors was created in twentieth-century Ireland; but the social conservatism of rural Ireland in no way weakened the political hold of nationalism. As the Anglo-Irish landed class withdrew, support for the Union became narrowly concentrated in the Protestant north-east; but the Home Rule MPs held their seats, waiting for the time when they would again hold the balance of power in the House of Commons.

In England Salisbury managed to avoid the expensive interventionism that he had adopted in Ireland. Even the entry of Chamberlain into his cabinet in 1895 had little impact on the Prime Minister's policy, which was to keep taxation low and avoid legislation as far as possible. However, Salisbury found himself increasingly struggling against the tide. During the 1890s, unemployment and poverty undermined confidence in the economic system; and royal commissions on housing and the elderly fostered demands for new government spending. Yet Salisbury believed that expenditure was already getting out of control, especially among local authorities, whose expenditure rose from £36 million in 1880 to £108 million by 1905. This pushed up local rates, thereby creating pressure on national government to relieve the burden by making more generous grants to local authorities. In 1902 local school boards were abolished, partly as a way of checking their spending; but even under county councils, education costs continued to rise.

In fact, state expenditure was by now on a long-term upward trend which no one could stop; from £93 million in 1870 it increased to £281 million by 1900. This involved a major growth in the number of state employees (civil service, local government, the armed forces) from 250,000 in 1851 to 550,000 in 1891 and to 960,000 in 1901. For several years the Chancellor of the Exchequer, Sir Michael Hicks-Beach, coped because trade and the death duties yielded extra revenue. But the demands of naval rebuilding and colonial campaigns upset the balance of revenue and expenditure. The outbreak of the Boer War in 1899 created a huge deficit which compelled the Chancellor to increase income tax and place special duties on such items as coal and imported grain. By 1901 Chamberlain had reached the conclusion that traditional Victorian finance had ceased to be viable. To remedy this he declared in favour of abandoning free trade in favour of tariffs in 1903. In Chamberlain's view tariffs would generate the extra revenue needed to finance social reform. Thus, by 1902, when Salisbury retired, the Conservatives were on the brink of a bitter internal split. Despite his political success, Salisbury had become out of touch with the social and political problems of British society; and his negative creed seemed dangerously obsolete to many in his own party.

14

British Society in Decline, 1873–1902

If the 1850s and 1860s may be regarded as the hey-day of Victorian Britain, then the 1870s mark the beginning of decline. Certainly, many contemporaries thought so. For it was in this decade that Britain's manufacturing superiority began to be undermined by American and German competition. Externally, Britain's position also appeared to be undermined by the Franco-Prussian War, which alerted the country to its vulnerability to the mass-conscript armies created by the European powers; this gave rise to a tradition of literature based on the fear that an invasion of southern England had become a real possibility. Britain's unpreparedness seemed all the more serious as revelations about the physical degeneracy of her urban male population appeared from the late 1880s onwards. Thus, when Queen Victoria's diamond jubilee was celebrated in 1897 the pomp and splendour barely concealed the underlying anxieties. The humiliations suffered by the army in the South African War after 1899 blighted the end of the century, and were widely interpreted as proof of the fashionable Darwinian notion that only those nations which struggled to adapt would survive. The British began to remind themselves that all great empires had succumbed to external pressure after a period of internal decay; by 1900 Britain appeared to have reached that stage.

THE ECONOMIC DEPRESSION

The 1870s and 1880s rang to the complaints of farmers and businessmen suffering from reduced profit margins, or even bankruptcy, as a result of the prolonged fall in prices. This gave rise to the idea that Britain experienced a 'Great Depression' from the early 1870s to the late 1890s. In many ways this was a considerable exaggeration, for the output of the economy grew by around 50 per cent in this period. It is true that Britain suffered a substantial and growing deficit on her visible trade, but this was not a new development. In 1900 for example, she imported £523 million of goods and exported £354 million. However, her surplus of £109 million from shipping and insurance, and £103 million earnings from foreign investments, left her with an overall balance of payments surplus of £33 million.

On the other hand there is evidence that Britain's economy had by now passed its peak. The rate of growth was slower than in the mid-Victorian era, and, more alarmingly, it was inferior to that of Germany and the USA. Thus, Britain's share of world output of manufactured goods fell from 22.9 per cent in 1880 to 18.5 per cent in 1900; in the same period the American share rose from 14.7 per cent to 23.6 per cent, and Germany's from 8.5 per cent to 13.2 per cent. Britain was inexorably being overtaken.

In fact, however, the traditional industries – cotton, coal, steel, shipbuilding – continued to make large profits, though their productivity fell significantly. The real problem lay in the concentration of the economy in a narrow range of industries that had been the base for the earlier industrial revolution. In 1870, for example, cotton and metal goods together generated no less than 70 per cent of all export earnings. Where the economy failed in the late nineteenth century was in exploiting the fast-growing industries on which the *next* stage of industrialisation was to be based: chemicals, motor cars, machine tools and electricity. All too often, British companies produced a wide range of these products but only in relatively small quantities; they thereby failed to gain the economies of scale and were less price-competitive than foreign producers.

Contemporaries found it tempting to identify scapegoats for Britain's loss of competitiveness. Farmers blamed outbreaks of disease and exceptionally bad weather. Some manufacturers complained that their rivals gained an unfair advantage by raising tariffs to protect their markets against British imports while dumping their own goods at below cost price in Britain. A famous book by E. E. Williams, *Made in Germany* (1896), reflected this widely felt grievance.

Yet the undoubted rise of protectionism across the world was only a marginal factor, at most, in the loss of British markets. No British government was, as yet, prepared to abandon the free trade system. Indeed, there were several compelling reasons for refusing to do so. First, the fast-growing population depended for its standard of living on importing the cheapest food available, and manufacturers knew that if food became dearer the pressure to raise wages would inevitably grow. Secondly, Britain gained great advantage from free trade because by maximising the level of *world* trade she boosted her earnings from finance, shipping and insurance; moreover, her purchases of food and raw materials from the less developed countries gave them the resources with which to buy her manufactured goods.

However, there is a case for saying that Britain cultivated the world economy at the expense of her own. Between the 1870s and 1914 she invested only 5 to 7 per cent of her gross national product at home, compared with around 12 per cent invested at home by Germany and the USA. The banks showed much less interest in providing investment for manufacturing industry in Britain than elsewhere. Yet the huge increase in overseas investment – from £1200 in 1870 to £4000 million by 1914 – showed the potential. Had this been diverted into the domestic economy, the technological innovation resulting from it would inevitably have raised the productivity of manufacturing industry significantly. Yet there was no institutional means of accomplishing this; and national policy remained in the hands of the Bank of England whose priority was the role of sterling and international finance, not manufacuring industry.

THE ENTERPRISE CULTURE

Historians have become increasingly attracted by the idea that Britain's economic performance in the late-Victorian era, and indeed in the twentieth century, reflected a decline in the skill and drive of her businessmen, and a general failure of British culture. It seems unlikely, in some ways, that in the first industrial nation entrepreneurial values and attitudes did not dominate society. However, we have already noticed that the middle class failed to impose its thinking on mid-Victorian society as fully as the prescriptive literature might suggest. Moreover, by the 1880s the middle classes were devoting less effort to influencing the upper class and more to joining with them. One expression of this was the expansion of the public schools, which were in fact private, fee-paying schools, where middle-class boys were educated alongside young aristocrats and aspiring to careers associated with the landed, rather than the manufacturing, class. Businessmen also showed a growing tendency to move away from their industrial base, to buy land and country houses and to pursue careers in politics. Certainly the honours system opened its doors to the bourgeoisie in this period. Hundreds of knighthoods were bestowed upon middle-class men, often in return for political services or financial contributions, and by 1900 four out of every ten new peerages were awarded to businessmen or professionals.

Such behaviour suggests that the middle classes were keen to emulate the lifestyle of their social superiors rather than to maximise success in business. It has been argued that amongst second- and third-generation businessmen this had serious implications for the economy. If success in manufacturing was not the chief goal but merely a means to helping one's family to rise in the social scale, then it is not surprising that late-Victorian entrepreneurs often failed to seize the opportunities for innovation and investment that were open to them.

However, this explanation for economic decline represents a considerable over-simplification. It assumes that the evidence about entrepreneurs points only to deterioration. In fact many highly successful businesses emerged in this period, notably in the manufacture of soap (William Lever), chemicals (John Brunner and Alfred Mond) and bicycles (Raleigh), in addition to the new chains of grocery shops (Thomas Lipton) and mass-market newspapers (Alfred Harmsworth of the *Daily Mail*). Also, the interpretation of the evidence about social climbing is problematical. Businessmen who became MPs or peers often continued to be successful entrepreneurs. Purchases of land and country houses represented an indulgence rather than a major diversion in their lives. Only a small minority of the sons of the middle classes went to public schools at this time, and those who did seem to have come from the professional rather than the business middle class.

POVERTY AND POPULATION

As early as the 1850s Victorian society had been startled by revelations about the extent of urban poverty, especially in London. But at that time it was widely expected that the continued spread of manufacturing industry would generate employment for all those who were able and willing to work. However, by the 1880s such optimism no longer seemed justified; industry had failed to absorb the workforce even though thousands of men emigrated every year. Traditionally poverty was handled in three ways: by charity, by self-help in the form of Friendly Societies, and by the poor law system. All three were increasingly regarded as inadequate by the end of the century.

According to the figures supplied by the poor law guardians, only 2 to 3 per cent of the population received assistance by the 1880s. This meant that many who suffered hardship refused to apply to the guardians because of the humiliating conditions likely to be experienced in the workhouse. Husbands and wives could be separated, uniforms had to be worn; and the elderly especially feared death in the workhouse, which meant the shame of being buried as a pauper. During the 1890s the role of the poor law system was severely discredited by the studies of urban poverty conducted by Charles Booth in London and B. S. Rowntree in York. Both agreed that 28–30 per cent of the population actually suffered from poverty, and Rowntree defined, in terms of weekly income, at what point a family fell into poverty. More fundamentally Booth and Rowntree challenged traditional assumptions about the causes of poverty; rather than blaming the moral failings of individuals they suggested that poverty often resulted from circumstances beyond the individual's control such as old age, casual or irregular labour, and cyclical unemployment.

As a result, the question of poverty and unemployment became a matter of concern amongst the educated middle classes. A generation of students including the architect of the welfare state, William Beveridge, devoted time to working with the poor in the East End of London and conducting academic surveys of working conditions. Some fresh ideas emerged from this activity, for example, the introduction of old age pensions, the provision of public-works schemes by local authorities, the feeding of schoolchildren, and the creation of a ministry in central government to be responsible for providing either work or benefits for the unemployed. Sidney and Beatrice Webb wished to break up the poor law system entirely and redistribute its functions to national government or to county councils.

Although politicians in London did little before 1900 to implement these ideas, they undoubtedly took alarm, partly because they feared that urban poverty would create fertile conditions for the spread of socialism. More fundamentally, they accepted that in the long run Britain was unlikely to be capable of maintaining her great Empire, her armed forces and her domestic industry on the basis of an impoverished and degenerate population. This focused attention increasingly upon the size and the quality of the British population. Although large-scale emigration to the colonies could be regarded as a source of strength to Britain, it had the effect of unbalancing the domestic population by leaving women in the majority. This meant that by 1871, for example, nearly three hundred out of every one thousand women in the 25–35 age group were unmarried. In fact the proportion of women who married fell slightly up to 1914.

Yet by the late 1870s the census of population had begun to reveal something even more worrying to the politicians. The birth rate, which had been at 34 per thousand people, began to fall to 28 by the turn of the century, and continued downwards to 1914. It was clear from the census returns that certain middle-class occupational groups were deliberately choosing to restrict family size. This may have been partly a response to the growing costs of rearing and educating children; it may also have been a reaction on the part of women to the physical dangers of childbirth; many died giving birth and many more ruined their health by repeated pregnancies.

The trend towards smaller families carried two distinct problems in the view of contemporaries. First was the fear that it might spread to the working classes, who were largely ignorant of the methods of birth control. If this eventually reduced the size of the British population it would undermine Britain's entire role as a great imperial power. Second was the fear that if the *middle classes* alone continued to have fewer children this would have the effect of reducing the intelligent and enterprising section of the population. This stimulated a fashionable interest in eugenics – the idea of improving the national stock by breeding from the best elements, and preventing reproduction amongst the physically unfit and mentally backward. Though not widely supported in the country, the eugenics movement was very influential amongst the political and intellectual elite around the turn of the century and is one of the most telling symptoms of the loss of national confidence which was so typical of the whole pre-1914 period.

NATIONAL DECADENCE AND NATIONAL EFFICIENCY

All these concerns about Britain's economy, population and Empire were crystallised by the outbreak of the war in South Africa in 1899. This had the effect of creating a mood of deep pessimism and exposing all Britain's institutions to critical scrutiny. It is not hard to see why. The start of the war revealed Britain's inability to defend her Empire competently. She had only 14,000 troops in South Africa and struggled to raise the 300,000 eventually required. During the first year, defeat followed defeat and the questions began to be asked: could Britain possibly have coped with a second colonial conflict; and how would she fare against a major European opponent?

These doubts were eloquently voiced by Rudyard Kipling in a poem called *The Islanders* in 1902, in which he suggested that the British were becoming a nation of effete spectators. Some confirmation of this appeared to come from the military authorities in 1902 when they revealed that six out of every ten men who had volunteered to fight in the war were considered physically unfit for the army. This, of course, simply fuelled existing fears that a race of degenerates had been bred in the slums of Britain's cities. The issue was kept alive by the appointment of a government committee on 'Physical Deterioration', whose report in 1904 recommended a series of measures to improve the health of children.

The belief in 'National Decadence' gave rise to a fashionable school of thought whose chief object was to promote National Efficiency. A favourite target of its criticism was the political system, which was alleged to be run by amateurs who were absorbed by party politics but not capable of operating a modern state. The young Winston Churchill declared: 'Germany is organised not only for war but for peace. We are organised for nothing except party politics.' From this arose the belief that more use should be made of experts and successful businessmen to run the national government departments. As Churchlll's remarks suggest, comparisons were increasingly made with other states. Germany won much admiration for her professional army, her scientific education, her social insurance schemes and her manufacturing efficiency. Even more alarming was the example of Japan, traditionally regarded as a backward, Oriental power, whose sweeping victory over the Russians in the war of 1904–5 came as a revelation to British opinion. Not the least worrying aspect was its potential impact on Indians, for whom evidence of the vulnerability of Europeans to Asiatic states proved to be especially unsettling.

National Efficiency attempted to promote their views by a variety of schemes such as the establishment of the Boy Scout Movement in 1907 under Robert Baden Powell. It was anticipated that the skills and training thus provided would prepare the future generation of British soldiers and make them more aware of the need for national defence. The government itself tried to infuse a more professional element into the army by setting up the Committee on Imperial Defence, in 1902, and a General Staff for the army, in 1904; until that time Britain had simply not had a regular system for military planning. On the home front, reformers hoped to promote National Efficiency by means of a series of social welfare measures such as the medical inspection of schoolchildren and the free provision of school meals, which would be funded by national government. They also favoured improvements in secondary education and a greater concentration on technical and scientific training in place of the education in Classics, theology and the arts which had dominated British universities. Their pressure bore some fruit in the form of A. J. Balfour's 1902 Education Act, which abolished the school boards and made the county councils responsible for providing both elementary and secondary education. Other ideas for social reform were implemented by the new Liberal government after 1906. However, no change occurred in the personnel of politics; not until the First World War were the party politicians to give way to an influx of experts and businessmen.

15

The Working Class and Socialist Revival

For many British workers the last thirty years of the nineteenth century brought significant improvements in living standards. This may seem a surprising suggestion in view of the evidence about poverty gathered by Booth and Rowntree (see p. 118) and the contemporary concern about the Great Depression. No doubt some businessmen suffered from lower profit margins and unemployment increased, though in the absence of comprehensive figures it is impossible to determine by how much. On the other hand, for the typical *employee* the key development was the 40 per cent fall in prices between the mid-1870s and the mid-1890s. Thus, although money wages either fell or remained stagnant, their real value increased because the cost of most essential items of consumption fell faster. This underlying improvement in real wages had political implications as well as social ones, for it raised expectations and fostered a greater assertiveness amongst organisations of working-men; it is no accident that this was the period in which the idea of an independent party for labour began to be taken seriously.

THE RISE IN LIVING STANDARDS

For the families of even unskilled manual workers lower prices of food made a dramatic impact on weekly budgets. The process began around 1873 when large imports of cheap wheat arrived from the United States of America and Canada. For the first time, the benefits of the abolition of the Corn Laws began to be felt. Within twenty years the price of bread had fallen by approximately half. As a result, the poorest families simply bought more bread, but many were now able to divert some of their expenditure on bread to other items of consumption. This coincided with a much more varied supply of food both from the Empire and from foreign countries during the 1880s, including sugar from Australia as well as the West Indies, beef and lamb from the USA, Argentina, Australia and New Zealand, tea from the new plantations in Ceylon and India, and cocoa from West Africa. The extra purchasing power enjoyed by working-class families also stimulated the production of a range of cheap consumer goods such as soap, jam, newspapers, and by the 1890s, bicycles.

In this way the typical modern British diet took shape. Though often criticised by middle-class investigators who believed people should concentrate on buying bread and potatoes, it undoubtedly represented an improvement in nutrition and in variety. It also raised expectations about higher material standards, which was to be a feature of social and political life throughout the twentieth century. On the other hand, these developments proved to be problematical in the long term. For example, they left Britain extraordinarily dependent upon imported food; by 1914 half of the meat consumed and two-thirds of the grain came from abroad. In an era of free trade and British naval dominance the supply could be taken for granted; but during the First World War, Britain's vulnerability to attacks on shipping became only too apparent.

THE GROWTH OF TRADE UNIONS AND CLASS CONSCIOUSNESS

How far were British workingmen able to take advantage of changing economic conditions during the late nineteenth century? In fact it proved surprisingly difficult. Despite Britain's early industrialisation, for example, trade unions were rather slow to establish themselves except on a limited basis. By 1880 about 750,000 men held union membership, or only one manual worker in every seven. Of course, other ways of using influence were open to them. Many of those workers who had a parliamentary vote keenly supported free trade and further reductions in the taxes on food; but it can hardly be said that they made a major impact on the political system during the 1870s. In addition, the loss of markets and growing competition faced by businessmen during this period led to repeated attempts to reduce the men's wages; it was thus a particularly difficult period for trade unions.

Moreover, the problems faced by organised workers went deeper than this. Men are much more easily recruited into unions when employed in large-scale factories and mills. Yet in spite of the early development of a factory system, British industry had not advanced as far in this direction as used to be believed; in fact by the 1880s the average workshop employed only 29 men. Thus many workers remained close to their employers and saw less need to form trade unions; and for several major occupations such as domestic service or agricultural labour, the fragmentation of the workforce and its acute dependence upon the favour of the owners severely undermined independent behaviour. Even where trade unions were established they repeatedly lost credibility during the nineteenth century owing to their inability to conduct strikes successfully. When faced with the threat of a strike, employers invariably locked their workers out or brought in men from elsewhere to break the strike. The availability of surplus labour crucially undermined the unions' efforts; this is why some unions actively promoted emigration schemes in the hope that those who remained at home would enjoy greater bargaining power. In the same way, trade unions felt handicapped in industries such as cotton textiles in which large numbers of women were employed. Since women were usually willing to work for lower wages than men, the unions felt that the owners deliberately used them to hold down the general level of pay.

As a result of these problems union organisation became essentially sectional, concentrated in certain skilled crafts, although two semi-skilled groups, the miners and cotton workers, did manage to build a substantial membership. The craft unions of the 1860s and 1870s charged high membership fees which enabled them to offer 'friendly society' benefits to members; these included sickness and injury payments and treatment by a doctor. Characteristically they also aspired to win recognition from the owners with a view to establishing regular collective bargaining. Union leaders fully understood that to strike in the face of an economic slump was fatal, and a bargaining system was a way of avoiding the outbreak of spontaneous strikes. Conversely, carefully timed and co-ordinated strikes in a phase of economic expansion often found employers more ready to make concessions. This seems to be the explanation for the brief periods of successful strikes and expanding union membership which were associated with the booms of 1889–90, 1896–7 and 1910–14. During the 1890s the union movement began to extend itself beyond the narrow range of skilled men to include such groups as dockers and gasworkers who formed new 'general' unions for the semi-skilled. As a result, total membership rose to 1.9 million by 1900 and to over 4 million by 1914.

Yet despite this development the British trade union movement can hardly be said to reflect a very pronounced class consciousness. By comparison with working-class organisations on the mainland of Europe the British were slow to develop a distinctive ideology, and in particular showed little interests in Marxist ideas. There are several explanations for this. Most politically aware workingmen appreciated the scope for improvement within the existing economic and political system. They enthusiastically supported free trade and the Gladstonian cry of 'Peace, Retrenchment and Reform'. Up to the 1880s there was little popular demand for state intervention, in fact almost the opposite, for the workers often regarded state institutions, such as the poor law and compulsory education, with fear and suspicion, while social workers, doctors and reformers were disliked for criticising the lifestyle of poor people. In this context the idea of a socialist society proved difficult to popularise. Many of the most ambitious workers looked less to the state and more to self-help strategies in the form of Friendly Societies, Co-operative Societies and trade unions, to improve their position.

Moreover, unlike their counterparts elsewhere in Europe, British workingmen did not suffer legal repression or feel completely excluded from the political system, at least from the 1860s onwards. By 1885 more than half the working-class adult males enjoyed a parliamentary vote. Some also played a part as elected councillors on school boards, county and parish councils, and on poor law boards of guardians after 1894 when the property qualification was abolished. This participation left a lasting impression on the twentieth-century Labour Party in that local government experience strengthened the pragmatic, non-ideological element in the working-class political elite.

It is also significant that by the 1860s middle-class radicals, such as John Stuart Mill, had undermined the traditional arguments against trade unions; they contended that union organisation, designed to press for better wages and conditions, was a perfectly legitimate, and even necessary, part of economic life. The effective management of their funds by trade unions was clearly recognised in the legislation of both Gladstone and Disraeli, which gave them legal status and the right to picket peacefully in support of strikes during the 1870s. By 1868 the unions had organised themselves as a single pressure group – the Trades Union Congress (TUC) – which tried to defend its members' interests nationally by seeking the help of politicians and influencing legislation.

The most striking advance came in 1874 when the first two workingmen were elected to the House of Commons. This had been possible since 1858 when the property qualification for MPs had been abolished. After the 1867 Reform Act some constituencies were effectively dominated by coal miners, and there the local Liberal Associations were persuaded to support the nomination of officials of the Miners' Federation, who enjoyed a straight contest against Conservative candidates. In this way Thomas Burt and Alexander MacDonald were elected in 1874; they took the Liberal Whip in parliament and were known as 'Lib–Labs'. By 1906 twenty-four such workingmen had become MPs. These developments had the effect of integrating several generations of workingmen into the political system and thereby of weakening any inclination to overthrow it.

LATE-VICTORIAN SOCIALISM

On the other hand, one should not exaggerate the obstacles to the emergence of a distinctive left-wing, working-class movement. During the 1880s confidence in both traditional economics and conventional political parties began to weaken, and new socialist organisations appeared: the Social Democratic Federation (SDF) (1883), the Fabian Society (1884) and the Independent Labour Party (1893). Yet to a large extent this reflected *middle-class* rather than working-class interest in radical ideas. The revelations about poverty and the evidence of Britain's manufacturing decline undermined their faith in the capitalist system and in the laissez-faire approach of governments. The leading Fabian Socialists, Sidney and Beatrice Webb, pioneered a distinctive socialist strategy based upon detailed investigations of working conditions, precise recommendations to governments, and infiltration of the system by working through elected local government; in this way they influenced the thinking of a whole generation of Liberals and even some Conservatives.

In addition, some workingmen began to see the shortcomings of Gladstonian Liberalism. While the experiment with Lib–Lab MPs satisfied the miners, it could hardly be extended to other workers who enjoyed less local influence on the Liberals. Moreover, several of the new unions were led by socialists, such as Will Thorne and Ben Tillett, who wished to emancipate labour from its client relationship with Liberalism. They began this process by persuading the TUC to adopt the eight-hour working day as a policy – against the opposition of the conventional Lib–Lab leaders.

However, as the members of the new unions represented only 10 per cent of total membership, they alone could not have imposed a new political strategy on the movement. During the 1890s many skilled workers were radicalised by the effect of unusually high unemployment and aggressive tactics by their employers. Also, some legal disputes in 1895–6 effectively undermined the legal status the unions had enjoyed since 1870. As a result, many traditional trade unions, who were usually suspicious of attempts by Socialists to use their funds for political purposes, readily contemplated a fresh political initiative to increase their influence in parliament.

The 1890s also proved to be the crucial decade for the men who were to emerge as the first generation of Labour Party leaders: Keir Hardie, Ramsay MacDonald, Arthur Henderson and Philip Snowden. All held radical Liberal opinions, but experienced difficulty in becoming Liberal MPs. This was because many local Liberal Parties, weakened by loss of funds, felt reluctant to adopt workingmen as candidates who would have to be subsidised both at and between elections; for until 1911 no salaries were paid to MPs.

Not surprisingly Hardie and MacDonald helped to form the new Independent Labour Party (ILP), whose politics were a pragmatic mixture of socialism, radical Liberalism and trade union demands. It took root in the industrial provinces – West Yorkshire, Lancashire and central Scotland for example; and drew its recruits from the more prosperous sections of the working class, men already well educated, politically aware and actively promoting self-help strategies for the workers. By contrast, the poorest sections of the working class remained too deferential and too absorbed by the daily problem of survival to take a very active, let alone a socialist, role in politics.

Although Hardie and MacDonald advocated Socialism, they were never sympathetic to Marxism; they neither expected nor wished to obtain power through class conflict or revolution. By opting for the parliamentary route they anticipated converting middle-class reformers to the creation of a socialist state. Nor did their socialism as yet include a socialist economic programme. Rather it showed the influence of Nonconformist religion and traditional Radicalism. Their vision of Socialism was expressed in moral terms as the creation of a society based upon brotherhood and co-operation rather than upon the selfish individualism of capitalism.

By 1899 the ILP and some of the trade unions had decided to launch a new organisation for the working class. The delegates at the TUC in that year voted to create the Labour Representation Committee (LRC). The new organisation came into being in 1900 and adopted the name 'The Labour Party' in 1906. At first it was a loose federation consisting of a National Executive comprising representatives of the unions, ILP, SDF and Fabian Society. Only two of its candidates were elected to parliament at the election of 1900. At first the LRC suffered a lack of resources because the unions continued to be suspicious of attempts to exploit their funds. They suddenly became more co-operative after 1901, however, when a notorious legal case – the Taff Vale Dispute – resulted in an employer forcing a trade union to compensate him for the costs of a strike. It now seemed imperative to gain enough influence in parliament to change the law. Yet the LRC still lacked a distinctive programme. Though some of its candidates were socialists, the party as a whole was not committed to socialism. Its programme reflected much common ground with Liberalism: free trade, land reform, graduated taxation, poor law reform, and old age pensions. However, this actually helped the LRC to make its *initial* breakthrough into parliament in 1906. The formal adoption of Socialism did not come until 1918.

16

The New Imperialism

By the 1860s the British Empire consisted of three distinct elements: the colonies settled by Europeans, in Canada, Australia, New Zealand and South Africa; the Indian Empire; and a large collection of territories scattered across Africa, Asia and the Pacific. Already extensive, the Empire was destined to expand rapidly during the 1880s and 1890s. This development would have surprised the mid-Victorians, for it was accepted that the settlers in Canada and Australia should enjoy self-government, and to that end they were being organised into larger federations. The disastrous attempt to retain control over the Europeans in the North American colonies made direct rule from London seem inconceivable in the long run. In a famous phrase, Disraeli had once described colonies as 'millstones round our neck'. This reflected the irritation of the London government at being dragged in to rescue British traders and settlers when they provoked native peoples by competing for their land. Even during the late nineteenth century, politicians found themselves regularly sending military forces to fight colonial wars they wished to avoid, and thereby acquiring extra territory for the Crown. To this extent the British were reluctant imperialists, keen to enjoy the commercial benefits of Empire without incurring the costs.

However, there is some evidence that during the 1880s and 1890s British imperialism changed in character. The entry of new powers, notably Italy, Belgium and Germany, into the colonial race forced governments to adopt bolder policies. The occupation of Egypt in 1882 helped to accelerate expansion, producing what *The Times* called the 'Scramble for Africa'. In addition, Britain's perceived economic difficulties encouraged some leading politicians to advocate a more deliberate exploitation of the material resources of Africa for fear that other powers would grab them.

IMPERIAL STRATEGY AND DIPLOMACY

It cannot be disputed that Britain acquired new territory at an extraordinary rate after 1882. The Egyptian coup triggered a conference at Berlin in 1884 at which Britain gained Nigeria, Somaliland and Bechuanaland. In 1889 Cecil Rhodes' advance into the 'Rhodesias' provoked a further settlement amongst the powers in 1890 which brought Zanzibar, Kenya, Uganda and Nyasaland into British control. At the end of the South African War in 1902 the Transvaal and the Orange Free State were absorbed into British South Africa. By that time the whole of Africa except for Abyssinia and Liberia had fallen under European control.

The most obvious motive for British expansion was strategic. For decades she had been acquiring buffer zones such as Burma and the Punjab to protect her vulnerable Indian Empire. Egypt occupied a vital point on the route to India and the Far East, especially after the opening of the Suez Canal in 1869. By extension it could be argued that Egypt's security required control of the Sudan, and that the East African coast was of strategic importance because a hostile power might threaten British shipping in the Indian Ocean.

However, these arguments are convincing only up to a point. Gladstone, for example, withdrew forces from the Sudan in 1885 without noticeably affecting British security. Nor was there any significant naval threat in the Indian Ocean. In any case the strategic arguments have less obvious relevance in connection with the landlocked African territories newly gained in this period.

Alternatively, governments may have acted simply out of a wish to maintain British prestige and status. However, though this is suggested by contemporary propaganda, prime ministers such as Gladstone and Salisbury adopted a far more realistic approach. They were often sceptical about the new territory, and actually helped rivals, notably Germany, to gain African colonies. The explanation for this lies in *European* diplomacy rather than in imperial strategy. After the Franco-Prussian War of 1870 there was a real danger that Europe would be dragged into a further conflict. Britain wished to keep the peace, and also needed co-operation from Germany, Italy and Austria especially over her position in Egypt. Such objectives could more easily be achieved by a series of agreements in which each power received a generous allocation of territory in Africa. In a sense the new colonies acted as a safety valve to relieve the

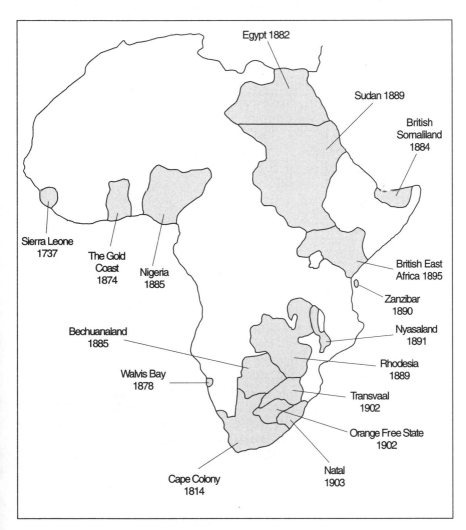

Map 4 British Territory in Africa c. 1902

tension building up in Europe itself. It mattered little to Salisbury and Gladstone that Germany gained large, but worthless, territories in Africa if this helped to maintain good diplomatic relations.

ECONOMIC IMPERIALISM

Until relatively recently it was widely believed that the underlying pressures behind Britain's expansion in the 1880s were essentially economic. In some ways this seems plausible. The original rationale for the Empire in India had been the exploitation of trade and subsequently the need to export British manufactured goods. Once Britain appeared to be losing some of her markets to foreign competition, such considerations gained additional force. Moreover, most European states and the United States had begun to restrict the entry of goods into their domestic market by adopting tariffs. There was a danger that this practice might be extended, particularly to China where Britain's lucrative trade was threatened by economic concessions granted by a weak Chinese government to other European powers.

Certainly several leading imperialists thought in terms of economics. For example, Lord Rosebery, who was both Foreign Secretary (1892–4) and Prime Minister (1894–5), argued that Britain was 'pegging out claims for the future' in Africa. Joseph Chamberlain claimed that the extension of British control in South Africa would secure the valuable mineral resources (gold and diamond mines) and open up opportunities for emigration from Britain's overcrowded cities. In a famous analysis published in 1902, *Imperialism: A Study*, J. A. Hobson argued that Britain was obliged to find new territories to serve as an outlet for the huge surplus of capital generated by her industry, which could not be absorbed by the domestic economy. Between 1870 and 1914 Britain's net overseas investment increased from £1200 million to £4000 million.

In spite of this evidence, however, the economic explanation for the new imperialism is not wholly convincing. British capitalists were far more cautious than Marxist theory suggests. In practice, over two-thirds of all foreign investment in this period went either to countries outside British control, notably the USA and Argentina, or to the older colonies such as Canada, Australia and India. Hardly any capital was attracted to the newly acquired African territories. Nor did they supply markets for British goods. The explanation is simply that territories such as Kenya, Bechuanaland and the Rhodesias were thinly populated and lacked communications and mineral resources. As a result, both the East Africa Company and Rhodes' South Africa Company failed to make profits for their shareholders. The one major exception to this was in the west African territories (Nigeria and the Gold Coast) where a highly profitable trade in cocoa and palm oil made the Royal Niger Company a viable commercial concern. It is only fair to point out that the mere *hope* of finding wealth provided sufficient motive for some enthusiastic imperialist entrepreneurs. Rhodes, for example, promised that more gold and diamonds would be discovered in the land north of the Transvaal. But unrealised hopes could sustain expansion only for a limited time. By the 1890s Lord Salisbury felt convinced that Britain had already secured the best economic assets in Africa.

NEW THINKING ABOUT EMPIRE

One novel aspect of late-Victorian imperialism was the contribution made by academics and politicians to the debate about the justification for Britain's Empire. For some this took the form of a more deliberately *moral* rationale, based on the assumption that Britain represented a superior form of civilisation and therefore had an obligation to extend the benefits of her rule to less developed societies. Rudyard Kipling, the leading poet of Empire, expressed this view in *The White Man's Burden* (1899):

> Take up the White Man's Burden,
> Send forth the best you breed.
> Go bind your sons to exile
> To serve your captives' need.
> To wait in heavy harness
> On fluttered folk and wild,
> Your new-caught sullen children,
> Half devil and half child.

This idea that the British should vigorously carry out a duty to rule half the world was strengthened by missionary activity, the campaign to suppress the slave trade in Africa, and by Darwinian thinking about race. Certainly during the 1990s some of the controversy passed out of imperial questions as both Liberals and Conservatives accepted that British rule could be morally justified by the improvements it brought to the lives of subject peoples.

Others began to reconsider the long-term purpose of Empire. In Sir Charles Dilke's *Great Britain* (1870) and J. A. Seeley's *The Expansion of England* (1883), the authors showed themselves aware of Britain's inferiority, in terms of population and resources, to the USA and Germany; as a result they began to contemplate unifying the colonies so as to enable Britain to match these larger powers. In the 1880s this idea was expressed as 'Imperial Federation'. Its leading advocates, Lord Rosebery and Joseph Chamberlain, hoped to achieve two objects: first, the creation of a customs-free imperial zone, protected by external tariffs, and secondly, the development of a common imperial defence policy. However, these aspirations conflicted with the nationalism of the white colonies, and increasingly with Indian demands for self-determination. During the next century the pressures to relax British control, both political and economic, was too strong; imperial federation thus remained a lost cause.

POPULAR IMPERIALISM

Perhaps the most striking symptom of imperialism during the last twenty years of the nineteenth century was the apparent growth of enthusiasm for Empire displayed by ordinary citizens. Popular imagination was stirred by the exploration of Africa by David Livingstone and others. This is underlined by the market for articles and books about imperial adventures. For example, the *Boys' Own Paper*, founded in 1879, soon sold one million copies and influenced an entire generation of young men. At a different level many British families enjoyed close and personal links with the Empire through sons and daughters who had emigrated. Of course, many of the quarter of a million annual emigrants left for the United States of America, but those who lived in the colonies gave their relations at home a direct interest in a supportive policy towards the Empire; imperialism could not be simply an abstract question debated by a handful of politicians.

Moreover, in this period the material benefits of Empire in the form of cheap and plentiful supplies of tea, sugar, cocoa and other tropical products, made a major impact on the diet of millions of people. This was reinforced by the advertising of these products, which frequently adopted a blatantly patriotic and imperialistic message. Such regular reminders about links with the colonies were probably more effective in influencing popular attitudes than the more direct political propaganda.

None the less, one should not underestimate the extent to which imperial triumphs and disasters dominated political debate. The war with Afghanistan in 1879, General Gordon's death at Khartoum in 1885, Lord Kitchener's victory in the Sudan in 1898, and the campaigns in South Africa during 1899–1902 inevitably attracted the nation's attention and were exploited for political purposes. The young Winston Churchill consciously prepared his own political career by means of several well-publicised exploits in colonial wars during the 1890s; he made some much-needed money from his written accounts, and won his first seat in parliament in 1900 as a man who had escaped from a Boer jail in South Africa. Of course, this does not mean that all sections of society became enthusiasts for imperial expansion. Patriotic opinion was quickly aroused whenever British nationals faced danger in far-off places, but it could also collapse suddenly, as it did after 1902.

THE 'BOER WAR': A TURNING-POINT

Imperial expansion reached a climax at the turn of the century as a result of the South African or 'Boer' War. This arose out of competition for land between the Zulu people, the Dutch or Boer settlers in the Transvaal and Orange Free State, and the British in Cape Colony and Natal. Since 1881 the British had been anxious to avenge a humiliating defeat by the Boers at the Battle of Majuba Hill. Imperialists hoped that this would be the means of establishing a British Federation over all the provinces of southern Africa. In this sense the British were the aggressors in the region. London governments primarily wished to maintain British influence because the Cape provided a base on the secondary route to India. But during the 1880s the discovery of gold and diamonds led to an influx of European speculators and settlers which played into the hands of British expansionists such as Cecil Rhodes. In 1889 he extended British territory to the north of the Transvaal, thereby largely encircling the Boers. Nevertheless, the Boers were not an expansive power and represented no real threat to British interests.

However, London's attitude effectively changed in 1895 when Chamberlain became Colonial Secretary. He gave tacit encouragement to Sir Alfred Milner, Britain's High Commissioner at the Cape, to contrive a breakdown in relations with the Boers in October 1899 which gave Britain an excuse to go to war. Unhappily the British suffered from delusions about their opponents, expecting to be able to defeat an ill-organised force of peasant-farmers with ease. In the event, they were obliged to wage a costly and protracted war until 1902. Although the British setbacks and victories helped Salisbury to win a general election in 1900 by rallying patriotic opinion, the long-term effect of the war was to burst the bubble of imperialism. The huge cost thoroughly destabilised the Conservative government during the early 1900s; the increase in the national debt from £640 million to £800 million led to higher taxation and eventually to a split in the party. But above all, the meagre results of the war largely destroyed the optimistic case for imperial expansionism. Indeed, although the Empire did grow still further as a result of the First World War, the imperial cause never fully regained the moral high-ground that it had occupied in the late-Victorian era. Emigration continued at a high level until 1914 but thereafter diminished; by the 1920s the British were visibly in retreat from their imperial heritage.

17

The Emergence of the Interventionist State, 1905–14

For most of the Victorian era the state continued to play a minimal role in the lives of the British people. It raised just enough revenue to run essential services – the police, justice, the civil service, and the armed forces – and to pay off part of the national debt. But taxation of income and wealth was still widely seen as inherently damaging to the economy, and redistribution as counter-productive. However, the old system was already under pressure; whereas in 1890 central and local government spent 9 per cent of gross national product, by 1910 they spent 13 per cent. During the Edwardian period the direct taxation of wealthy people increased state resources significantly and the national government began to supplant local authorities in the field of social welfare by introducing old age pensions, medical services for children, maternity benefits, health and employment insurance.

For the first time, pressure from the working classes became a major factor in the extension of state interventionism. Indeed, although some of the Edwardian innovations attracted controversy at first, it is significant that no political party proposed to abolish any of them, only to improve and extend them. In this way a real turning-point was reached in the relationship between the people and their government; it gradually began to be seen positively as a provider of certain material benefits, not simply as an oppressive or inquisitorial agent in the lives of the people.

THE MOTIVES BEHIND SOCIAL REFORM

Like all major changes the Edwardian reforms can be explained at several different levels. To some extent they were a reflection of long-term changes in ideas. During the 1880s and 1890s Fabian Socialists and New Liberals had responded to evidence about poverty by advocating state intervention and an extension of national taxation with a view to redistributing income from the rich to the poor. Working-class reformers had also begun to demand certain reforms, for example, old age pensions; and the Women's Co-operative Guild began to urge government to promote the health and welfare of the mothers on whom the fitness of the population ultimately depended. This is a reminder that the motives behind reform were not simply humanitarian. The Boer War had focused the attention of the right-wing on the need to strengthen the domestic population in the national interest. For this reason, inteventionism actually began during the declining years of the Conservative Government under A. J. Balfour, with the 1902 Education Act and the 1905 Unemployment Workman's Act. This latter measure promoted the establishment of the famous Royal Commission on the Poor Laws, whose members included Beatrice Webb. Its report in 1909 underlined the need for a government to take some responsibility from the local poor law guardians, who simply lacked the resources to cope with unemployment.

In fact the Unionist statesman Joseph Chamberlain, once a radical Liberal, did much to publicise the idea of old age pensions. When he launched his campaign for tariff reform in 1903 one of his arguments was that tariffs on imported goods would give governments the extra revenue needed to finance such social welfare measures. Moreover, his campaign offered something even more radical than welfare. In effect he claimed that if government protected the domestic market from foreign imports it would secure employment for British workers – something that Victorian governments would scarcely have done.

Chamberlain's campaign was a serious challenge to the free traders in all parties. It effectively ensured that questions such as living standards, unemployment and welfare would move to the top of the political agenda in the Edwardian period. The Liberals were obliged to address these questions partly to defend free trade, but also to retain their working-class vote in the face of the emergence of the Labour Party. However, the Liberals' advocacy of social reform is by no means fully explained by electoral expediency. The four hundred Liberals elected to parliament in 1906 were not obviously threatened by Labour; and their commitment to old age pensions, poor law reform and the taxation of wealth had grown out of the intellectual revisionism of the 1890s. Since Gladstone's demise, the party had undergone a change of personnel and, with it, taken on the ideas of Hobson, Booth and Rowntree. Experiments conducted by local authorities in dealing with poverty during the 1880s and 1890s had increasingly convinced them that local resources were quite inadequate to the scale of the social problems afflicting Britain; therefore they now looked to the state to take over much of the burden.

In this sense the new Labour Party was not the cause of the social legislation of the Edwardian years; but it certainly helped to accelerate the process. After the 1906 election, Labour and Liberal MPs often joined together in demanding such measures as pensions and free school meals. No doubt political motives loomed large in the minds of Lloyd George and Winston Churchill, who did not wish the government to be outflanked by Labour. But this is not a sufficient explanation. For there was, as yet, no convincing proof that social reform was really popular, and no government could predict in advance of legislation what the response of the working class would be.

THE BREAK WITH VICTORIAN PRINCIPLES

From the perspective of the late twentieth century it is easy to underestimate the extent to which the Edwardians considered state social reforms to represent a challenge to traditional thinking and practice. For example, those who received assistance from the poor law authorities automatically lost their right to be voters, a rule which remained in force until 1918. By contrast, after 1906 those parents whose children received free school meals, and all those who were eligible for old age pensions after 1908, retained any political rights for which they were otherwise qualified. The pensions became available to men and women aged 70 years if their income fell below a certain level. No contributions were required, a concession which violated the conventional belief that people should be given a stimulus to lead thrifty and responsible lives; the reason was that those most in need of pensions, especially women, were often not able to make contributions during their working lives. Another novel feature was that the pensions were entirely freed from the stigma attaching to the poor law system; for they were paid at post offices and given as a right once the initial application had been made. Not surprisingly, pensions proved to be immediately popular.

On the other hand, not all the innovations were immediately welcomed, though familiarity usually brought approval in time. For example, when the government introduced Labour Exchanges in 1908 many workers felt suspicious initially. But the minister, Winston Churchill, and his adviser William Beveridge, took care to avoid antagonising the men. Thus, attendance was purely voluntary; some trade unionists were employed in operating the new system; and men were quite free to reject jobs offered at below the wage rates negotiated by the unions. As a result the number of men applying to Labour Exchanges increased rapidly.

Lloyd George's most ambitious reform was the 1911 National Insurance Act, which attracted criticism at first because it imposed contributions upon the workers as well as on their employers and the state. However, the principle of contributions was a very familiar one to a generation accustomed to Friendly Societies and trade union benefit schemes. The fear was that there would be competition between the existing schemes and the government's system. Lloyd George dealt with this by allowing existing Friendly Societies to become approved agents of the state scheme, through which their members' benefits could be paid. The health insurance was radical in the sense that it was *compulsory* for all workers below a certain income level. Once contributions had been made, the insured person received benefits as of right, including a weekly payment when too ill to work, free treatment from a doctor, and a maternity benefit for married women. This began the process of getting medical and material assistance to those members of the community who most needed it.

Unemployment insurance also guaranteed weekly cash payments as a right. But the scheme was applied only to relatively well-paid men in building, shipbuilding and engineering. Clearly the motive here was to save the respectable and deserving workman from being driven to the poor law by cyclical unemployment beyond his control. Despite the initial controversy it soon emerged that four out of every five of these insured workers had not previously enjoyed any insurance against unemployment; and a quarter of them made a claim during the first year of the scheme. In this way, though such reforms were not a response to working-class demand, they began to win acceptance after they had been implemented.

On the other hand the initiatives taken by the Liberals fell far short of a comprehensive programme of welfare. Only 2.5 million men had unemployment insurance; most women and children fell outside the health scheme; only 668,000 people qualified for old age pensions because the age had been set at seventy; and six out of every ten local authorities failed to provide school meals until it became compulsory to do so in 1914. However, to dwell too much on these limitations is to introduce an inappropriate standard associated with a much later historical period; the relevant comparison is with the Victorian period. During the Edwardian years the government clearly accepted a degree of responsibility to provide a minimum standard for its citizens, which it had not previously done. For example, expenditure on social services rose from only £5 million in the late 1880s to £33 million by 1913. Although the old poor law system remained intact until 1929, as a safety net for those who fell between the new state schemes, it began to deal with fewer people; the elderly in particular could now avoid a term in the workhouse. In the process, attitudes towards the state began to change slowly but significantly. Government welfare began to be taken for granted; and in future the debate was to be not over whether social welfare was desirable, but over how to extend and improve it.

THE 'PEOPLE'S BUDGET'

Radical innovations in social policy would scarcely have been feasible without changes in national taxation. This was already a problem because the Boer War had left the government with a much larger national debt. The orthodox response to this was to set aside funds to pay off part of the debt each year so as to lower future interest payments. When the Liberals took office in December 1905 it appeared initially that the new Chancellor, H. H. Asquith, would follow this approach. But financial retrenchment was *not* to be the hallmark of Liberal policy. In fact Asquith prepared the ground for change by requiring every citizen and employer to make an annual return of his income, by taxing 'unearned' income at a higher rate than earned income, and by devising a 'super tax' on incomes above £5,000. In effect, Asquith had adopted the principle that the rate of taxation paid should be graduated according to each individual's ability to pay. This met the complaints of radicals that the traditional reliance upon revenue from indirect taxes on consumption taxed the poor disproportionately. In this way, Asquith made a major break with Gladstonian finance.

These foundations were built upon by David Lloyd George in his famous 'People's Budget' of 1909. Though conscious of the need to refute the tariff reformers' challenge to free trade, his immediate need was simply to meet an anticipated deficit of £16 million in the next financial year. This gave Lloyd George the perfect opportunity to achieve a lasting change in policy by taxing very wealthy people more heavily. For example, he raised revenue on motor cars and on petrol, which were then used only by the rich; he increased the rate of income tax and introduced the super tax; and he proposed new levies on the value of land. Nor did reform stop in 1909; in his 1914 budget for example, Lloyd George increased still further the rates for income tax, super tax and death duties.

In combination these innovations represented a landmark in twentieth-century British politics and public finance. They opened up new resources for governments and decisively shifted the basis of national finance from indirect taxes on consumption to the direct taxation of incomes, and thereby placed more of the burden on the wealthy. Some of the extra revenue went into the pockets of the poor, the best example being the £8.5 million spent on non-contributory old age pensions; but at the same time the Chancellor managed to find additional money to rebuild the navy almost every year. However, apart from the extra duties charged on alcoholic drinks and tobacco, Lloyd George's new taxes were not paid by the workingmen or even by most middle-class employees. This was because no one paid income tax at all unless their annual income rose above £160. The new super tax affected only 25,000 people, for example. Thus, there is no doubt that the effects were to redistribute income, if only slightly. The budget inaugurated a long-term redistribution which was continued during the First World War and in each succeeding decade down to the end of the 1970s.

FREE TRADE AND COLLECTIVISM

Historians, aware of the decline of the Liberal Party after 1918, have sometimes assumed that the experiments with state interventionism before 1914 had already alienated the middle classes who remained attached to laissez-faire and Victorian views about taxation. However, this danger was more hypothetical than real. In effect the Edwardian Liberal governments contrived a judicious mixture of collectivist or interventionist initiatives with individualism and private enterprise. Liberals were not becoming Socialists; they did not aspire to acquire the ownership of industry for the state. Even The Labour Party remained uncommitted to socialism until 1918. Moreover, both Labour and the Liberals were firmly wedded to traditional free trade principles. This was obviously popular because it guaranteed cheap food for consumers. Also, much of business continued to support free trade as the best way of maintaining a supply of cheap raw materials, helping to maximise export markets, and reducing pressure on wages at home.

It was precisely the combination of free trade on the one hand with social and financial reform on the other that enabled the Liberals to command support across the boundaries of social class. Many employers felt the need to improve the health and education of the British labour force, and recognised that judicious state intervention was necessary in sectors that had been badly served by private investment. In his 1909 budget Lloyd George proposed to tackle this problem by setting aside an annual sum of money for the Development Commission. This was to invest in schemes of land reclamation, forestry, transport and experimental farming, thereby creating employment and remedying some of the shortcomings of private investment. In addition, the government was becoming a major employer in its own right. Whereas, in 1901 some 960,000 people held jobs in the civil service, local government and armed forces, by 1911 the total stood at 1,270,000. Above all, the state now planned to remedy the defects in the labour market by means of the Labour Exchanges, which were intended to improve the mobility of workers and reduce casual employment.

Perhaps the most direct challenge to the rights of individual businessmen came in the form of legislation affecting working hours and wages. Coal miners, for example, won both an eight-hour day and a minimum wage, albeit after a major strike in 1912.

In 1909 the Trade Boards Act had set up local committees empowered to impose minimum wages in the 'sweated trades' where pay had always been extremely low. Finally, during 1913–14 Lloyd George promoted a 'Land Campaign' which, among other things, included proposals for regional tribunals whose task would be to raise minimum wages for agricultural labourers. He also envisaged state subsidies to build houses in rural areas, another form of expenditure well calculated to counter any downward turn in the trade cycle. Although the implementation of these ideas was interrupted by the outbreak of war, it is clear that by 1914 the British government had moved decisively away from the limited, negative view of the state that had characterised the Victorian period, towards a new combination of interventionism and private enterprise; in this way the twentieth-century pattern of politics was born.

18

The Edwardian Crisis

Edwardian Britain has traditionally been seen as a time when politics and society suffered from fundamental divisions which threatened to destroy the system of parliamentary government; a series of controversies over the House of Lords, Ireland, women's suffrage and industrial strikes were thought to involve a violent challenge to the authority of the elected government and to the forces of law and order. The unexpected outbreak of war in August 1914 could, from this perspective, be seen as a welcome and opportune diversion for a society that was becoming ungovernable.

However, this is at least an exaggeration, and in some ways a basic misrepresentation of the period. We can understand how the pessimistic interpretation originated in the demoralisation within the Conservative Party after its divisions over tariff reform and its crushing defeat at the election of 1906. The Party was not accustomed to being kept out of power, and the alliance between the Liberals, the Irish and Labour was interpreted by some on the right as a subversive plot. But it would clearly be unwise to inflate the injured feelings of one displaced elite into a general malaise in British society.

THE LIBERAL REVIVAL AND LABOUR

The return of free trade to the top of the agenda after 1903, and the revival of Nonconformity, stimulated by Balfour's 1902 Education Act, helped to restore the Liberals as the dominant force in politics up to 1914. They scored a landslide victory at the election of January 1906, winning 401 seats to only 157 for the Conservatives.

Yet, in spite of this, it has traditionally been assumed that the Liberals were in decline and being replaced by the Labour Party in the Edwardian period. In fact, after its establishment as the Labour Representation Committee in 1900, the Labour Party, as it called itself from 1906 onwards, did achieve a breakthrough by winning 29 seats in 1906 and 42 in December 1910. The Liberals fell from their 1906 peak by losing over 100 seats in 1910; but they still retained office until 1915.

Essentially, the traditional view suffers from the benefit of hindsight. Because we know that the Liberals experienced a disastrous decline after 1918, it is only too easy to find the causes of their downfall in the pre-1914 period and exaggerate their weaknesses. However, in recent years research has undermined this interpretation in several ways. First, it has shown how far the Liberals adapted their programme and ideology to appeal to the working class and to tackle social issues; and secondly, it has revealed that the Edwardian Labour Party was much weaker electorally than once supposed.

This point is underlined by the manner in which Labour's breakthrough was achieved. In 1903 the LRC Secretary, Ramsay MacDonald, reached a private agreement with the Liberal Chief Whip whereby each party would withdraw some of its candidates to help the other at the next election. This was seen by the Liberals as a way of avoiding any split in the anti-Conservative vote. But for Labour the pact proved absolutely vital, for most of the 29 MPs elected in 1906 had no Liberal opponent and received most of the Liberal vote. Subsequently the reappearance of a Liberal candidate usually resulted in Labour falling to the bottom of the poll. This suggests that Labour's independent support was, as yet, quite limited, and consequently the Party maintained the pact at two more general elections in 1910. The increase in its MPs did not reflect extra popular support, but simply the decision of the Miners' Federation to affiliate to the party in 1908; this meant that technically the 'Lib–Lab' members were now Labour MPs. After 1910 Labour defended four of its seats at by-elections and lost every one of them. In fact, if any party can be said to have been gaining ground up to 1914 it was not Labour but the Conservatives.

The reason the pact worked so well, apart from sheer electoral expediency, was that it reflected the common ground between the two parties. Most of the leading Labour politicians, such as MacDonald, Keir Hardie and Arthur Henderson, were essentially working-class Liberals; they advocated free trade, Irish Home Rule, parliamentary reform, social welfare and graduated taxation of wealth, especially land, just as the radical Liberals did. As yet, Labour was simply not sufficiently distinctive, ideologically, to be capable of outflanking the Liberal government. Indeed, in the long term this was to be its strength, for it enabled Labour to inherit much of the tradition of British Liberalism.

However, in the short term the closeness between Labour and the Liberals caused friction within the Labour Movement because many of the local ILP activists, who were more Socialist, felt their parliamentary leaders had become too tame and loyal to the government. At the local level it was a little demoralising to be confined to contests in only 50 constituencies in 1906 and a maximum of 78 in January 1910. Could Labour not afford to expand beyond the confines of the electoral pact?

In some sense this began to happen, in that in the by-elections between 1911 and 1914 many more three-cornered fights occurred. By 1914 Labour was considering contesting 117 seats. Moreover, the expansion of trade union membership added to the funds from which the Party hoped to draw. In 1913, unions were allowed to collect a regular political levy from their members and establish a political fund; as a result, by 1914 Labour had just reached the point at which, at last, it could exploit the resources of the union movement.

On the other hand, none of this demonstrates that Labour had actually undermined the Liberals before 1914. In any case Mac-Donald had no intention of abandoning co-operation with the Liberals, as yet, because he appreciated that to do so would put Labour seats at risk. The Liberals continued to win elections in working-class constituencies, and most union members still voted Liberal rather than Labour. The implication of this is that the prime catalyst of the Liberal decline was the First World War.

INDUSTRIAL MILITANCY

The more excitable members of the political establishment believed that behind the rather moderate Labour Party stood a militant trade union movement whose membership had grown from 1.9 million in 1900 to 4.1 million by 1914. Whereas there had been 300 to 400 strikes each year between 1902 and 1906, there were 800–900 during the 1911–14 period. The success of many of these strikes encouraged more men, especially the unskilled, to become union members. As a result, the movement began to lose much as its old, sectional character; there were more sympathetic strikes in which one group of workers refused to return to work until their colleagues' grievances had been met. The most alarming example of this attitude was the 'Triple Alliance', comprising miners, railwaymen and transport workers, formed in 1913. Although the Triple Alliance did not strike before 1914, it seemed to threaten the government with something approaching a general strike, in which much of the economy would be paralysed. However, the general strike remained a remote notion for most British workers. Very few union leaders advocated syndicalism in this period. Those who did were arrested by the authorities – for example, Tom Mann who was charged with inciting soldiers not to fire on strikers in 1912 and Jim Larkin who was imprisoned for sedition in 1913.

On the other hand, while the involvement in strikes helped to promote working-class consciousness, this does not prove that militancy heralded a general rejection of parliamentary government. Indeed, there is little evidence that the strikes were at all political; rather they reflected traditional, material motivation. The fall in the real value of wages as a result of inflation around the turn of the century provided the underlying impetus to militancy in this period. Unions were also provoked by the infamous Taff Vale case in 1901, which made them legally liable for the costs of strikes to employers; when this threat was lifted by a new law in 1906 a rash of strikes immediately broke out. Finally, the boom in the economy after 1909 created conditions in which workers could bargain more effectively with their employers.

So far from being alienated from politics, the working class began to be drawn more closely into the system in the Edwardian period. One symptom of this was the unions' readiness to establish a political fund to finance the Labour Party in 1913. There were, in fact, solid reasons for thinking that the system could be made to yield gains for the workers. During strikes, government ministers such as Lloyd George frequently intervened to put pressure on employers to recognise the representatives of the men and to negotiate with them. Many concessions were also won by legislation, including the 1906 Trade Union Act, minimum wages for several groups, and the eight-hour working day for miners.

THE CONSTITUTIONAL CONFLICT

It is arguable that the main challenge to parliamentary government came not from the working class but from the upper-class Conservative elite, which failed to reconcile itself to being excluded from office. Ever since the widening of the electorate in 1867 the Conservatives had drawn comfort from the power enjoyed by the hereditary House of Lords to veto radical policies put forward by a government which represented the votes of the poorest sections of the community. However, this strategy had not been tested very often, except over Irish Home Rule, because the Conservatives had themselves been in power in the late-Victorian period.

After their landslide victory in 1906 the Liberals believed the House of Lords would defer to their popular mandate. Yet it rapidly emerged that this was not the case, for several Liberal bills were rejected or mutilated during 1906–8. But in 1909 the peers overplayed their hand by rejecting Lloyd George's budget. This was done partly because they felt outraged at the proposals to tax land, and partly because they saw that the new taxes made the case for introducing tariffs irrelevant.

Rejection of the budget presented the Liberals with their long-awaited opportunity to attack the peers. Lloyd George had by no means expected rejection, but gladly took advantage of it. The Liberals argued that the action represented a breach of the constitution and that it was a selfish act by wealthy men who were chiefly trying to evade a fair share of taxation. In view of the indisputable need for both naval rebuilding and the provision of old age pensions – which were too popular for the Conservatives to renounce – it was impossible for the peers to question the need to raise extra revenue. Lloyd George gleefully resurrected the old radical charge that landowners were idle parasites living off the hard work of businessmen and manual workers. He threatened them with even more revolutionary charges: 'who made ten thousand men the owners of the soil and the rest of us trespassers in the land of our birth?' Ostensibly this was the language of class warfare; in reality he was exploiting the issue to help retain working-class votes for the Liberals.

In order to overcome the peers' veto the Liberals were obliged to hold an early general election in January 1910; inevitably they lost many of the seats won in the special circumstances of 1906. But the peers had presented them with a popular issue, and so they retained office with the support of Labour and the Irish Nationalists. This enabled them not only to pass Lloyd George's budget, but to reform the powers of the House of Lords so as to reduce its capacity for obstructionism in the future. Such a reform bill could not pass the House of Lords unless hundreds of new Liberal peers were created. The King agreed reluctantly to this but only on condition that Asquith won another election first. This the Prime Minister duly did in December 1910. As a result the peers accepted the Parliament Act of 1911, which removed altogether their powers over financial legislation and allowed the House of Commons to over-ride their veto on ordinary legislation by passing a disputed measure in three successive sessions.

The outcome was an immense triumph for parliamentary democracy. For although the hereditary membership of the House of Lords had been left intact, the role of both the institution of the upper house and of peers as individuals diminished significantly after 1911. Even the Conservatives declined to choose leaders from amongst the peerage; and they failed either to restore any of the lost powers or to make membership of the upper house more representative as they had promised in 1911.

THE IRISH HOME RULE CRISIS

The constitutional crisis had many indirect consequences, however. In the first place, it greatly demoralised the Conservatives who believed that their one effective defence against attacks upon private property had vanished. Right-wing Tories blamed their party leader, A. J. Balfour, for this and forced him to resign in 1911. His successor, Andrew Bonar Law, proved to be a weak leader who failed to restrain the unconstitutional ideas of his extremists.

In the second place, the crisis restored the balance of power to the 82 Irish MPs in the Commons. Therefore Home Rule returned to the top of the agenda. Between April 1912 and May 1914 the third Home Rule bill was passed three times through the Commons, thereby overcoming the opposition of the peers. Unfortunately the delay allowed the opponents of Home Rule to foment an increasingly violent agitation. The Unionists, who represented Protestant opinion in the north-east of Ireland, claimed that an all-Ireland parliament would reflect the views of the Catholic majority and would damage the trade between Ireland and the mainland. The English Conservatives also argued that Britain still required control of Ireland for strategic reasons. But their main immediate motive was to exploit the Irish issue as the best means for reuniting their own party and undermining the entrenched Liberal government by the threat of force.

However, the government refused to be easily moved. Four-fifths of the Irish constituencies had consistently voted for Home Rule, and Asquith now relied for his majority on their support in parliament. Therefore he could nor risk backing down. In response, some of the Protestants organised the Ulster Volunteer Force, ostensibly to resist a Dublin parliament by physical means. Bonar Law used his authority as Tory leader to give support and respectability to this threat of violence. In January 1914 the situation deteriorated alarmingly when a cargo of 35,000 rifles was landed on the Irish coast for use by the Ulster Volunteers. Soon a rival Nationalist force, known as the Dublin Volunteers, emerged, and with it the prospect of a full-scale civil war. In this situation the authority of the Asquith government was undermined by disloyalty on the part of some army officers stationed in Ireland; in March 1914, 57 officers at the Curragh offered to resign rather than enforce the Home Rule policy in Ulster. The failure to court-martial these men was a serious error, for it put in doubt the army's capacity to prevent civil war in the event of Home Rule being implemented. Fortunately the outbreak of the First World War in August interrupted these events.

THE SUFFRAGETTES

Throughout the period between 1905 and 1914 leading politicians came under pressure from the 'militant' campaign for women's enfranchisement led by Mrs Emmeline Pankhurst and her daughter Christabel. The argued that a change of tactics was fully justified because women had been trying to win the vote since 1866 by constitutional means without success. 'The argument of the broken pane of glass is the most important argument in politics,' Mrs Pankhurst claimed. The 'suffragettes' as they were called, to distinguish them from the nonviolent suffragists, determined to use militancy in order to gain new publicity for the women's cause, to arouse public opinion in their support and to make the life of the Liberal government so intolerable that it would have to introduce a women's suffrage bill. They pointed out that men had resorted to violence to obtain political reforms throughout the nineteenth century, and that their tactics were no more than a continuation of an established British tradition.

Militancy passed through several stages up to 1914 when it was abruptly abandoned. It began in 1905 with interruptions to the public meetings held by cabinet ministers, and interventions at by-elections designed to persuade voters to reject government candidates. But after a few years the novelty wore off and the police began to use increasing violence to suppress surffragette interventions. Thus, from 1908 onwards the women avoided physical confrontations and, instead, attacked property; windows were broken, post boxes and ministers' houses set on fire, and politicians ambushed at railway stations and on golf courses. But the most emotive tactic adopted by the suffragettes was to undertake hunger-strikes when imprisoned for these offences. At first this secured an early release, but the authorities then resorted to forcible feeding in prison, which severely damaged the health of several suffragettes.

For a Liberal government such repressive measures undoubtedly caused great embarrassment. On the other hand, the suffragettes never mobilised enough public sympathy or inflicted sufficient damage to property to force the authorities to back down. Indeed, the Pankhursts' cardinal error was to alienate the Labour Movement, which might have provided them with the numerical weight they lacked. By 1914 deadlock had been reached in the struggle for moral advantage between the suffragettes and the government. Significantly, the Pankhursts took the first opportunity presented by the outbreak of war to cease campaigning, with their claim to the vote as yet unattained.

INTO WAR

In spite of this succession of crises and challenges the Liberal governments steadily surmounted their difficulties, achieved extensive reforms and retained office in three elections during the Edwardian period. In this sense the claim that parliamentary government had been undermined by violence appears unconvincing. In fact, with the exception of the Irish Question, none of the controversies involved a serious attempt to use force to challenge the authority of parliament. The women and the organised working class were chiefly concerned to participate in the system rather than to overthrow it. The sense of crisis flourished primarily within the ranks of the landed class and the Conservative Party, which felt aggrieved at being attacked as a class, subjected to high taxation and excluded from power. In effect, Edwardian politicians were employing the *rhetoric* of class warfare rather than the reality.

This is not to deny that Asquith's Liberal government appreciated the domestic advantages of going to war in 1914. The wave of strikes abruptly subsided, suffragette agitation ceased, controversial legislation was suspended for the duration of the war, and even the Irish declared their support for the British cause. However, none of this influenced the decision by the cabinet to enter the war in August 1914. Most Liberals loathed the prospect. Yet they accepted reluctantly that war had become inevitable as a result of Germany's determination to support Austria. Moreover, they saw that if the cabinet had split over entry into the war, the only consequence would have been that either a Conservative or a Coalition government would have taken its place. It seemed wiser to retain office united, and thereby to preserve as much as possible of the domestic achievements of Liberalism. Had the First World War been as short as expected, these expectations might well have been borne out.

19

The Continental Commitment, 1890–1914

Until the end of the nineteenth century Britain managed to maintain her traditional policy of 'splendid isolation'. This meant relying on the navy to defend communications with the colonies, protect food supplies and deter any Continental enemy from attempting to invade the British Isles. On rare occasions when a superior land power threatened to dominate the European mainland, Britain reverted to the tactic of building an alliance with the weaker states. But on the whole she preferred diplomatic isolation; this really meant that while she maintained relations with the other powers, she avoided giving binding commitments to join in a war. In short, Britain had friends but no allies and hence, no entanglements. This was not, of course, wholly true. For example, Britain had given guarantees to maintain the territorial integrity of Belgium. But such promises were, as Salisbury commented, only to be upheld if it suited Britain's current interests to do so.

RETREATING FROM ISOLATION

However, during the 1890s governments increasingly regarded diplomatic isolation as a dangerous liability; for Europe had become divided into two alliance systems – on the one hand, the Triple Alliance of Germany, Austria and Italy, and on the other hand, the Dual Alliance of France and Russia. Although Britain was not the target of these alliances, in practice she found herself disadvantaged by them. This was because she had no reliable supporters when her interests were threatened by another power. Throughout the 1890s Britain clashed over colonial issues, particularly with France and Russia, but even with the United States. The Indian Empire was regarded by her Viceroys as vulnerable to attack from across the north-west frontier. But with her limited forces Britain simply could not guarantee to meet all the possible challenges by herself. Even the Royal Navy, whose gunnery, training and tactics were very poor in the 1890s, was losing its numerical lead as France, Russia and Japan expanded their fleets. Whereas in the early 1880s Britain's capital ships equalled those of France, Russia, Germany, Italy, Japan and the USA combined, by 1897 she had 62 to their 96 battleships.

The implication to be drawn from Britain's military weakness was that she must seek diplomatic support. From time to time the government did win co-operation from Germany and the other Triple Alliance powers over Egypt and the Mediterranean. But an insoluble problem was posed by Russia's expansion in the Far East at the expense of China, which put Britain's lucrative trade at risk. It was in this context that Joseph Chamberlain and others proposed an alliance with Germany in 1898. The combined strength of the two countries would have been sufficient to force the Russians to disgorge any further gains, much as had been done at the Congress of Berlin in 1878. However, this would have exacerbated Germany's fears of a two-front war with both Russia and France, which was worth the risk only if Britain was willing and able to give Germany support. On balance, Salisbury judged that it would be a mistake to support Germany; for as the strongest Continental power she might simply be encouraged to make another attack upon France in the future. As a result, Britain reached the turn of the century still in isolation, but feeling vulnerable.

THE IMPACT OF THE BOER WAR

Despite Chamberlain's efforts to reach an alliance with Germany, relations between the two countries were steadily deteriorating after the demise of Bismarck in 1890, which paved the way for a more expansionist policy. The German naval laws of 1898 signalled an attempt to build a first-class fleet capable of fighting the Royal

Navy in the North Sea and thus posing a direct threat to the security of the British Isles. By 1900, popular literature about hypothetical invasions, which had traditionally cast the French or the Russians as the enemy, had begun to identify Germany in this role.

Above all, it was the war in South Africa between 1899 and 1902 which brought British fears about security to a climax. The war exposed how friendless Britain had become and it revealed the inadequacies of both her armed forces and her military planning. When the war broke out Britain had only 10,000 troops in South Africa; but eventually she was obliged to raise 300,000 in a humiliatingly slow campaign to overcome her enemy. It was apparent that if another colonial conflict had occurred at the same time Britain would have been unable to cope with it.

Thus, although Britain emerged victorious, the government came under acute pressure to reform and modernise national and imperial defence. In spite of the reforms of Gladstone and Edward Cardwell, the army still lacked professionalism. In 1902 A. J. Balfour's government responded by creating the Officers' Training Corps, the Committee of Imperial Defence and, in 1904, the General Staff; this latter body introduced an element of advance planning into the army for the first time in its history. Even so, many thought Britain's resources inadequate. A new pressure group, the National Service League, appeared at this time, to campaign for compulsory military training for all adult males. Though this was normal practice in most European countries, the British condemned it as a 'Prussian' method, preferring to rely upon the voluntary recruiting system until 1916. Significantly no political party was prepared to advocate conscription until after the outbreak of the First World War.

Meanwhile the navy reorganised itself in several ways. Under Admiral Sir John Fisher the scattered fleets were rationalised and increasingly concentrated on two fleets, one at Gibraltar and the other in the English Channel and North Sea. The most dramatic technical innovation came in February 1906 with the launching of the *Dreadnought* battleship. It carried more big guns and travelled faster than any other battleship afloat. But if the *Dreadnought* flattered British pride, it also gave new cause for concern; for all existing ships had been rendered obsolete at a stroke. The possibility that Germany might build to the same standard, but at a faster rate, dominated the period up to 1914.

THE TRIPLE ENTENTE

Although Britain had reorganised her military and naval forces to an impressive extent by 1914, she nevertheless continued to rely upon diplomatic methods for defending her interests. But the failure to obtain an alliance with Germany led directly to the adoption of an alternative expedient – the alliance with Japan in 1902. This treaty proved to be a real turning-point in that it committed Britain to joining Japan in a war if she were involved with two other powers. Since Japan was planning to tackle Russia this was becoming a real possibility. In the event, the Japanese easily defeated the Russians in the war of 1904–5 without involving any other powers. But both Britain and France, who was Russia's ally, perceived the dangers of being dragged in. The French were also dismayed at the evidence of Russia's weakness, and consequently felt even more vulnerable in the face of German military might. For her part Britain now felt much the same about the rapidly growing German navy. As a result of these mutual fears the two states began to draw together, initially by resolving the relatively minor colonial disputes that had divided them for so long; this was the basis of what became known as the Anglo-French Entente of 1904.

However, Lord Lansdowne, the Foreign Secretary, gave no promises of military support to the French; the Entente was in no sense an alliance. None the less, in practice it gradually acquired the significance of an alliance simply because Germany chose to put it under pressure by challenging the French claims to Morocco in 1905 and in 1911. To Sir Edward Grey, Foreign Secretary in the new Liberal government at the end of 1905, this appeared to be the act of a bully. As a result, he agreed that Britain and France should begin to hold naval talks.

Subsequently Grey carried this new policy even further by signing an entente with Russia in 1907. This was a frank recognition on the government's part that it could not expect to defend India by military force and should therefore seek a diplomatic accommodation with the Russians; the effect was to leave Britain in control of the foreign policy of Afghanistan and thereby prevent any Russo-Afghan secret deal. But the crucial implication of the entente was that Britain and Russia recognised that their rivalry in Asia had become overshadowed by the greater problem posed by German military might in Europe.

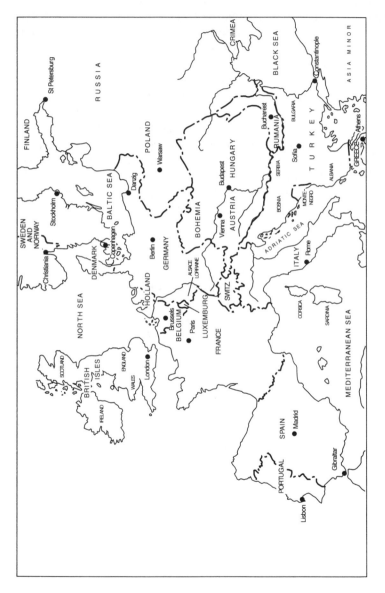

Map 5   Britain and the European Powers in 1871

The completion of the 'Triple Entente' represented a major diplomatic defeat for the Germans, who regarded it as encirclement by three hostile powers. But Germany mishandled her response. In 1911 she again challenged France's attempt to take over Morocco. This greatly alarmed the British government; even Lloyd George, who was still best-known for his opposition to the Boer War, issued a public warning to Germany not to assume that she could disregard Britain's interests by taking high-handed action against France. But although the 1911 crisis brought war nearer, Grey none the less remained reluctant to commit Britain to military support for France or Russia. This is why he continued to refuse to give either a binding commitment, for fear that it would simply encourage them to risk a conflict with Germany. Peace remained his ultimate objective.

PLANS FOR WAR

During the Edwardian years the press and the politicians became obsessed by the need to strengthen the navy for fear of a surprise invasion of the British Isles. Popular newspapers encouraged their readers to report on suspicious behaviour by German 'spies' who were believed to be working as waiters, barbers and clerks. Imaginative accounts such as *The Invasion of 1910* (1906) by William Le Queux also sold well. Boy Scouts patrolled the cliff tops of southern England; and young women began to train in first aid and nursing under the Voluntary Aid Detachments.

Clearly the Liberal government, though anxious to economise on military spending, could not afford to ignore the rising tide of war fever, especially when it seemed to reflect the judgement of professionals about the threat posed by the German navy. In 1909 the Conservatives, assisted by the press, manufactured a naval scare by claiming that Germany was building battleships at a faster rate than Britain. The cabinet accelerated the *Dreadnought* programme and, in fact, retained a comfortable lead over Germany until 1914. In 1910 it passed an Official Secrets Act, which was designed to make it easier to arrest anyone suspected of spying, a highly illiberal measure which passed through parliament without controversy.

The result of the invasion fears was a concentration of ships in the Channel and the North Sea where they could defend France's northern coastline too; meanwhile it was understood that in the Mediterranean the French navy would support British lines of communication. In the event of a war the navy hoped to implement its traditional strategy of blockading the enemy's ports, strangling her trade and waiting for a decisive battle. But all this was irrelevant, for no amount of naval activity could prevent the fall of Paris, which was highly vulnerable to the German armies that stood ready to advance through Belgium and northern France almost immediately on the outbreak of war. Sir Edward Grey's policy was by now founded on the assumption that it was in Britain's national interest to save France from another defeat at the hands of Germany. That this also involved an infringement of Belgium's territorial integrity was of only marginal significance. A German invasion of France would give her access to extra shipbuilding capacity and the use of a long coastline facing the south-east of England.

For this reason Grey responded to French pressure for a more than purely naval commitment on Britain's part. This involved a radical reorganisation of Britain's army, which was undertaken by Richard Haldane; he created a professional army known as the Field Force or Expeditionary Force, which was to be mobilised within fifteen days, and a Home Force or Territorial Army composed of partly-trained men who would not fight until some months later. Although it suited the government to portray the Field Force as a necessary means for dealing with future *colonial* wars, it was, in fact, designed for use in Europe. Thus, by 1914 Britain had abandoned her traditional policy in favour of a real, if informal, commitment to military intervention. Her war plan meant despatching the Field Force as quickly as possible across the Channel to assist the French forces in checking the advance of the Germans towards Paris; the crucial strategic problem had been diagnosed and, as subsequent events were to prove, an effective answer found.

BRITAIN'S ENTRY INTO WAR

Despite these deliberate preparations there was nothing inevitable about Britain's entry into the war in August 1914. Most of the

Liberal ministers detested the whole idea, and the backbenchers kept up their attack on the Foreign Secretary for failing to maintain good relations with Germany. However, as the Liberal and Labour critics preferred to rely upon the navy for national defence, rather than the army, they could not easily resist the additional expenditure on *Dreadnoughts*. Moreover, when Haldane visited Germany in 1912 to seek an agreement to end the naval race, he failed to secure any concessions, which undermined the left-wing critics at home. In fact, they largely failed to influence British policy. This was partly because after the Liberals lost their overall majority in 1910 a serious split over foreign affairs might have upset the government and put at risk all the domestic reforms achieved since 1906. In any case, their fears were to some extent allayed by Grey's skill in avoiding major conflicts; in 1912–13, for example, when several of the Balkan states became involved in a war, he managed to confine it to a regional affair without dragging in the leading powers.

Thus, when the Austrian Archduke was assassinated at Sarajevo in July 1914 the British initially expected that at worst this would lead to another regional war in south-east Europe, which would not require their intervention. However, the Russians' insistence on supporting Serbia against Austria's threats, and the readiness of the German government to back up Austria, made an international war unavoidable. None the less, half the Liberal cabinet remained opposed to British participation, which is why the government initially refused to commit itself to any course of action. On 2 August, Grey managed to persuade the ministers that Britain had entered into an obligation towards the French, and thus it was decided to offer naval protection if Germany threatened France's northern coast. This was a crucial half-way step towards war. On 3 August, Grey's speech in parliament succeeded in winning general support from all parties for the commitment to France. This made it politically possible for the cabinet to issue an ultimatum to Germany on the next day to the effect that she should not violate Belgian territory. This is by no means an indication that the British went to war for the sake of Belgium, though the ruthless invasion by Germany certainly helped the government by giving it a moral cause.

Thus, although two ministers resigned, the Liberal government remained largely united, as did the party generally. Anti-war meetings swiftly collapsed and the country embarked upon war in a mood of euphoria. Of course, this reflected the widely held belief that the fighting would be over by Christmas; the excited crowds that thronged London's streets would have been sobered had they realised that over four years of fighting, involving a scale of casualties previously unknown, lay ahead.

20

The Impact of the Great War

'All over Europe the lights are going out. We shall not see them lit again in our time.' Thus spoke a gloomy Sir Edward Grey on the eve of Britain's entry into the First World War. In many ways his prophecy seems to have been justified by the political, economic and social changes arising from the conflict. During the 1920s and 1930s it proved all too tempting to blame every failure, from moral decline to high unemployment, on the 'Great War'. Nowadays, however, a less apocalyptic view is taken. Many of the wartime charges were ephemeral; others grew out of pre-war developments which simply culminated during wartime.

COALITION GOVERNMENT

In the political sphere the impact of the war was undoubtedly dramatic. It destroyed the Edwardian pattern of Liberal government by alliance with Labour and the Irish; and it left behind it a three-party system of politics which led to over twenty years of Conservative dominance.

Initially Asquith's government coped well with war. The anti-war movement, largely collapsed amid patriotic euphoria; hundreds of thousands of men volunteered to fight for their King and Country; and a party-political truce removed most of the controversies from the agenda. By appointing Lord Kitchener as Secretary of State for War, Asquith went some way to putting his government above partisan criticism for a time.

However, by early 1915 much of this had been undone by the disappointment over Britain's achievements at sea and on land. The Royal Navy proved to be vulnerable to attack by submarines and mines, and thus spent much of its time waiting at bases in the far north of Scotland. The army succeeded in preventing the fall of Paris, but from 1915 onwards became trapped in trench warfare. The offensives launched first by Sir John French and later by Sir Douglas Haig in France invariably failed to gain more than fragments of territory. But it was easy for them to blame the government for failing to supply them with sufficient high explosive shells to drive the Germans from their trenches. As a result, Asquith's ministers soon suffered from claims that they had not prepared adequately for war, an unjust charge but difficult to refute convincingly.

Moreover, the government's five-year term of office was due to expire by December 1915, and it seemed unlikely that the Liberals would be able to win an election in the absence of military victory. This explains why Asquith agreed to form a Coalition government with both Labour and the Conservatives in May 1915. As a result, elections were simply postponed until December 1918.

However, the coalition had disastrous effects on the Liberals, for many of those who had reluctantly supported entry into the war now felt little loyalty to a government that introduced illiberal policies such as press censorship, military conscription and protectionism. As the war dragged on and casualties mounted, left-wing Liberals increasingly criticised the pre-war naval race with Germany and the entanglement with Russia and France. Some joined anti-war organisations such as the Union of Democratic Control, which campaigned for a negotiated compromise to end the war rather than complete victory. This brought them into collaboration with Ramsay MacDonald, the former Labour leader, who had resigned owing to his opposition to the war. MacDonald shrewdly perceived that the war was effectively forcing middle-class Liberals into alliance with working-class radicals. In this way a major realignment of political forces began to develop.

Meanwhile some right-wing Liberals co-operated with their Conservative colleagues. Surprisingly Lloyd George took the lead in demanding innovations such as conscription which offended many Liberals. By December 1916 he and Bonar Law were insisting that Asquith reorganise his government by instituting a smaller and more efficient war cabinet. This eventually led the Prime Minister to resign, whereupon the King invited Lloyd George to form an alternative government. This was another damaging step for the Liberal Party because two-thirds of its MPs, including Asquith himself, refused to join and withdrew to the Opposition benches. The split lasted officially until 1923, but in effect for much longer. British Liberalism never fully recovered.

THE END OF LAISSEZ-FAIRE?

The crisis of wartime helped to accelerate government intervention in the economy which had already begun under the Edwardian Liberal regime. The cause lay in Britain's decision to abandon her traditional naval strategy in favour of a massive commitment to a land war. During the autumn of 1914 and the spring of 1915 young men flocked to the recruiting stations, partly out of patriotic response to Kitchener's appeals, partly through dissatisfaction with their civilian employment, and partly out of a youthful desire for a brief adventure abroad. Eventually Britain put over five million men in the field, an unprecedented number.

This had the immediate effect of creating an insatiable demand for all kinds of military supplies. Industry therefore moved resources out of some traditional industries – in the process sacrificing export markets in textiles, for example – in order to concentrate on producing the steel, coal, ships and munitions required by the war effort. Whenever this production was interrupted by labour shortages, strikes or insufficient power, the government intervened. It took over the railways and coal mines and established a Ministry of Munitions, which owned or managed most of the engineering companies. It also negotiated deals with the trade unions to allow unskilled workers to fill the role of skilled men, and with employers to accept some limitations on profits. In addition the unrest amongst civilians grew so disruptive that measures were taken to maintain living standards, including the imposition of controls on house rents, subsidies on essential food items, and a system of food rationing. Inevitably government expenditure rose rapidly so that by 1917 it amounted to 60 per cent of gross national product by comparison with a mere 7 per cent by in 1913. Although most of this was financed by raising loans, around one-third came from higher taxation, notably income tax, which rose to four times the pre-war level by 1918.

At the time, it appeared that such extensive state intervention in the economy had finally killed the Victorian tradition of laissez-faire. But many of the innovations proved to be ephemeral; after 1918 a reaction against wartime taxation and controls developed; and by 1920 the cabinet had abandoned almost all restrictions on industry. On the other hand, the war had given concrete form to the hitherto vague ideal of a socialist state. Fabian Socialists, especially, were encouraged by the practical demonstration of state control, and demands for the nationalisation of certain industries, such as coal and the railways, won wide support among trade unions. Nor was it possible to effect a complete return to pre-war policies; for example, though income tax was reduced in the 1920s, it remained much higher than before 1914 because the state now carried greater commitments in the form of social welfare policies. Even employers appreciated the advantages of closer collaboration with the government; for the war had given them guaranteed profits, government contracts and protection from foreign competition. In this way traditional competitive capitalism retreated in the face of twentieth-century corporatism.

TOTAL WAR AND SOCIAL CHANGE

For millions of ordinary people the war years proved to be a uniquely disruptive and unsettling experience. Many moved home either to go abroad or to work in munitions factories; expectations of marriage were dashed; the wealthy had to make do with fewer servants; and middle-class girls escaped the control of chaperones. In the army, junior officers were thrown together with working-men, shared their suffering, and often adopted more liberal political views as a result.

Contemporaries, indelibly influenced by the deaths of three-quarters of a million British men, saw the war in negative terms. But historians have increasingly emphasised the positive, long-term significance of mass participation by both soldiers and civilians of both sexes. Some argue that participation raised the status of groups like women and forced the political establishment to make economic and political concessions to reward ordinary people and satisfy their expectations. By 1916 the idea of social reconstruction after the war had become fashionable; its spirit was famously captured by Lloyd George's promise to build homes 'fit for heroes to live in' in 1918. This mood generated several notable reforms including the 1918 Education Act, which raised the school-leaving age to fourteen, the 1918 Maternity and Child Welfare Act, which required local authorities to establish clinics and appoint health visitors, and the 1919 Housing Act, which initiated house-building by local authorities with the aid of state subsidies.

On the other hand, much of this reform was short-lived; post-war cuts in taxation soon killed the housing and education measures. Other wartime measures were essentially continuations of pre-1914 developments; for example, the 1911 scheme for employment insurance was extended to the majority of the working population in 1920.

As a group, women appear to have been major beneficiaries of wartime participation. Thousands of young women cheerfully abandoned low-paid work in domestic service for the higher pay and status of employment in munitions factories. The grant of the vote to 8.4 million women in 1918 symbolised their attainment of full citizenship. However, none of this changed women's role in society. The vote was given to women over thirty years of age, thus excluding the young munitions workers. As soon as the war ended, most women workers were rapidly forced to surrender their new employment, so that their role in the inter-war labour force was no greater than before 1914. Society continued to regard women primarily as wives and mothers. Indeed the war actually strengthened this view by underlining the need to raise new families to replace those who had been killed.

It is true that the aspirations of the post-war generation resulted in a further fall in average family size; two children became typical during the 1920s. This was regarded as a way of maintaining family living standards and improving the health of women. But smaller family size by no means indicated a retreat from marriage itself. Of course, high casualties amongst young males led to fears of a 'Lost Generation'; but in the long run more young men remained at home because of the permanent reduction in emigration from 1914 onwards. Thus, by the mid-1920s *more* men and women married than before 1914, and a trend towards earlier marriage became established. In successive generations the trend towards marriage continued until the 1970s. Paradoxically the political emancipation achieved by women coincided with a reaffirmation of their traditional role; twentieth-century British women were *more* likely to become wives and mothers than their Victorian and Edwardian. predecessors. Thus, in so far as the war helped to foster aspirations to family life it was a force for stability and conservatism in society rather than a disruptive or subversive one.

LLOYD GEORGE'S WARTIME PREMIERSHIP

The rise of David Lloyd George to the premiership in December 1916 was one of the least expected but most significant events of the war. It had major long-term implications for the political system; and more immediately it revolutionised the system of government. Lloyd George replaced the traditional twenty-man cabinet with a new War Cabinet of five, who met daily to make quick decisions affecting the conduct of the war. He also created new ministries for Shipping, Food, Air, Information, Labour, and Pensions, each designed to tackle an obstacle in the war effort or to appease political interests. These posts were frequently filled by businessmen and experts rather than party politicians in the belief that their relevant skills or knowledge would improve administrative efficiency.

Such innovations effectively enhanced the patronage and status of the Prime Minister. Indeed, even after 1918 most British prime ministers found it convenient to retain much of Lloyd George's system. The role of the House of Commons declined, while that of the Prime Minister grew.

In one sense, however, Lloyd George's position was unusually vulnerable. He did not command a formal majority in parliament, nor did he even lead a political party. In effect he relied upon the Tory leader, Bonar Law, to secure the co-operation of his party; in addition, a minority of the Liberals and most of the Labour MPs supported him, at least until the summer of 1917 when the Labour leader, Arthur Henderson, left the cabinet. The Conservatives tolerated Lloyd George because the alternative leaders seemed worse, and because they themselves did not command enough working-class support to feel confident about governing the country alone. Yet they continued to dislike and distrust him, as they showed when they refused to support him in his controversies with the generals. As a result, Lloyd George failed to impose his ideas on military strategy on Sir Douglas Haig, the Commander-in-Chief; Haig's resignation would almost certainly have destroyed the government.

On the other hand, Lloyd George did succeed in forcing the Conservatives to accept domestic reforms as the price for his premiership. This enabled him to resolve the issue of parliamentary reform that had dogged the Edwardian governments. During 1917 and 1918 a bill was passed to extend the vote to all men over twenty-one years, and to women over thirty years who were either local government voters or married to local government voters. Consequently the electorate increased from 7.9 million to 21.4 million, of whom 40 per cent were women.

In the circumstances of 1918 such a social transformation of the political system naturally alarmed the Conservatives. Already several European countries had succumbed to revolution; and the wave of strikes and workers' soviets in Britain suggested that the contagion might be spreading. Conservatives accepted that the election had to be fought as soon as the war had ended, and for this reason they agreed to maintain an alliance with Lloyd George and thus extend the Coalition into peacetime. This proved to be wise, for Lloyd George's status as 'The Man Who Won the War' gave them a major asset at the election. For the Prime Minister the alliance offered his only chance of retaining office. In the event, his premiership lasted until 1922, but in the process it perpetuated the division in the Liberal Party and allowed the Conservatives to enter upon twenty years of almost uninterrupted power.

THE WORKING CLASS AND THE WAR

Before 1914 the left in Britain had expected war to disrupt the economy, create unemployment and thus provoke working-class unrest. In fact, these fears were to a large extent misplaced. Certainly wartime inflation caused hardship, especially during 1914–16, but on the whole, working-class families gained in both material and political terms. The underlying reason for this lay in the fact that the insatiable demands of the military machine created a shortage of labour. As a result, workers began to enjoy a full week's work and overtime. Others abandoned low-paid occupations for more skilled jobs. In the process the trade unions could bargain more effectively and increase their political status. Not surprisingly their membership rose, from 4.1 million to 6 million by 1918.

The combination of higher wages for men, better employment for women and the payment of allowances to the dependants of servicemen had the effect of raising the incomes of many families. To some extent this improvement was cancelled by increased food prices, though by 1917 the government had subsidised most basic items of consumption and ensured a fairer share by means of rationing. As a result the health and life expectancy of civilians actually improved during the war; in particular, infant mortality rates continued to improve, falling from 142 per thousand live births in 1900 to 82 by 1920.

Wartime experience also seems to have raised the expectations and promoted the class consciousness of many British workers. This manifested itself in the pattern of industrial militancy. During 1914–16 the number of strikes fell, partly under the influence of patriotism and partly because many organised workers were absent at the front. However, the trend was soon reversed; strikes increased each year from 1917 to 1920. This reflected a common feeling amongst workers that their own contribution to the war had not been matched by those in the wealthier classes who were enjoying huge profits by supplying government contracts. This was even more true of demobilised soldiers, who realised that they had missed the high wages available at home, and were anxious to catch up after 1918. This made the post-war years a time of unusual industrial militancy until rising unemployment forced the men back onto the defensive.

These developments in the labour force had important political repercussions. It was not until the summer of 1917 that the Labour Party, which had been a loyal participant in both Coalition governments, made its bid for real independence as a result of the expulsion of Authur Henderson from the cabinet. Ramsay MacDonald and the Fabian Socialist Sidney Webb drew up new policy statements for the election and devised a new constitution which included an official commitment to state ownership of the means of production and distribution for the first time. This offered a symbolic break with Liberalism. Of more practical importance was the decision to recruit an individual membership to complement the indirect trade union membership, and to organise a local Labour Party in each constituency. This prepared the way for an increase in parliamentary candidates – from 78 in 1910 to 388 in 1918 – which, by implication, meant abandoning the electoral pact with the Liberals. By 1918 Labour had good reason to feel confident about this initiative, for the Liberals were divided and demoralised by the rivalry between Asquith and Lloyd George. Moreover, the reform bill of 1918 had enfranchised all adult male workers as well as many women. An historic turning-point had arrived.

Certainly the general election held in December 1918 produced a breakthrough for Labour, though the results fell far short of expectations. Lloyd George's Coalition government scored a massive victory with 526 seats and 54 per cent of the vote. Most of the new members were Tories, swept in by the vengeful, nationalistic mood of the voters and by the Prime Minister's prestige. Labour's 22 per cent share of the poll and 61 seats represented only a modest improvement on the pre-war maximum of 42 seats. But by comparison with the collapse of the independent Liberals this was an impressive performance. It left Labour as the largest party of Opposition, and thus, as the alternative government. In this change lay the long-term significance of the war.

21

The Inter-War
Economic Depression

By 1918 the general mood in Britain was for a return to pre-war conditions. Nowhere was this stronger than in economic affairs, where orthodox economists, politicians and businessmen eagerly anticipated the re-establishment of the pound as the leading currency, the recapturing of world markets and the return of the City of London to its traditional role. However, this optimism reflected a misplaced confidence in the Edwardian economy, which had suffered from declining productivity and a narrowly based export sector. It also ignored the way in which the war had exacerbated existing weaknesses so as to make it almost impossible for Britain to recover her previous influence over the world economy.

In effect, the war years had driven economic resources into coal, steel, shipbuilding and engineering in order to supply the armed forces. But this created opportunities for the United States, India and Japan to expand their production of textiles and other goods to fill the gaps left by Britain. Subsequently it proved difficult for Britain to recover the lost markets. There were several reasons for this. Many countries resorted to protectionism; the depressed state of the world economy limited the demand for traditional British products; nationalism undermined British markets in India; and industries such as coal were simply too inefficient to be competitive. Finally, the steep fall in the price of food and raw materials during the 1920s greatly reduced the income of many agricultural and colonial states which had formerly bought manufactures from Britain. Moreover, Britain had sold off many of her foreign assets during the war so that her earnings from investment as well as from shipping and insurance were inadequate to cover her visible trade deficit. She had been forced to raise huge loans, notably in the United States, to whom she now owed £1150 million. As a result, Britain was no longer in a position to stimulate the world economy and restore a high level of trade. Only the United States could now play that role, but she declined to do so.

In domestic finance the war had also left the government with little room for manoeuvre. The conventional aim of balancing the budget had been abandoned and the Treasury had effectively lost control of finances. After 1918 it was determined to regain its influence. But government borrowing had increased the National Debt from £650 million to £8000 million and, as a result, the state paid £325 million, which represented a quarter of its revenue, in interest charges on the National Debt. Yet political pressure to reduce the high levels of wartime taxation competed with the costs of house-building, pensions for ex-servicemen and their families as well as unemployment benefits and interest payments on the National Debt. In this situation the governments of the 1920s opted for caution, lowering taxation and curtailing expenditure in the hope that a recovery of the export markets for British industry would resolve their dilemma by boosting revenue and reducing unemployment.

CHURCHILL AND THE CURRENCY

It is no exaggeration to say that the Treasury and the governments of the 1920s regarded the currency as the most important issue of economic policy. During wartime the Bank of England had been forced to accept that it could not back the currency with gold; paper banknotes had been issued; and the value of the pound had fallen. After 1918 it was widely believed that Britain should return to the 'Gold Standard' and that the value of the pound ought to be exactly the same as before the war – 4.86 American dollars. However, the authorities hesitated over implementing this policy for several years. In 1920 the pound stood at only 3.40 dollars, though it had risen to a point close to the pre-1914 level by 1924. This encouraged the Chancellor of the Exchequer in the new Conservative government, Winston Churchill, to take the fateful step of returning to gold at 4.86 dollars in 1925.

This policy aroused relatively little debate except between Treasury officials and unorthodox economists such as J. M. Keynes. Neither Conservative nor Labour Chancellors doubted the wisdom of the return to the Gold Standard. They expected it to restore the role of the pound in world trade, thereby bringing benefits to the City of London and to manufacturers. However, the effects were seriously damaging. By raising the value of the currency the Chancellor made British exports more expensive and thus hindered manufacturers from recovering export markets; this is why unemployment fell only slowly during the 1920s. In addition, the maintenance of the pound at its new level meant that Britain had to attract foreign funds by putting up the Bank Rate, which in turn deterred manufacturers from investing in their businesses. Worst of all, most employers, especially in the export sector, attempted to become more competitive by reducing costs, which meant cutting wages. Fears about a general attack on wage levels aroused the trade unions to organise the General Strike of 1926.

As a result of this policy the British economy grew more slowly than those of other western countries during the 1920s. The General Strike had the effect of checking major reductions in wages. Thus by 1929, industry was seriously handicapped and the balance of payments deficit was becoming worse. Meanwhile, the costs of unemployment had steadily undermined the government's control of the budget. The pressing need to balance the budget by imposing expenditure cuts broke up the Labour government in August 1931. However, although the new National Government was formed with a view to defending the pound, it wholly failed to do so. In September 1931 Britain again went off the Gold Standard and her currency was effectively devalued. This was, in fact, the first step on the road to recovery, though as unemployment increased during 1931–3 this was far from obvious.

THE UNEMPLOYMENT PROBLEM

The inter-war period began in optimism as businessmen offered consumer goods that had not been available for four years; this created a brief boom in 1919–20. But when this collapsed, unemployment rose sharply to 2 million, or 17 per cent, in 1921. Thereafter unemployment remained high until 1940. Its causes were to some extent cyclical; as world markets shrank during the slump of 1929–33, Britain's unemployment rate rose to a peak of 22 per cent, or about 3 million. Although the situation improved considerably between 1922 and 1928, and again between 1934 and 1939, unemployment never fell below 10 per cent.

The stubborn persistence of unemployment at 10 per cent suggests that the underlying problem was *structural*. This seems clear from the regional concentration of unemployment in Yorkshire, Lancashire, north-east England, Scotland and Wales where the economy was dominated by coal, steel, shipbuilding and textiles. For example, in 1921 unemployment in shipbuilding stood at 36 per cent, and at 27 per cent in engineering, compared with 17 per cent nationally. The town of Jarrow in County Durham, which was almost wholly dependent on ships, suffered 67 per cent unemployment by 1934; but towns in south-east England engaged in light engineering had only 3 or 4 per cent out of work at that time.

The orthodox remedy for unemployment was bleak. In the view of many economists and businessmen unemployment would remain high until wages fell significantly. Politicians and trade unionists argued that the available supply of jobs should be reserved for those who needed them – by which they meant men, especially ex-servicemen. To this end most of the women who had entered industry during wartime were ejected in 1919–20. This reflected the conventional assumption that working men had to support a family of dependants from their wages, whereas women's earnings simply represented marginal additions to income, which could be spent on luxuries. On the contrary, many widows now acted as the chief wage-earners in the family; and as the depression wore on, wives often found it necessary to take paid employment to replace their husbands' income. Another traditional remedy for unemployment had been emigration. But after 1918 emigration never returned to its former level in spite of encouragement from the government. In fact, the depression affected the colonies and America so badly that by 1930 more people were returning to Britain than were leaving.

Most of the controversy surrounding unemployment was provoked by the schemes for supporting its victims rather than ideas for curing the condition. In 1920 the system of unemployment insurance pioneered by Lloyd George in 1911 had been extended to cover 12 million workers. This still excluded domestic servants and agricultural labourers, and in practice women were denied benefits

if they refused to accept jobs as servants. Some politicians considered that the benefits removed the incentive to search for employment, and consequently payments were withdrawn from anyone
who was judged not to be genuinely seeking work. In fact, many
young men migrated from Wales, the North and Scotland to the
expanding towns of south-east England. However, this could never
be a complete solution to unemployment, partly because the growth
industries failed to generate sufficient new jobs, but also because
employers invariably avoided the skilled, unionised, male labour
force of the old industrial areas. They preferred to employ very
young men or women who would accept lower wages. In any case
the skills of the male workers were inappropriate in the consumer
goods industries that sprang up in the South. Consequently, it was
not until 1940, when the economy had been stimulated by the
demands of war, that unemployment at last fell below 10 per cent.

ECONOMIC RECOVERY IN THE 1930s

Alternatives to the economic strategies of the Treasury ranged from
socialism to Keynesianism, though their advocates were largely
marginal figures between the wars. In the immediate aftermath
of the war many Labour and Liberal politicians wanted to impose
a special levy on capital, designed to reduce the National Debt at
a stroke. The Independent Labour Party proposed state control of
the banks, investment in public works schemes to boost employment, and raising the school-leaving age. But the most original and
comprehensive alternative programme emerged from the mind of
J. M. Keynes, who first attained prominence by attacking post-war
governments for extracting financial reparations from Germany and
for returning to the Gold Standard. Keynes challenged the assumption that unemployment could be dealt with by trying to restore
export markets. Instead he proposed a series of measures including
devaluation, low interest rates, and tariffs which were designed to
stimulate the *domestic* market for British goods. But his most significant policy involved a major counter-cyclical programme of state
investment in road-building, land drainage, housing and telephone
installation to create new employment and raise demand for goods.
    Although Keynes's complete analysis did not appear until 1936
when he published *The General Theory of Employment, Interest and*

Money, his ideas achieved wide currency during the late 1920s, partly as a result of his collaboration with Lloyd George on the Liberal Party's economic plan, *Britain's Industrial Future* (1928). Moreover, after 1931 many politicians who had originally disparaged Keynesian ideas, began to adopt them. On the left, the influential trade union leader Ernest Bevin argued that the application of counter-cyclical policies by President Roosevelt in the USA proved that unemployment could be tackled effectively by the state. On the right, some younger Conservatives such as Harold Macmillan advocated a 'middle way' between private enterprise and socialism; they supported reformist pressure groups such as 'Political and Economic Planning, formed in 1931 with a view to persuading governments to adopt a more interventionist policy. In their discussions lay the origins of the consensus policies of the post-1945 era.

Meanwhile, power lay with the National Government (1931–1940). It was ostensibly committed to balancing the budget and defending the value of the currency, but proved to be much more flexible in practice. Although unemployment grew worse for the first two years of the new government's life, by 1934 an improvement set in; from 3 million, unemployment fell to 1.5 million by 1937. Moreover, the output of the economy increased much faster than it had during the 1920s, largely as a result of expansion in house-building, motor cars, vacuum cleaners and other electrical appliances, and the aircraft industry.

Neville Chamberlain, who served as Chancellor of the Exchequer until 1937, went some way to meeting the Keynesian strategy, though he never acknowledged this. For example, attempts to balance the budget were abandoned, and the £70 million of expenditure cuts and taxation increases adopted in the crisis of 1931 were reversed. After 1932 Chamberlain's budgets were in fact mildly inflationary; by 1934, partly for political reasons, taxation had been lowered again and even the reductions in unemployment benefits had been reversed. Extra expenditure on rearmament after 1935 gave a further stimulus to the economy.

More importantly the failure to maintain the value of the currency released the economy from the handicap it had suffered since 1925. By March 1932 the pound had fallen to 3.40 dollars, a substantial devaluation which helped to maintain exports and to restrict imports, if only temporarily. Moreover, devaluation relieved the government of the need to maintain high interest rates; as a result, investment became more attractive, especially for the housng industry, which enjoyed a boom for the remainder of the decade.

Finally the National Government seized the opportunity for which the Conservatives had been waiting since the Edwardian period, to abandon free trade. During 1931 and 1932 it imposed a general 10 per cent duty on imports and took powers to impose duties of up to 100 per cent on selected items. This, however, had limited effects. It probably encouraged new investment in steel which enjoyed the benefit of a 33 per cent protective tariff; but other traditional industries had diminished too greatly to be easily revived. Suppliers of electrical goods captured the domestic market, but tariffs effectively propped up the less efficient manufacturers. Finally, it proved difficult to use the tariff policy to promote Empire trade as Chamberlain hoped. Although Empire produce was given the advantage of lower duties on entry to Britain, there were few reciprocal concessions. Most colonies insisted on protecting their own manufacturers against British competition, and so the ideal of Empire free trade remained a dream. Consequently, the triumph of Chamberlainite protectionism proved to be a brief one; after 1945 the western economies, including Britain, aspired to return to free trade.

22

The Rise of Labour, 1918–29

By 1918 the war had reduced British politics to a chaotic condition. The Liberals, Labour and the Conservatives were all to a greater or lesser degree divided; and in Ireland the Home Rule Party had been completely outflanked by the extreme Republican forces represented by Sinn Fein, whose elected representatives refused to attend the London parliament. All the conventional parties regarded the huge new electorate as volatile, partly because many new voters were young and female, and because of the unsettling effects of military service on those who had recently returned from France. Christabel Pankhurst fuelled the politicians' worst fears by establishing a new Women's Party; but fortunately for them this was disbanded soon after her failure to win election in 1918.

THE COLLAPSE OF COALITION

By far the most conspicuous symptom of change in British politics was the remarkable survival of Lloyd George's wartime Coalition until 1922. For several years it seemed likely that this would generate a new Centre or National Party drawing upon elements of Conservative, Liberal and Labour support. However, the huge majority enjoyed by the Coalition's supporters in 1918 was deceptive; it obscured the fact that the whole enterprise was essentially an expedient to keep Lloyd George in power and to assist the Conservatives to make a difficult transition from war to peace.

Inevitably the government began to disintegrate as Conservatives discovered that it was not, after all, necessary for them to endure Lloyd George's rule indefinitely.

Four issues particularly antagonised Lloyd George's Tory supporters. First, they launched an Anti-Waste campaign which succeeded in forcing the government to reduce income tax and abandon its housing and education reforms. Secondly, they objected to the concessions made to the Indian National Congress now agitating under Gandhi's leadership for self-government. Thirdly, they condemned the extensive sales of titles by the Prime Minister's personal agents; huge sums paid for knighthoods and peerages went into the Lloyd George Fund, thereby depriving the Conservative Party of some of its sources of income. Finally, after a protracted war fought between the British army and Republican forces, the government negotiated a settlement with the Irish leaders in 1921 which gave independence to three-quarters of the country, leaving only Ulster as part of the United Kingdom. Defence of the Union had been so central to the Tory Party's ideology since the 1880s that this defeat caused despair and disillusionment which was bound to destroy what remained of its loyalty to the Coalition. But the more concessions Lloyd George made to right-wing critics the more he embarrassed his Liberal followers, some of whom began to seek reunion with their old party.

The final blow to the Coalition came when its electoral appeal began to fail. As the Labour and Liberal vote recovered at by-elections, it became obvious to Conservatives that Lloyd George had ceased to be an asset to them. Consequently, at a meeting in October 1922 the MPs repudiated the alliance in order to be able to stand as an independent party at the next election. Lloyd George resigned immediately, never to return to power. Bonar Law, who had retired as Tory leader owing to poor health in 1921, was recalled. He became Prime Minister, called an immediate election and won it comfortably. Wartime coalitionism was thus decisively replaced by a return to three-party politics.

THE DEVELOPMENT OF THE LABOUR MOVEMENT

The underlying object of the Coalition had been to contain the growth of the Labour Movement, which appeared to have been greatly strengthened by the war and the new democratic franchise. Right-wing Conservatives, increasingly obsessed by the perceived threat of Bolshevik subversion, professed to see the British Labour Party as an agent of revolutionary forces. However, such alarmism was far from justified. By 1920 the trade unions claimed 8.3 million members and the number of strikes rose sharply, resulting in the loss of 35 million working days in 1919, 26 million in 1920 and 85 million in 1921. Militancy had been stimulated partly by the evidence of extensive wartime profiteering by businessmen and by the determination of the government to relinquish controls over the coal mines and other industries rather than taking them into permanent state ownership. The sudden slump during 1920–21 and the inevitable rise in unemployment exacerbated tensions in the working class.

In this deteriorating situation some workers felt attracted by direct action as a means of pressurising a government which was too strongly entrenched to be moved by parliamentary methods. Syndicalism achieved some influence, for example, in the Triple Alliance of 1921. But before the planned strike of the Triple Alliance took place, the transport and railway workers withdrew, leaving the miners on their own. In spite of this, the government took the threat of a general strike seriously enough to begin organising an emergency system for maintaining supplies if it ever took place. The most famous example of direct action occurred in 1922 when the opponents of the government's anti-Russian policy organised the dockworkers to refuse to load a ship which was to carry arms to help the forces fighting the Communist regime.

However, these were untypical cases. On the whole the union leaders adopted strike action for purely material objectives, not as a political weapon. They fully endorsed the parliamentary route to power via the Labour Party. By 1922 there were grounds for optimism about this strategy. While the Coalition had become discredited and the Liberals remained bitterly divided between Asquith and Lloyd George, Labour had emerged as the obvious alternative government. By this time the popular reaction against the war and the pre-war arms race boosted the reputation of Ramsay MacDonald, who was widely seen to have been justified in his courageous stand against the war.

Despite his left-wing credentials, however, MacDonald's ideology placed him firmly in the radical Liberal tradition. Although the Party adopted a Socialist commitment in 1918, it failed to devise a practical proramme for nationalisation of industry, and under MacDonald's influence it retreated from the idea of imposing a levy on capital to reduce the National Debt. Philip Snowden, who dominated Labour's economic thinking in the 1920s, upheld free trade, balanced budgets and the Gold Standard. Thus, while Labour promised to reduce unemployment, it was more precise about social policies than about economic remedies: maintaining unemployment benefits, introducing pensions for widows, building council houses and extending the school-leaving age, for example.

For a party still struggling to establish itself, the common ground with Liberalism represented a great advantage. In the 1920s many able Liberals, including Charles Trevelyan, Richard Haldane and Christopher Addison, joined the Labour Party, attracted by its support for disarmament, social welfare reform and free trade. A number of Conservatives, such as Sir Oswald Mosley, disillusioned by the failure of orthodox policies to reduce unemployment, also gravitated to Labour, seeing it as the best hope for the future progress of ordinary people. In this way Labour soon became more than simply a working-class party.

The advance of Labour manifested itself from 1919 onwards in extensive gains in local government elections which continued throughout the decade. In many towns this reversed the pattern of Edwardian politics by driving the Liberals into pacts with the Conservatives. This advance was sustained by a major increase in resources available to the party. As a result of trade union expansion, 3.5 million members paid to become affiliated members of the Labour Party. The larger unions frequently put forward their officials as parliamentary candidates by offering to pay the costs of their election campaigns. The number of Labour candidates rose from 388 in 1918 to 571 – for 615 seats – by 1929; and the local Labour Parties increased from only 150 before 1914 to 527 in 1922 and over 600 by 1924. At last Labour had become a party on a national scale, completely eclipsing the Liberals, though its resources remained inferior to those of the Conservatives.

THE FIRST LABOUR GOVERNMENT, 1924

In spite of Labour's advance, the Conservatives held office for the entire inter-war period except for nine months in 1924 and between

1929 and 1931. Although they won only 38 per cent of the poll at most of these elections, they won most of the seats because Labour and the Liberals divided the non-Conservative vote relatively evenly between them. In fact, Labour's rise to power was a steady, not a dramatic one: from 22 per cent of the vote in 1918 the party won 29–30 per cent in 1922 and 1923, 33 per cent in 1924 and 37 per cent in 1929.

With such slender popular support Labour could not have formed a government in 1924 but for certain errors committed by the Tory leader, Stanley Baldwin. After succeeding Bonar Law in 1923 he called an election in the same year in order to win a popular mandate to introduce tariffs, which he believed to be the best way of increasing employment. However, the voters, especially the women, reacted almost as strongly as they had in 1906; free trade was still preferred because it was the guarantee of cheap food supplies. Consequently the Conservatives returned only 258 MPs to 191 for Labour and 159 for the Liberals. No party enjoyed a majority, but the Liberals quickly joined with Labour to force Baldwin's resignation. King George V then exercised his constitutional rights to invite MacDonald to form a government. This was an important decision, for the King had shown confidence in Labour despite its lack of experience in office and the absence of a majority; this helps to explain why most of the working-class movement continued to support the monarchy as an institution above party politics.

Though surprised by the turn of events, McDonald knew that he had to accept the invitation, otherwise Labour would be accused of being unfit to govern. He handled the opportunity with considerable skill. Resisting the temptation to offer a deal to the Liberals, he deliberately chose to form a minority government whose life would inevitably be brief. In doing this MacDonald hoped to achieve two objects: to demonstrate Labour's competence and to enhance its status in relation to the Liberals, now firmly excluded from office.

Much depended upon the personnel in MacDonald's new cabinet. He himself occupied the Foreign Office, and he appointed several experienced former Liberal and Conservative ministers. His Chancellor of the Exchequer, Snowden, reassured the financial interests by introducing a cautious budget in which there was no attempt at imposing state controls or taxing the wealthy. This, of course, disappointed many Socialists, who had hoped for an attack upon unemployment. However, by offering few targets to the Opposition parties, the government managed to retain office for the first nine months of 1924. In the autumn, when the Liberals and Conservatives decided to challenge him, MacDonald accepted the inevitability of defeat, resigned and called yet another election. The 1924 election put the Conservatives back in power with 419 seats while Labour lost 40 of its 191 seats; but this setback was less significant than the total defeat suffered by the Liberals, now reduced to only 40 MPs. As the Liberals became marginalised Labour emerged as the only realistic alternative to the Conservatives.

THE GENERAL STRIKE, 1926

Stanley Baldwin, who served as Prime Minister from 1924 to 1929, represented a conciliatory and liberal brand of Conservatism. He aspired to uphold the Disraelian tradition by enacting social reforms, such as widows pensions in 1925, and political reforms such as the equal franchise for women in 1928. Above all, he accepted Labour as a reputable governing party and sought to avoid class confrontation: 'Give Peace in Our Time Oh Lord!' was his response to the threat of industrial strikes. However, Baldwin's strategy was gradually undermined by his failure to reduce unemployment and by the return to the Gold Standard in 1925. It was this latter policy, which appeared to the trade unions to herald a general reduction in wages, which precipitated the General Strike of 1926.

The origins of the General Strike may be traced back to 1921. The onset of long-term unemployment at that point began to reduce union membership and put organised labour on the defensive. The coal miners, however, were anxious to counter-attack. Their industry stood at the centre of the economic–political problems of the inter-war period. One-third of its output had been exported before 1914, but productivity had diminished and export markets had been lost. As a result, by 1925 the coal owners insisted that they must cut wages, which comprised 70 per cent of their production costs. The miners successfully persuaded the Trades Union Congress that the attack on their wages was only the first step to an attempt to lower the wages of all industrial workers. In order to avert this threat the union leaders agreed to organise a general strike. Baldwin, however, hoped to avoid this by setting up a commission of enquiry into the coal industry and, meanwhile, maintaining the miners' wages by means of a subsidy from the government. This postponed the General Strike for nine months until May 1926.

In the event, the strike lasted for only nine days. Despite being very solidly supported by millions of workers and their families, it was abruptly called off by the TUC without any attempt to negotiate terms for the men as they returned to work and with no concessions for the miners. This extraordinary outcome can be explained only by the mentality of the TUC leaders. Men such as Ernest Bevin, the leader of the giant Transport and General Workers Union, never endorsed the ideology behind the general strike. Rather, they accepted it reluctantly in the hope of averting wage cuts for their own members; they never believed it was realistic to maintain the miners' wages, and therefore called the strike off once they felt they had shown a measure of solidarity and before the funds of their own unions became exhausted.

On the face of it this amounted to a resounding defeat for the trade union movement. This was certainly true for the miners, who remained stubbornly out on strike for six months before being forced by poverty to accept greatly reduced wages. However, seen in the broader context the results were more positive. The response to the strike had been sufficiently emphatic to make an impression upon employers, who largely refrained from imposing the lower wages they had believed to be necessary. In fact prices fell faster than wages during the late 1920s and early 1930s. Of course there were far fewer strikes after 1926 and the number of trade union members dropped; from a peak of 8.3 million in 1921, membership sank to 5.2 million by 1926 and to 4.4 million by 1933. Clearly most of the fall *preceded* the General Strike and thus must be attributed to long-term unemployment.

For the Prime Minister the defeat of the General Strike was in one sense a triumph. However, by embittering the workers and exacerbating class antagonism it undermined his political strategy. In 1927 Baldwin gave way to pressure from his right-wing colleagues to introduce the Trades Disputes Act, which made sympathetic strikes illegal and made it more difficult for the unions to collect the political levy. Although this reduced the Labour Party's income temporarily, it only had the effect of uniting the industrial and political wings of the movement in their determination to win the next election and repeal the legislation.

'WE CAN CONQUER UNEMPLOYMENT'

By the end of the 1920s it had become obvious that the government's economic policy had failed to solve the problem of unemployment, which by 1929 stood at 1.1. million. The issue was brilliantly exploited by Lloyd George who had taken over the leadership of the Liberal Party in 1926. His collaboration with J. M. Keynes and other economists resulted in the publication of the Liberal Yellow Book, *Britain's Industrial Future* (1928). This was an extraordinarily detailed economic programme designed to pull Britain out of the depression by massive schemes of government investment to create employment and increase consumer demand. In a famous summary produced for the election under the title 'We Can Conquer Unemployment', Lloyd George claimed that he could reduce unemployment to normal proportions, by which he meant about half a million, within a year. The revival in Liberal fortunes in by-elections during the late 1920s suggested that the public were convinced. By contrast, Baldwin offered a conventional policy under the slogan 'Safety First'.

Although Lloyd George's bold attempt to focus upon unemployment put the Conservatives at a disadvantage, he himself was easily ridiculed by both the other parties as the man who had already discredited himself by extravagant promises. In fact, it was MacDonald who benefited from the unemployment issue despite his failure to devise a precise economic policy. Many voters assumed that Labour would tackle unemployment by methods similar to those advocated by Lloyd George. As a result the Labour Party returned 288 MPs at the election compared with 260 for the Conservatives and 59 for the Liberals. However, this proved to be a poisoned triumph, for MacDonald was entering office at a time when Europe was soon to be engulfed in a major financial crisis which was to alter the British political scene for a decade.

23

Political Stability in the 1930s

The 1930s has traditionally been regarded as a bleak decade for the British people, dominated by social distress, the collapse of the Labour government, the sudden upsurge of fascism, and the growing threat of another European war. Yet by comparison with many other societies the British escaped the worst effects of the economic depression. The manifestations of political violence were on a small scale and the parliamentary system never seemed in serious danger of being overthrown. Why was this so?

THE ORIGINS OF THE NATIONAL GOVERNMENT

After Ramsay MacDonald's return to office in 1929 it rapidly became clear that he had no medium-term policy for dealing with the crisis of capitalism. Unemployment rose steadily from 1.1 million in June 1929 to 2.5 million by October 1930. The Prime Minister, derided by Churchill as 'the boneless wonder', seemed to be a prisoner of the orthodox economic views of his Chancellor, Snowden, and the treasury. In February 1930 a junior minister, Sir Oswald Mosley, resigned office after failing to persuade the cabinet to adopt an interventionist policy to create employment. Behind the scenes Lloyd George attempted to negotiate an agreement with MacDonald, offering him Liberal support in Parliament in return for a bolder attack on unemployment.

But by the summer of 1931 the Prime Minister could prevaricate no longer. Britain's balance of payments deficit had provoked the withdrawal of funds from London in anticipation of a devaluation of the pound. Thus the pressure to restore confidence forced the government to devise expedients for balancing the budget. A committee under Sir George May warned that the budget deficit for 1932 would be £120 million and recommended economies of £97 million. However, this was rejected by the Trades Union Congress because it included a proposed reduction of 10 per cent in unemployment benefits. As a result the cabinet split and MacDonald was obliged to resign.

At this stage King George V intervened in order to persuade the leaders of the three political parties to form a coalition, which became known as the National Government. Its immediate object was to lead the country through the economic crisis, defend the currency and balance the budget. MacDonald was to remain as Prime Minister. This proposal was, however, rejected by most Labour MPs and by Lloyd George, but supported by the Conservatives, most of the Liberals, led by Sir Herbert Samuel, and by fifteen Labour MPs.

Contrary to expectations the National Government lasted from 1931 to 1940. The explanation for this lay with the Conservatives. Although reluctant to join originally, Baldwin soon saw the advantages of a National Government. It enabled him to maintain his own leadership of the party and restrain its right-wing elements. It helped Conservatives to achieve their long-standing aim of introducing a policy of protectionism. And it created highly advantageous conditions for winning a general election. Indeed, the new government moved quickly to hold an election in October 1931 while the Labour Party was still too demoralised by the defection of MacDonald to offer a coherent alternative. As a result, in October 1931 the National Government secured 556 seats and Labour was reduced from 288 to a mere 52. This placed the government in a position of immense power. MacDonald remained as Prime Minister until 1935; he was followed by Baldwin (1935–7) and by Neville Chamberlain (1937–40).

During these years the National Government was bitterly attacked by the left over the effects of its policies on the working-class, and from within its own ranks by Churchill over the failure to re-arm in the face of the threat from Germany. But it was vulnerable only for a brief period between 1931 and 1933 when the economic depression grew steadily worse and unemployment continued to rise. This situation presented an opportunity to extra-parliamentary forces on the far right to challenge the conventional politicians.

THE BRITISH UNION OF FASCISTS

During the 1920s one or two extreme right-wing organisations appeared in Britain including the Imperial Fascist League. They were essentially symptoms of the fears about Bolshevik subversion and nationalistic attacks on the Empire. But their support was too small to make them more than a marginal factor in politics. However, the formation of the British Union of Fascists (BUF) in 1932 posed a far more serious challenge. Its leader, Sir Oswald Mosley, had been a junior officer in the war and a Conservative MP, but had joined the Labour party in 1926. His oratorical skill, physical presence and intellectual powers made him a formidable politician. He appealed to disillusioned men who had fought in the war and now felt themselves neglected. He capitalised on the apparent inability of the conventional liberal parliamentarians to cope with the inter-war economic depression, and claimed that when the National Government failed, his movement would step in to save Britain from Communism. Indeed, one of the attractions for Conservatives was Mosley's frequently demonstrated boast that his Blackshirt stewards could prevent the disruption of political meetings by left-wingers. What made the BUF so alarming for the National Government was the possibility that if Mosley carried out his threat to enter his own candidates at the next general election it seemed certain that he would split the National vote and possibly let Labour back into power.

Between 1932 and 1934 the BUF recruited thousands of enthusiastic members especially amongst young people. Mosley also campaigned in depressed areas such as Lancashire where he claimed that the former markets of the cotton textile industry could be recovered by suppressing Indian manufacturing. In this way the fascist appeal varied from one region of the country to another according to local grievances. However, the BUF's ideology and programme also owed something to the influence of the larger and better-established fascist movements on the Continent.

Mosley visited Italy, received financial support from Mussolini, and adopted the idea of the corporate state. Later in the 1930s the BUF also emulated the German National Socialists in attacking the Jewish community, which it treated as a scapegoat for the economic failures of the country.

But despite its rapid growth, the BUF lost momentum in 1934. This has usually been attributed to the reaction against the violence used by the fascists, notably at a mass rally at Olympia in London. The violent methods alienated many of the respectable Conservatives and major newspapers such as the *Daily Mail* which had given Mosley favourable publicity. Although the BUF continued its campaigns it never seemed likely to pose a serious threat to the parliamentary system after 1934. In retrospect it has been tempting to conclude that fascism was fundamentally alien to British society because the democratic culture was so long-established. However, this is almost certainly too complacent a view. The influx of thousands of young men into the BUF, attracted by its quasi-military style, was unmistakeable evidence that violence continued to be part of the political tradition in Britain. Mosley's ambitions were thwarted less by the political culture than by economic factors. Britain suffered far less from the depression than other countries. In particular she escaped the inflation that destroyed the value of middle-class savings and incomes, and thus created support for fascism in Germany. As a result, Mosley never fully capitalised on the potential support for his movement. The economic recovery from 1934 onwards confined the BUF to the margins and the drift towards war with Germany made Mosley appear increasingly a traitor in British eyes.

THE FAILURE OF THE LEFT

Another part of the explanation for the survival of the National Government lay in the fragmented and demoralised condition of the left in Britain after 1931. For some Socialists the betrayal of his party by Ramsay MacDonald and the timid economic policy of his government called into question whether it was realistic to achieve socialism by parliamentary methods. They argued that any radical economic programme would inevitably be frustrated by a crisis engineered by financiers. However, such doubts concerned small groups of socialist intellectuals in the Independent Labour Party and the Socialist League more than the rank-and-file workingmen. The mainstream of the Labour Movement remained committed to parliamentary methods. If a repetition of the events of 1931 was to be avoided, the Labour Party had to devise a more practical economic programme. During the 1930s Labour adopted the nationalisation of 14 industries and a scheme for compensating the former owners – a major advance on earlier proposals.

Labour also achieved a partial recovery from its defeat at the election. A new leader, George Lansbury, took over from 1931 to 1935. When he resigned in disagreement with the party's defence policy he was succeeded by a middle-class Socialist, Clement Attlee. Meanwhile the Party won by-elections at the expense of the National Government and increased its individual membership from 280,000 in 1932 to 419,000 by 1934.

However, the Party's position in parliament was so hopeless that some on the left looked to alternative means for defending the interests of the working class. Yet none of these proved wholly realistic. For example, the trade union movement continued to lose membership until 1934. Its leaders largely avoided challenging the employers; instead a tacit understanding arose between the two sides of industry whereby the unions accepted reductions in the size of the labour force while the employers increased the wages of those who remained in work. In this way the trade unions abandoned the cause of the working class as a whole. Naturally there were some attempts to fill the vacuum created by this decline. The British Communist Party increased its membership from 2500 in 1930 to 18,000 by 1939. However, many of the new recruits were not workingmen but middle-class intellectuals who had been moved by the Spanish Civil War and the international threat of fascism.

The most famous expression of working-class discontent was the Jarrow March of 1936. The town of Jarrow in north-east England had been created largely by its shipbuilding yards, and their collapse put two-thirds of its men out of work. The organisers of the march presented their case very skilfully by restricting it to 200 men so as to avoid mass confrontations with the authorities. On arrival in London the marchers delivered a petition to parliament and gave three cheers for the King before returning to their homes. In this way they won respect and sympathy for their dignified protest, although without achieving any immediate concessions.

By contrast, the demonstrations and marches of the National Unemployed Workers Movement (NUWM), led by Wal Hannington, were on a much larger scale. This organisation was deliberately designed to recruit the unemployed workers who had been neglected by the trade unions. Although the NUWM rapidly recruited 50,000 members and succeeded in mobilising many more at public rallies, it never posed a serious physical threat to authority. Its demands were far from radical. Essentially the NUWM wanted a restoration of the unemployment benefit that had been reduced in 1931 and the abandonment of the family Means Test. The Means Test was one of the most detested aspects of inter-war policy; it meant that an unemployed worker could be refused payments if an investigation showed that his wife or his adult children were in employment. The effect of this, according to many contemporaries, was to encourage people to inform on their neighbours and to force sons and daughters to leave home. Although the government stubbornly persisted in using the Means Test, it did show itself sensitive to criticism of the level of welfare benefits. For example, when it tried to introduce a new, uniform scheme of benefits, to be administered by the Unemployment Assistance Boards, in 1934, it was shocked by the popular outcry. As a result the scheme was abandoned and a more generous one was adopted in 1936.

THE RISE IN LIVING STANDARDS

The major underlying explanation for the apparent passivity of the British people during the 1930s is that their material conditions were far less grim than the contemporary political debates would suggest. Indeed, in recent years historians have considerably revised the traditional view, which was heavily influenced by contemporary work such as George Orwell's *The Road to Wigan Pier* (1937). This book was based on the author's own experiences in some of the most distressed parts of industrial England; but the sense of shock registered by Orwell tells us as much about his own background in a wealthy upper-class family as about working-class experience. Nor is the book simply an objective record, but rather a mixture of narrative and political opinion made readable by Orwell's skills as a novelist.

The basis for the revisionist view of the 1930s consists in the improvement in real wages during this period. Throughout the 1920s and the first half of the 1930s prices fell substantially faster than wage rates; as a result those in work, who formed the majority, enjoyed, on average, a rise of 17 per cent in real wages between 1924 and 1935. The effects of this were apparent in the expansion of the consumer goods industries; for example, domestic appliances such as vacuum cleaners, motor cars, cosmetics, women's magazines, and radios. There was also a huge growth in the entertainments industry; the number of visits to cinemas rose from only 36,000 a year to 8 million. Above all, the British people enjoyed a revolution in the provision of housing. This was partly due to the building of 1.1 million homes for rent by local authorities. They were built to a very high standard which included the provision of indoor bathrooms and toilets, larger kitchens, extra bedrooms, hot water and improved ventilation. As cheap electricity became available in two out of every three homes between the wars, the daily lives of housewives, who were largely confined to the home, became less burdensome. In addition 2.5 million homes were constructed by private builders for sale. With low interest rates and a fall in the costs of building materials, these new houses were bargains eagerly sought after by young married couples. The habit of home-ownership reflected a major change in British society. Before 1914 only 10 per cent of all homes had been owned by their occupiers, but by the 1960s a majority were being purchased by means of long-term loans from building societies.

The rise in the standard of living during the inter-war years can be measured in other ways. For example, life expectancy for women rose from 55 years in 1910 to 66 years by 1938. The infant mortality rates continued their long-term decline from 82 per thousand births in 1920 to 55 by 1938. This reflects the higher consumption of fruit, vegetables and eggs, the availability of pure water supplies by local authorities, and the provision of subsidised milk for young children and mothers by some local councils. After 1918 local authorities were required by law to establish clinics to assist pregnant women, and during the 1930s a higher proportion of babies were born in hospital. The state also assisted, with an extension of the existing system of welfare benefits, notably after 1925 when pensions were introduced for widows, and old age pensions became available at the age of 65 not 70 years.

Perhaps the most important factor in improving women's health
was largely beyond the influence or control of governments. This
was the reduction in family size, which had begun amongst some
middle-class couples in the 1880s but now spread throughout the
community. By the late 1920s married women, on average, experienced 2.2 live births by comparison with between five and six for
their predecessors in the mid-Victorian era. Although contra-
ceptive methods had become better known during the war when
condoms were widely distributed to the troops who went to France,
most couples adopted traditional methods. The key to the change
lay less in methods than in aspirations and attitudes. By reducing
family size young couples hoped to raise their family's standard of
living and to preserve the health of women. They responded eagerly
to the publication of *Married Love* by Marie Stopes in 1918. In this
she argued that the deliberate spacing of pregnancies would enable
married couples to enjoy their sex lives more, promote the health of
wives, and also serve the needs of the state by ensuring that a higher
proportion of babies survived. Although the politicians chose to
avoid this issue, a quiet social revolution was accomplished by
ordinary people without official or even medical assistance.

In the light of these improving social conditions the survival of
the National Government is readily explained. For the majority
of the population the period of deflation enabled them to enjoy
a higher standard of living. Once the economic recovery had set
in during 1934 it proved very difficult for the Opposition to offer a
credible alternative. The Labour Party never succeeded in refuting
the charge that its return to power would provoke another economic crisis. Thus, although the Labour vote rose from 30 per cent
to 38 per cent at the election of 1935, this produced only 158 seats;
much of the working-class vote as well as almost all the middle-class
had stayed loyal to the National Government. Not until 1938–9,
when confidence in foreign policy began to be undermined, did it
really lose public support; it took the traumatic defeats during the
early stages of the Second World War to trigger a major swing of
opinion to the left.

24

The Era of Appeasement

At the peace treaties of Versailles and Sèvres, Britain largely secured her objectives. First and foremost the German navy no longer existed. The German threat to Belgium and France had been lifted by enforced disarmament and by the demilitarisation of the Rhineland. By dismantling the Turkish Empire Britain strengthened her position in the Middle East where she occupied Palestine, Transjordan and Iraq. In south-eastern Europe the creation of several new states provided a barrier to Russian expansion. Not only had the British Empire survived the war, but it had been augmented by several former German colonies now entrusted to Britain as mandated territories.

This is a corrective to the assumption that Britain occupied such a weak position between the wars that she had no alternative but to appease the fascist dictators. No doubt the aggrandisement of Japan, Italy and Germany during the 1930s eventually undermined the strategic position of the western powers, but this reflected the incompetent diplomacy of Britain and France rather than any inherent military weakness. During the 1920s Britain and France together enjoyed great military and political strength in Europe; the withdrawal of the United States into isolationism and the distraction of the Soviet Union by internal problems allowed them to uphold the peace settlements if they wished to do so; unfortunately they themselves were confused and ambiguous about this central objective.

THE REACTION AGAINST WAR

As a result of Britain's involvement in a land war in support of France during 1914–18 she had suffered the deaths of 750,000 men.

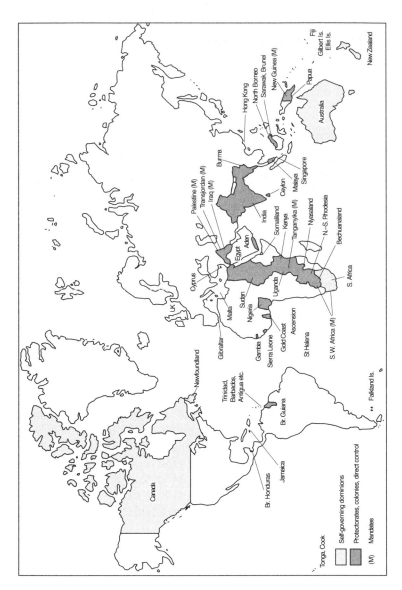

Map 6   The British Empire in 1919

This inevitably triggered a reaction in favour of returning to her traditional policies; in particular, the arms race with Germany, and the 'secret diplomacy' that had entangled Britain with France and her war of revenge, were widely regarded as errors. The fashionable alternative in the 1920s involved disarmament and participation in the League of Nations as a means of resolving disputes by arbitration.

In fact, however, inter-war governments felt suspicious of the League because they believed it threatened their sovereign powers and was potentially a means for attacking imperialism. Lloyd George had agreed to the establishment of the League largely as a concession to the American President, Woodrow Wilson. On the other hand, the governments of Baldwin, MacDonald and Chamberlain took some care to appear sympathetic towards the League of Nations because it attracted widespread public support. The League of Nations Union built up a membership of 400,00 and its lecturers and canvassers were active throughout the period.

Britain began to disarm promptly in 1919, not because of public opinion but because the Treasury regarded the massive military establishment as insupportable. As a result, the size of the army fell from 3.5 million men to 1 million in 1919 and to a mere 200,000 by 1924. Total expenditure on defence stood at £700 million in 1919–20, but had been cut to £115 million by 1922 and remained around that level until 1935–6.

The Chief implication of this policy was that Britain had no intention of putting an army on the mainland of Europe again. The navy suffered less extensive economies because of its continuing role in protecting imperial and commercial communications. Meanwhile the Royal Air Force increased its share of expenditure. This can be explained in terms of the impact made by the attacks by airships and aircraft during the war. It was widely assumed that Britain had now lost her traditional advantage as an island power. 'The bomber will always get through', as Baldwin put it. In a future war the enemy was expected to concentrate on bombing Britain's urban population and manufacturing industry with the result that civilian morale would collapse and her capacity to supply the war effort would be destroyed. As a result, from 1922 the government began to build new squadrons of fighter and bomber aircraft in the hope that this would deter an aggressor and prevent an invading force from crossing the English Channel.

During the later 1920s and early 30s popular fears about another European war reached a climax. One symptom of this mood was the huge demand for literature about experiences during the Great War. Many participants published their memoirs or reflections at this stage: Robert Graves, *Goodbye To All That* (1929), Siegfried Sassoon, *Memoirs of an Infantry Officer* (1930), and Vera Brittain, *Testament of Youth* (1933). All emphasised the futility of the war and its devastating effects in destroying a generation of young men. For a time it appeared that the country might become pacifist. In 1933 the students at Oxford University shocked their elders by voting for a motion which repudiated the idea of fighting for 'King and Country' as the volunteers had done in 1914.

In fact, opinion was reaching a turning-point. Hopes were very high around 1932 that the Disarmament Convention meeting at Geneva would succeed in lowering tension. But the withdrawal of first Japan and then Germany both from the disarmament talks and then from the League of Nations thoroughly alarmed British opinion. It was in this situation that the League of Nations Union conducted the famous 'Peace Ballot' amongst eleven and a half million people during 1934–5. Its purpose was to demonstrate to the government that popular support for the League was so strong that it would be dangerous for ministers to let the League down in its efforts to prevent territorial aggression. However, the crucial question in this ballot revealed a three-to-one vote in favour of applying both economic and *military* sanctions against aggressor states. This was a most emphatic indication that the public were far from being pacifist; for voters were fully aware that a new challenge now faced the League in the form of the threat posed to Abyssinia by the ambitions of the Italian fascist leader Benito Mussolini. Because many people felt that the League could not afford to fail to defend another of its members, they were prepared, very reluctantly, to risk the use of force to check an unjustified act of aggression.

THE APPEASEMENT OF GERMANY

No sooner was the ink dry on the Treaty of Versailles than British politicians began to argue that Germany had been treated too severely. As a result, British statesmen devoted the next twenty years to attempts to remove her grievances. For example, her reparations payments were greatly reduced, she was admitted to the League of Nations, and in 1926 Britain and France withdrew early from the Rhineland. In this period, appeasement was not a matter of controversy in Britain. It seemed both just and necessary, for by removing the humiliations which had been heaped upon the new parliamentary regime in Germany – the Weimar Republic – it was hoped that a stable and prosperous state could be established. In this way the pressures that had driven imperial Germany to war in order to resolve internal instability would not arise again.

Even in the 1920s, however, appeasement was a somewhat flawed strategy, for it never went far enough to restore Germany as a great military power, and it stopped short of incorporating all the German people into the German state. These fundamental objectives were espoused by the respectable statesmen of the Weimar Regime, not just by the far right. Moreover, by 1933 appeasement appeared to have failed in the sense that Weimar had been replaced by the Nazi regime. This development posed a major dilemma for British statesmen. Hitler's rise to power provided plentiful evidence that Germany's expansive, aggressive ambitions represented a real threat to British interests. This was how Winston Churchill interpreted the problem; the logic seemed to be that appeasement had now become futile and that Britain should co-operate with France and even Russia to build up a defensive alliance to check this new threat to the stability of Europe. However, few British politicians were, as yet, ready to follow the lead of a man who was widely regarded as an ambitious warmonger. The government drew a different lesson from the rise of Hitler: that appeasement should be *accelerated*. Neville Chamberlain, the arch-appeaser of the decade, summed up this thinking when he said: 'If only we could sit down at a table with the Germans and run through all their complaints and claims with a pencil, this would greatly relieve all tension.'

Today it is easy to overlook how widely Chamberlain's view was accepted during the 1930s. Initially it was not clear how evil a system the Nazis were creating. The treatment of the Jews, for example, aroused little criticism in Britain, partly because anti-semitism was prevalent in British society if less extreme than elsewhere in Europe. Above all, many British people were inclined to overlook the unpleasant features of Nazi Germany because they were more worried about the threat posed by Stalinist Russia to the weak, unstable countries of east and central Europe. A strong fascist Germany represented a much-needed bulwark against Communist expansion, at least to many politicians, and if this meant that Germany absorbed central Europe, then this seemed a price worth paying. If Churchill's case for resisting Hitler carried little conviction this was partly because he appeared to be a blatant opportunist, waging an essentially personal campaign in order to seize the party leadership from Baldwin. The Labour and Liberal critics of appeasement regarded Churchill as a warmonger and as a reckless politician who lacked judgement. Even Conservatives such as Anthony Eden, who resigned as Foreign Secretary in 1938 because of disagreement with Chamberlain's policy, refused to join with Churchill for fear that the case against appeasement would be damaged by association with him.

REARMAMENT

Throughout the 1930s the Chiefs-of-Staff of both the army and the navy protested that their resources were inadequate to meet their responsibilities. Not only were British troops occupied in maintaining order in India, Palestine and Transjordan, but in 1926, when Britain signed the Locarno Agreements, she also committed herself to defending the territory of Belgium and France. However, since no expeditionary force now existed, this was a dangerous promise; the government hoped that by simply giving a pledge they would create an atmosphere in which it would never have to be backed up.

Meanwhile the navy faced awkward technical problems as well as a lack of resources. The war had exposed the vulnerability of big battleships to attack from the air as well as by mines and submarines. In the Far East the rise of the Japanese and American navies wholly eclipsed the local British forces. Yet Britain allowed her alliance with Japan to lapse with nothing to put in its place except the vain hope that in an emergency American support would be forthcoming. As an alternative, the government began to construct a naval base at Singapore, but the work was repeatedly interrupted. At the Washington Naval Conference in 1921, Britain, the USA, Japan, France and Italy agreed to restrict the size of their fleets, but this did nothing to alleviate Britain's relative weakness in the Far East, and moreover, it contributed to the collapse of the shipbuilding industry.

Inter-war governments largely failed to co-ordinate their military planning with their diplomacy as had been done so effectively before 1914. As a result the armed forces became an obstacle to foreign policy, for they undermined every initiative with the warning that they could not possibly cope with three likely opponents – Japan, Germany and Italy. It gradually became clear that appeasement could not be pursued from a position of weakness. An opportunity to rectify the situation came in 1934 with the report issued by the Defence Requirements Committee. It advised that the government must decide on its priorities; in particular, Germany, not Japan, should be regarded as Britain's chief opponent. To this end, the committee recommended an expansion of the Royal Air Force and the creation of a new expeditionary force. However, this programme was frustrated by Neville Chamberlain, as Chancellor of the Exchequer, on the grounds that a major increase in spending would jeopardise the fragile economic recovery. In fact, this was a plausible excuse to avoid the re-emergence of an army which might drag Britain into another major war in Europe. Consequently rearmament concentrated upon building additional bomber squadrons for the air force. The defenders of appeasement claimed that by doing this they effectively prepared for the eventual struggle with Germany; but this was far from being Chamberlain's intention at the time. Indeed, Germany's expenditure on rearmament increased faster than Britain's in the later 1930s. Even worse was the reaction of other powers to Britain's half-hearted rearmament programme. France, Germany and the Soviet Union concluded that the refusal to create an expeditionary force implied that the government would always avoid intervention on the Continent whatever demands Hitler might make.

THE COLLAPSE OF APPEASEMENT

Until 1935 the British and French governments believed that they could isolate Hitler by fostering friendly relations with Mussolini. Unfortunately the 'Stresa Front', as it was known, had the effect of convincing the Italian leader that the French and British would acquiesce in his ambition to take over the African state of Abyssinia. In a sense Mussolini was correct, for the government took the view that no vital British interest was at stake in the Abyssinia question. However, the Foreign Secretary, Sir Samuel Hoare, had publicly declared Britain's support for the League of Nations' role in resisting aggression; as there could hardly have been a more blatant example of unprovoked aggression towards a member of the League, public opinion clearly expected the government to inter-vene. This drove a reluctant government from its original intention, and some half-hearted sanctions were imposed against Mussolini; but they had little effect and were abandoned as soon as the govern-ment felt it had discharged its responsibilities.

Yet the Baldwin government had succeeded in getting the worst of both worlds. On the one hand it had exposed the League to a humiliating failure. On the other hand it had alienated Mussolini and driven the two fascist dictators into one another's arms. The direct result was that in 1936 Hitler took advantage of the divisions among the western powers to send his troops into the Rhineland. This proved to be a decisive moment because it destroyed France's strategic position and encouraged Hitler to believe that the west would always back down in the face of his initiatives.

When Neville Chamberlain succeeded as Prime Minister in 1937 he was determined to accelerate the appeasement policy by remov-ing Germany's outstanding grievances as quickly as possible. In so doing he revealed how seriously he misunderstood his opponent. Chamberlain took up the question of Germany's lost colonies and offered to restore those that were under British control. Signifi-cantly, Hitler failed to accept the proposal. In fact the African territories were of little intrinsic value; they served Hitler's purpose as symbols of the injustice done to Germany at Versailles.

However, Hitler was suffciently encouraged by Chamberlain's attitude to accelerate his territorial aggrandisement in central Europe. When he occupied Austria in March 1938 the move was greeted with relief in Britain on the grounds that it resolved another rankling German grievance. But the next demand, for the incorporation of 3.5 million Germans living in the Sudetenland area of Czechoslovakia, proved more contentious. From the outset Chamberlain took the view that the Germans ought never to have been included in the Czech state, that there was no practical way of preventing their absorption into Germany, and that it would not be in Britain's interests to try. But he refused to recognise that France had pledged herself to defend Czechoslovakian territory, and did his best to pressurise both the Czechs and the French to concede Hitler's demands.

In fact Chamberlain was fundamentally wrong about the possibility of deterring Hitler. When the British Foreign Secretary, Lord Halifax, challenged Chamberlain's policy the German leader backed away. But to many people it appeared that, unless a compromise could be found, a war was likely. Chamberlain played on these fears in a notorious broadcast in which he said:

> How horrible, fantastic, incredible it is that we should be digging trenches and trying on gas masks here because of a quarrel in a far-away country between people of whom we know nothing.

He quickly regained the initiative by engaging Hitler in direct negotiations which resulted in the partition of Czechoslovakia under the terms of the Munich Agreement. On his return to Britain Chamberlain triumphantly claimed to have brought 'Peace with Honour'. But although this was greeted with enormous relief by a country that had been anticipating war, the underlying significance of Munich was that it began to turn the tide decisively against appeasement. Opinion had been changing since the invasion of Abyssinia in 1935. When the Spanish Civil War broke out in 1936 many of those on the left, once strongly inclined to pacifism, recovered their faith in the idea of a just war and volunteered to fight against Spanish fascism. The climax came in March 1939 when Hitler's troops occupied the remainder of Czechoslovakia, thereby providing the most dramatic proof of the failure of Chamberlain's Munich policy. As a result the British government offered guarantees to Poland and Romania, which were expected to be the next victims of German expansion. This was widely seen as a step towards war; by September 1939 only the Prime Minister and a few dedicated appeasers still clung to the illusion of peace.

25

The Impact of the Second World War

In some ways Britain's experience during the Second World War appears to have been a repeat of the First World War. The conflict put severe strains on her economic resources and undermined her export markets; it involved the active participation of the civilian population and, in particular, drew women into the labour force in unprecedented numbers; and it destroyed the credibility of the pre-war government. Yet this war proved to be of greater significance because many of its effects were long-lasting. This time the Empire did not survive unscathed, and within two years of peace India had been lost. The material benefits won by ordinary people were not snatched away after 1945; on the contrary, social reform was greatly extended and entrenched for decades to come. This was largely because the great patriotic upheaval generated by the war weakened the right wing and gave the Labour Party a large majority for the first time, which it used to introduce the welfare state and to nationalise one-fifth of British industry.

THE RISE OF CHURCHILL

From the outset it was apparent that the Prime Minister's heart was not in the war. Although Britain had recently given a guarantee to Poland, nothing was done to prevent the rapid dismemberment of that country by German and Russian forces. Indeed, for several months Britain held back in the hope, at least on the part of

Chamberlain, that the war might be confined to eastern Europe. This explains why the first nine months of the conflict was dubbed the 'Phoney War' in Britain. But it had the effect of isolating the Prime Minister, for the overwhelming majority of the people and the politicians had by now concluded that a war to eliminate Hitler and his regime was a just one. Inevitably the question arose whether Chamberlain was capable of leading the nation in these circumstances.

The government's public reputation suffered from the retention of all the leading politicians associated with appeasement. The only change was the appointment of Churchill as First Lord of the Admiralty, the post he had held in 1914. This enabled Churchill to attract support from the press because, in contrast to the other ministers, he projected an image of energy and excitement about the war effort. Chamberlain, however, had calculated that Churchill would destroy himself by the kind of recklessness he had displayed in the First World War; and he was correct up to a point, for Churchill energetically promoted the disastrous campaign to send Allied troops to Norway to prevent Germany obtaining iron ore supplies. Its failure in April 1940 led the House of Commons to hold a major debate on the conduct of the war in May. But it was Chamberlain not Churchill who found himself under attack. When the government's majority was reduced from 200 to 81 the Prime Minister felt obliged to resign, and so, at the age of 66, Churchill succeeded him.

This upset was more than just a personal triumph for Churchill, for it restored the Labour and Liberal Parties to office in a new coalition government. Churchill initially occupied the same position as that of Lloyd George between 1916 and 1918. He led a three-party coalition but was not the leader of any party himself, at least not until Chamberlain retired in the autumn of 1940 when the Conservatives reluctantly made him their leader. Like Lloyd George, Churchill was, for a time, strengthened at home by the scale of the military crisis enveloping the country; for during the summer of 1940 German forces broke through the Allied line in northern France, forcing Britain to evacuate 338,000 troops from Dunkirk. The Germans went on to capture Paris in June. Not only was Britain left alone to resist Hitler, but, as the coast of France and Belgium was now in enemy hands, much of the British population and industry fell within range of German bombing.

At this stage Churchill captured the popular imagination with his stirring broadcasts and speeches. But the 'Battle of Britain' was won largely by the investment already made in fighter planes that imposed a heavy toll on the German bombers. In addition, it soon became clear that the fears about the effects of bombing on civilian morale and industry had been exaggerated. Bombing was very inaccurate, and the population did become resigned to the routine measures taken to minimise its destructive effects. The experience of regular air raids also helped to unify the nation in its common suffering. When Buckingham Palace took several hits in a raid, a relieved Queen Elizabeth commented: 'Now we can look the East End [of London] in the face.' In speaking thus she reflected a growing feeling that the sacrifices required by the war should be equally shared.

THE 'PEOPLE'S WAR'

The withdrawal of troops from the European mainland and the start of the Battle of Britain had the effect of concentrating attention on the civilian population. In anticipation of mass bombing, the government immediately evacuated 1.5 million children from urban areas to the countryside. Altogether 60,000 civilians lost their lives during the war and many more were injured. The older generation of people who remembered the hardships of the First World War now argued that something should be learned from that experience; both the immediate suffering and the prospective gains ought to be borne fairly. This critical, egalitarian attitude was the start of a major shift of political opinion to the left. It manifested itself in a very cynical view towards government and to the propaganda circulated by the Ministry for Information; advice about saving food and preparing meatless meals was much resented by housewives who bore the brunt of war. They suffered especially from the damage caused by bombing, to one in every three houses in Britain.

Workers suddenly realised that after the years of mass unemployment their labour was in great demand. It was only the war that drove unemployment below 10 per cent for the first time in twenty years. In fact, by 1941 the government estimated that Britain now required an additional 2 million workers in order to sustain the war effort. The best means of achieving this was to conscript women by age groups and to direct them to key industries. As a result, by 1943, 46 per cent of all women aged between 14 and 59 years had taken up paid employment. Nearly half a million young women joined the female branches of the army, navy and air forces, in addition to those who served in the Land Army, the Auxiliary Territorial Service and the Air Raid Precaution. This participation gave women a higher status, if only temporarily, and also put more money into their pockets. However, it is not at all clear that the experience emancipated women from their traditional role any more than the First World War had done. By 1945, surveys showed that three-quarters of all women workers wished to abandon employment. As a result the marriage rate resumed its upward trend soon after the end of the war; there was a 'baby boom' during 1946–7, but then the birth rate returned to the level of the late 1930s. In this sense the war did not significantly change long-term patterns of behaviour or aspirations in British society.

On the other hand the war made a major short-term impact on the politicians in the coalition government. They felt obliged to offer several concessions in order to maintain the morale of civilians who suffered increasing material deprivations due to the interruption of food supplies and the destruction of housing. For example, they swiftly introduced rationing for most food items and gave free milk to young children and pregnant women. In 1941 the hated Means Test was abolished. Allowances were paid to families whose chief breadwinners had joined the armed forces, and an Emergency Medical Service was created. The Minister for Labour, Ernest Bevin, himself a union leader, raised the minimum wages of workers in several low-paid jobs; and employees generally used their new scarcity value to bargain for better wages. Indeed, average weekly wage rates increased by 80 per cent during the war, while the cost of living rose by only 31 per cent.

These short-term improvements in living standards were by no means sufficient to satisfy popular expectations, as the cabinet recognised by appointing Sir William Beveridge to chair a new committee on post-war social welfare policy. Moreover, the entry of several leading Labour politicians into Churchill's cabinet greatly strengthened pressure for reform. Thus, in the later stage of the war several important innovations were passed, notably R. A. Butler's 1944 Education Act, and the Family Allowances Act in 1945.

Family allowances were a long-standing feminist objective; but even for non-feminists the idea of making small weekly payments to mothers in respect of second and all subsequent children was seen as an economical means of making motherhood less of a burden. Although the measure failed to check the downward trend in the birth rate, it certainly eased the task of household management for millions of married women after 1945.

THE COSTS OF WAR

Pre-war appeasers had been right about the appalling burden the war would impose upon Britain. Government expenditure rose from £1.4 million in 1939–40 to £6.1 million by 1944–5. Much of this was paid for by higher income tax, which increased from 25 per cent to 50 per cent. However, as early as 1941 Britain found herself compelled to seek financial assistance from the United States. This took the form of the 'Lend Lease' agreements, which lasted until 1945. By that time Britain had largely exhausted her reserves of gold, dollars and overseas investments, and her debt had risen from £500 million to £3500 million. From the perspective of the 1980s some right-wing historians have condemned the whole war effort as inefficient and as responsible for subsequent British economic decline. As in the First World War, the desperate need for extra manufacturing output led to a neglect of productivity; high profits were made by employers and high wages earned by workers. However, it would be unrealistic to assume that the co-operation of the labour force could have been achieved without making concessions, especially in view of the militant mood prevailing during the war. In fact Britain's capacity to mobilise her workforce, male and female, gave her a decisive advantage over the autocracies of Germany and Russia and was crucial to her eventual success. Nor is an assessment of the economic impact of war complete if it examines only the costs. For the war greatly stimulated subsequent developments including radar, jet propulsion, antibiotics and atomic energy, which contributed significantly to economic growth from the late 1940s onwards.

From the perspective of Britain's imperial and military strength the Second World War also appears to have been disastrous because it overstretched the country's resources so dangerously. While the British Isles faced the possibility of invasion, communications in the Mediterranean and across the Atlantic suffered from submarine attack, and in the Far East Britain's position collapsed in the face of Japanese expansionism. As in the previous war the Empire rallied in support of the motherland; India, for example, contributed no fewer than 2.5 million troops. Yet despite all this effort, India became a major liability. Britain had neglected her eastern Empire for many years, but now she had to pay the price. The base at Singapore, which had never been adequately defended, fell to the Japanese in 1942, rapidly followed by Hong Kong, Malaya and Burma. India itself seemed destined to be invaded at a time when the Congress had launched a civil disobedience campaign and Indian soldiers had begun to desert to the Japanese. In this desperate situation Churchill's brave declaration seems hopelessly unrealistic: 'I have not become the King's first minister', he said, 'in order to preside over the liquidation of the British Empire.'

Events were, in fact, largely beyond his control. In return for American financial help President Roosevelt insisted on some definite progress towards independence for India. Britain did, in fact, make concessions in several for her colonies. The Jamaicans were given adult suffrage, and promises of self-government were extended to Malta and Ceylon. In March 1942 Churchill sent Sir Stafford Cripps, a Socialist, to India to offer a complicated deal involving post-war self-government. The significant thing about this initiative was that the Indian National Congress turned it down because, in Gandhi's words, it was 'a postdated cheque on a failing bank'. Consequently there was deadlock between the British and the nationalists for the rest of the war. Although British forces eventually repulsed the Japanese, they had suffered a terrible blow to their prestige throughout Asia and Africa. The Indian subcontinent had certainly become ungovernable by the closing stages of the war. Even without the war, India had already advanced a considerable distance towards self-government; 30 million Indians enjoyed the vote and had full control over provincial government from 1937 onwards. Much of the civil service had also been placed in Indian hands by 1939. Thus the way had been prepared and the British political will to rule the country had been decisively broken; the war simply accelerated events.

THE ORIGINS OF CONSENSUS

Churchill's dominance at home was never as complete as his public prestige seemed to suggest. As the war progressed, the Conservative Party largely ceased to function and it allowed the Labour ministers in the coalition to dictate policy on the domestic front. Labour's role was ambiguous because, on the one hand, its leaders occupied prominent positions, especially Clement Attlee, Herbert Morrison, Ernest Bevin and Hugh Dalton; but the backbench MPs who formed the official Opposition felt fairly free to criticise the government. In spite of the concessions made on social policy, by October 1944 the National Executive Committee (NEC) of the party had lost patience and decided that as soon as Germany had been defeated Attlee and the other ministers should leave the coalition. In this the NEC reflected a mood of rising expectations in the country which can be dated to 1942. In that year the first British military successes in North Africa, and the mobilisation of both American and Russian might, now pointed to an inevitable victory for the Allied powers. As a result the people began to contemplate life after the war and thus to focus on material improvements.

Radical opinion was crystallised by the publication of the famous report by the Beveridge Committee in December 1942. This included a comprehensive set of proposals on social security designed, in Beveridge's own words, to conquer the five giants – Want, Ignorance, Squalor, Idleness and Disease. No fewer than 630,000 copies of the report were sold, and the government became worried that its popularity had raised expectations too soon. However, even Churchill accepted the need for social reform. Politicians and civil servants had by this stage tacitly abandoned inter-war financial policy in favour of a Keynesian approach. In 1944 the government published a White Paper on employment which effectively committed it to adopting Keynesian methods to maintain full employment by adjusting the level of state expenditure and taxation. The acceptance of full employment as a goal complemented the Beveridge Report because if unemployment remained low then the costs of implementing the social reforms would be manageable.

Thus it is apparent that the mood of the country had moved to the left several years before the 1945 general election took place. Opinion polls, a novel feature of the late 1930s and early 1940s, indicated that the people feared a return to high unemployment after the war, and that their priorities were improved housing and the implementation of the Beveridge Report. In the light of this agenda the Labour Party appeared more credible than the Conservatives. Their record in the wartime government helped Attlee and his colleagues to eradicate the reputation for incompetence that the party had earned in 1931. Even Labour's proposals for the nationalisation of industry no longer alarmed the voters, for these measures were regarded as an extension of the interventionism that had proved necessary in winning the war. Young voters and servicemen proved to be particularly pro-Labour in 1945; they formed a new political generation whose views had been influenced by 1930s unemployment and the poor record of the National Government in preparing for the war.

Conversely the Conservatives were hopelessly disadvantaged by association with Chamberlain's appeasement policy. Although Churchill's personal reputation no doubt helped his party, he continued to be regarded more as an individual than as a party leader; he had, after all, been a rebel against his party throughout the 1930s. To this extent the rejection of Churchill at the election was not so surprising. The Labour Party increased its share of the vote from 38 per cent in 1935 to 48 per cent, which brought 393 seats, an overall majority for the first time. This landslide ensured that the effects of the war would be extended into peacetime, not swept aside as they had been after 1918.

26

The Era of Consensus, 1945–59

The twenty years following the end of the war have been widely regarded as a period of political consensus whose origins lay in the mood of unity and egalitarianism generated during the struggle with Germany. Despite party controversies, most of the central post-war policies were bi-partisan in character; and the emphatic result of the 1945 election served to warn the Conservatives that if they repudiated the consensus they would be marginalised for a long time. This is not to suggest that the parties agreed on everything. Rather, they accepted five major assumptions about domestic and external policy: first, the implementation of the 'welfare state'; second, the pursuit of full employment; third, the acceptance of the 'mixed economy', which meant a substantial measure of state ownership in the overall context of private enterprise; and fourth, the incorporation of the trade unions into the process of government. In wartime this had taken the form of collaboration to maintain industrial output, and the entry of union leaders such as Bevin into the cabinet. In peacetime, co-operation was less formal. Governments usually intervened in industrial disputes, especially those in the public sector, in order to seek a compromise, which frequently meant conceding demands for higher wages. The final aspect of consensus was foreign and defence policy. Both Labour and the Conservatives accepted decolonisation, supported the Commonwealth, and advocated British membership of NATO and the development of an independent nuclear deterrent. The corollary was that both parties showed virtually no interest in the early moves towards European unity.

The external aspects are a reminder that consensus did not involve simply concessions to socialism by Conservatives, as some right-wing critics claimed in the 1970s; it also meant a move to the right by Labour in defence and foreign policy by comparison with its inter-war programme. Of course, both the left-wing of the Labour Movement and the right-wing of Conservatism dissented from consensus politics; but both found themselves marginalised for several decades. The leadership of the parties differed more in emphasis and in degree rather than over fundamental principles; as a result, by the 1950s the political debate turned not on whether full employment or the welfare state was desirable, but over which party was more competent to implement these policies.

THE WELFARE STATE

Clement Attlee's government enjoyed two great advantages which few other Labour governments have had: it came to power with a clear idea of what it wished to achieve, and its large majority enabled it to enact its programme in full – 75 Acts of Parliament were passed in 1945–6 alone. Unquestionably its greatest achievement was the welfare state, Although many of the reforms owed a great deal to earlier schemes of state welfare, the new programme made a definite break with the past, partly because it was so *comprehensive* in scope and because it attempted to provide a *universal* level of support acceptable to the entire population.

Strictly speaking, two aspects of what came to be seen as the welfare state pre-dated the Labour government. The Education Act which raised the school-leaving age to fifteen was passed in 1944, and the Family Allowances Act, which paid five shillings a week to mothers for every second and all subsequent children, was passed in 1945. The National Insurance Act of 1946 raised the weekly benefits for unemployment, sickness and old age to a common level. This, of course, retained the principle introduced in the Edwardian period of linking benefits to contributions. In 1948 the National Health Service came into operation after much controversy between its architect, Aneurin Bevan, and the British Medical Association. This made health care available on the basis of need, not ability to pay; it incorporated large sections of the population, such as women, who had previously been neglected; and it amalgamated the existing voluntary, poor law and local authority hospitals into a single, national system. Finally, the government extended the inter-war policy by subsidising the building of local authority houses for rent. Between 1945 and 1951, 1.35 million new homes were built altogether.

However, the welfare state never fully lived up to its ideals. Poverty was far from being abolished, and, as old age pensions were not linked to the cost of living, their value was somewhat eroded by inflation. Thus, by the mid-1950s 1 million people were receiving National Assistance in order to subsidise their inadequate incomes. For Socialists it was also a matter for regret that the reforms failed to eliminate private health care and private educa-tion, which continued to offer advantages to the wealthy.

ECONOMIC PLANNING

One of the effects of the Second World War was to make the idea of economic planning fashionable in Britain; as a result, food rationing, price controls and import quotas were widely accepted as necessary, at least for several years. However, Socialist intellectuals such as Hugh Dalton, who became Chancellor of the Exchequer, intended to carry planning much further than this. For example, Dalton deliberately limited the resources available for house-building in order to construct more new factories. He also promoted a regional economic planning policy in the hope of avoiding the wastage of human resources concentrated in the old industrial areas; thus, 51 per cent of all new factories were constructed in the depressed areas during the 1945–51 period. The most conspicuous form of Socialist planning was the programme of nationalisation, which included the Bank of England, coal, railways, gas, electricity, long-distance transport and steel. At the time, nationalisation proved, in most cases, to be uncontroversial. This was partly because utilities such as gas were already under municipal ownership, and also because generous compensation was paid to the former owners. It had become blatantly clear that private enterprise had failed to generate the investment necessary to modernise coal and the railways, so that the state had to intervene in the interests of the economy as a whole.

In the period up to 1948 Dalton achieved considerable success in the face of formidable difficulties. Britain had emerged from the war facing debts of £3500 million, and with a balance of payments crisis; her exports were equivalent to only 46 per cent of their pre-war value. This is why the government concentrated on building factories rather than on supplying consumer goods, and why it appealed for women workers to return especially to the textile industry. Remarkably, it achieved a balance of trade surplus and rapid economic growth, combined with low inflation and full employment. However, the planning strategy suffered from serious shortcomings even in the early stages. For example, little attempt was made to impose a wages policy, although the government enjoyed considerable success simply by persuading the trade unions to moderate their demands. In addition, the ministers themselves seemed unsure about how far government control should go. By 1948, nationalisation was coming to a virtual halt as ministers argued over whether or not to nationalise steel. By 1951, they had brought about one-fifth of the economy into public ownership. There was no strong wish to go further, and by 1949 many of the economic controls surviving from wartime were scrapped by the President of the Board of Trade, Harold Wilson. Beyond this the Labour Government relied less upon planning than on indirect Keynesian methods for managing the economy.

Unfortunately much of the success of the economic strategy was squandered by misjudgements and by events beyond the government's control during the late 1940s. A severe shortage of coal during the winter of 1946-7 hampered the export industries. Also, by 1948 the dollar loans that Britain had raised in the United States had begun to run out, and the recession in America had reduced Britain's foreign earnings. This posed a fresh threat to the balance of payments, which led to speculation against the pound. In this situation the Socialist ministers revealed their conservatism by declining to take the opportunity to devalue the pound in 1948 when industry would have been able to take immediate advantage of it. Instead they delayed, and were forced to devalue the pound from 4.0 dollars to 2.9 dollars in 1949. Although this proved to be a highly beneficial measure in the long run, its short-term effects were disastrous politically. Fearful of the inflationary pressure caused by devaluation, the Chancellor, Sir Stafford Cripps, and his successor, Hugh Gaitskell, curbed domestic spending and raised taxation.

At the same time Bevin's commitment to supporting the United States in the Cold War led him to demand an increase in defence expenditure from £2.3 billion to £4.7 billion by 1951. The result was to turn the balance of payments surplus into a deficit and to undermine the entire political standing of Attlee's government.

THE CONSERVATIVE REVIVAL

The loss of power by the Labour Party in 1951 was far from inevitable; rather, it arose from political misjudgements. Attlee decided to hold an election in February 1950 at a stage when the country was experiencing the bad effects of the deflationary policy of Cripps but before the advantages in terms of faster economic growth had materialised. In the event, Labour won the election but by a majority of only five. Subsequently, the Chancellor, Gaitskell, further weakened the economy and the government's standing by his ruthless determination to finance rearmament at the expense of consumption. Attlee unaccountably held a second election in 1951. Although Labour won more votes than the Conservatives, they retained fewer seats. Churchill therefore returned to office with a majority of seventeen.

In retrospect it became clear that the election had been mistimed by Attlee; had he hung on a little longer he would have won. By 1952 the ending of the Korean War had allowed Britain to reduce her defence expenditure and to resume economic growth. This was accelerated by the devaluation of 1949, by the reduction in trade barriers under the General Agreement on Tariffs and Trade, by the shift in the terms of trade in Britain's favour, and by the earlier decision to concentrate resources in manufacturing..

The Conservatives were, thus, very lucky to have recaptured power in 1951. The new Chancellor of the Exchequer, R. A. Butler, took care to capitalise on the growing sense of prosperity after the years of austerity under Labour. To this end he stimulated the economy by reducing income tax in 1953, and again in 1955 shortly before another general election. During the 1950s as a whole, unemployment remained around 2 per cent and, on average, money wages doubled. But were these policies of any ideological significance? Although Churchill had used the rhetoric of individualism in 1951 to suggest that Conservatives would set the people free from the burdens of the Socialist state, his government largely followed the consensus established under Attlee. Conservative ministers maintained full employment, increased expenditure on the welfare state and conciliated the trade unions by supporting large wage increases in the public sector. Only the most marginal attempts were made to reverse Labour policies. For example, the steel industry was returned to private ownership, but otherwise the state sector was left intact, and income tax, though reduced a little, remained at an historically high level. The long-term process of redistributing income from rich to poor continued.

There are three main explanations for this loyalty to consensus politics. First, the war had thoroughly discredited the record of the National Governments and brought to the forefront Conservatives such as Macmillan and Butler who were critical of the social effects of unrestricted capitalism and were determined never to return to high unemployment. Secondly, the 1945 election had been a severe shock to the party; even the recovery in 1950–1 had left them with *fewer* votes than Labour, so that they feared that any major departure from Attlee's policies would lose them public support. Thirdly, Churchill put his own authority behind consensus. He was, after all, rather detached from the Conservative Party, which had not wanted him as its leader in 1940. He enjoyed coalition government. Nor had he forgotten his own Edwardian hey-day as a Liberal social reformer, and he even attempted to bring Liberals into his post-1951 government. As a result Churchill was determined to keep unemployment low, maintain welfare and conciliate the trade unions. This meant that he marginalised the right-wing Conservatives and promoted the more liberal ones, thereby helping to ensure that in the future the party leadership would stay close to consensus politics.

THE RISE OF MACMILLAN

During the 1950s Churchill's colleagues grew increasingly restless because of the decline in his intellectual and physical powers. But he seemed determined to enjoy his last years of power for as long as possible. At last in 1955 he gave way to Anthony Eden, long the heir-apparent, who held a swift general election and secured a majority of seventy seats. But Eden's grip and judgement were less

sure than this initial triumph suggested, for despite his long experience in foreign affairs, he walked into a major fiasco over the
Suez affair in 1956. The ignominious withdrawal of British troops
from Egypt thoroughly undermined Eden's credibility, and he was
obliged to resign.

The domestic importance of the Suez Crisis was very great, for it
brought to power one of the most influential twentieth-century
Conservatives, Harold Macmillan. His experience as a junior officer
during the First World War and his period as the MP for a northern, industrial constituency suffering high unemployment had made
Macmillan a rebel against his party leaders in the inter-war period.
He had concluded that uncontrolled capitalism did not work, and in
a famous book entitled *The Middle Way* (1938) he advocated a
combination of private enterprise and state intervention in social
and economic affairs. Macmillan thought of himself as upholding
the Disraelian tradition of Conservatism, but in practice he was
simply giving expression to the new consensus. During the early
1950s he associated himself closely with the interests of consumers
as the Minister of Housing who succeeded in building 300,000
houses a year.

Macmillan showed considerable skill in restoring both his party's
fortunes and the morale of the country in the aftermath of Suez.
Like Baldwin, he managed to steer the Conservatives away from
their traditions in external affairs. In particular, he accelerated the
process of decolonialisation and in 1961 he made Britain's first
application to join the European Economic Community. Once the
immediate humiliations of 1956 had been forgotten, the government restored its fortunes by concentrating on the promotion of
higher material living standards. Higher real wages, easy credit
and the growth of consumer goods industries resulted in a much
wider distribution of luxuries in British society than ever before.
The most conspicuous symptoms of this were the rapid spread of
home-ownership, which Conservatives called the 'property owning
democracy', the popularity of foreign holidays, and the purchase
of motor cars, which rose from 1.5 million in 1945 to 5.5 million
by 1960.

The consumer boom, however, fostered inflation and a deteriorating balance of payments. In order to check this trend the Chancellor of the Exchequer, Peter Thorneycroft, proposed to restrict
expenditure for 1958–9. Macmillan, however, refused to risk a

deflationary policy which would raise unemployment and undermine the consumer boom. When Thorneycroft resigned, Macmillan blithely dismissed it as a 'little local difficulty'. Thus the 1959 budget became another irresponsible bid for votes by means of £370 million of tax cuts. This enabled the Conservatives to erase the memory of Suez and confidently hold an election in 1959. In a notorious phrase Macmillan claimed that 'most of our people have never had it so good'. By winning a third successive victory and by an even larger majority, it seemed to contemporaries that the Conservatives had re-established themselves as the natural party of government.

27
The Decline of British Power, 1945–74

In 1962 many British politicians reacted with outrage when the former American Secretary of State, Dean Acheson, remarked that Britain had lost an empire but not found a role. Yet his comment was a perfectly fair one. In the aftermath of the Second World War, Britain succumbed to an illusion that she could remain one of the world's great powers. At the time, this was understandable; Churchill had only recently settled the peace apparently on an equal footing with Roosevelt and Stalin; Britain still possessed a huge Empire; and the 'special relationship' with America made her feel like an equal partner in the Cold War. Certainly the aim of Ernest Bevin, the Foreign Secretary after 1945, was to maintain Britain's status as one of the three major powers, and to this end he was prepared to strain the British economy to breaking point. By 1950 Britain still had an army of 900,000 men, something unheard of in peacetime, and she spent 14 per cent of her gross national product on defence.

However, this proved to be a vain endeavour. Britain's economy emerged from the war burdened by debt and lost markets; her resources were not comparable with those of the USA or the Soviet Union; and her failings in investment and productivity led to her being overtaken by the other west European economies during the 1950s. Thus, despite the nationalistic rhetoric of successive prime ministers, by the 1960s and 1970s Britain found herself compelled to re-adjust her view of her role and status in the world, so that by the 1980s she was no more than a middle-ranking power.

THE LOSS OF EMPIRE

'If we lose India', Lord Curzon once declared, 'we will fall straight away out of the ranks of the great powers.' Yet by 1947 India and Pakistan had won independence, and by 1948 so had Burma and Ceylon. The break was accomplished comparatively painlessly. Why was this? Part of the explanation may be found in the long-term preparations for self-government; successive reforms in 1909, 1920 and 1935 had extended Indian participation in government. By the 1920s many British leaders had accepted that Gandhi and the Congress had established a moral claim to determine their own destiny which Britain could not indefinitely deny. The battle to stop this trend of policy had been fought in the Conservative Party in the 1930s when the imperialists, led by Churchill, had been decisively defeated by the reformers, led by Baldwin. Thereafter it was essentially a matter of *when* Britain would give independence, not whether. The process was accelerated by the psychological blow suffered by Britain during the war, and by the widespread conflict within India between Muslims and Hindus, which began to make the country ungovernable by 1945. The new Labour Government was not keen to abandon the Empire, but its priorities were domestic not imperial. Thus, Attlee broke the deadlock by appointing Lord Mountbatten as the last Viceroy with a simple mandate to quit India by January 1948. Mountbatten accomplished the task even more speedily by partitioning the country between a Muslim majority state and a Hindu majority state and forcing the Indian princes to join one or the other.

For Britain the willingness of the new Indian state to remain a member of the Commonwealth gave a welcome impression of continuity; the Commonwealth created an illusion that she still enjoyed world wide influence but on a less formal basis than before. Moreover, the loss of India did not result in a sudden collapse of the rest of the Empire, which continued largely intact until the 1960s. There were two main reasons for this. The first was economic. In 1950, 48 per cent of all Britain's exports were sold in Empire markets, and politicians believed that the living standards of British workers still depended on these traditional links. In the 1950s the government expressed its policy in terms of 'trusteeship'. It argued that Africa stood in need of investment and that its nationalist movements were very undeveloped. Therefore Britain still had a role to play both in promoting economic growth and in enacting political reforms that would eventually allow power to be handed over to a competent successor regime.

The second reason for the maintainence of the Empire was political-strategic. As the Cold War developed, from 1948 onwards it seemed to the British and American governments essential to curb the expansion of Soviet influence in the Asian and African continents. Thus, instead of urging the British to withdraw, the Americans became keen for them to retain their naval bases and influence around the world. The British system of communications, stretching from the Mediterranean to the Far East, was maintained until the late 1960s, even though much of the original rationale for it had gone. The Cold War strategy led Britain into several colonial wars during the 1950s in order to check Communist subversion in Malaya and Kenya and nationalist forces in Cyprus. These rearguard actions proved to be costly but did achieve a measure of success, in that when independence was finally granted to Malaya and Kenya, the successor regimes were pro-Western in character.

THE BURDEN OF DEFENCE

Even before the onset of the Cold War, Bevin and Attlee assumed that Britain must maintain her existing defence role. The withdrawal of American troops from Europe during 1945 to 1947 had already underlined the point. For them and their successors, the symbol of Britain's determination to be a Superpower was the development of her own atomic weapon, which they believed to be justified by the overwhelming numerical superiority of Soviet forces in Europe. As a result, defence expenditure increased from £2.3 million to £4.7 million in 1951. When the Churchill government decided to develop the 'H' bomb in 1954 it was claimed that this weapon would 'make us a world power again'. Clearly the political and even psychological pressures behind this policy were as strong as any military or strategic ones.

In practice, however, Britain could not sustain the burden of European defence without massive American support. Although her defence spending fell from 14 per cent of gross national product in 1951 to 8.2 per cent by 1955, the costs remained excessive for her weakened economy. Germany, with much stronger economic growth, devoted only half as much to defence. Harold Macmillan, who served as both Chancellor and Foreign Secretary in the 1950s, claimed: 'it is defence expenditure which has broken our back'. On the other hand, within the Conservative Party support for maintaining the three armed forces at a high level remained a serious obstacle to retrenchment.

However, the aftermath of the Suez Crisis gave Macmillan the opportunity to impose cuts in defence. During 1957, troops were withdrawn from Germany, and the army was reduced from 690,000 men to 375,000. Ministers argued that nuclear weapons could be justified as a more economical means of deterring Soviet aggression than conventional forces with their high manpower costs. Unfortunately Britain found it increasingly difficult to obtain a method for delivering her nuclear bomb. By the late 1950s her 'V' bombers became obsolete and the missile 'Blue Streak' was abandoned in 1960. As a result Macmillan bought the 'Skybolt' missile from the USA, only to find that it, too, was abandoned in 1962. Britain obtained Polaris submarines as an alternative, but these events exposed in humiliating fashion the hollowness of British claims to possess a truly independent deterrent.

None the less, the political case for a nuclear deterrent had become so entrenched that the new Labour Prime Minister, Harold Wilson, continued to retain it after 1964. He also fought to preserve Britain's military bases throughout the Indian Ocean and the Far East, partly because President Johnson, on whose co-operation Britain depended to support her ailing currency, insisted that she should keep them. Eventually, however, the costs of imperial defence systems in the post-imperial era became too great. By 1967–68 Wilson had concluded that the economy could no longer support the burden. By 1970, troops had been withdrawn from Singapore and Malaya and, in effect, Britain's role east of Suez was abandoned.

THE IMPACT OF THE SUEZ CRISIS

By far the greatest single challenge to Britain's imperial role was that posed by the dispute over the Suez Canal in 1956. As late as 1951, 40,000 British troops remained in Egypt, but after the coup by Gamel Abdel Nasser in 1952, Churchill agreed to withdraw them within two years. Britain and the United States hoped that they would be able to rely on Turkey and Iran to maintain their strategic position in the Middle East. However, Churchill's successor, Anthony Eden, over-reacted to Nasser's increasing reliance on the Soviet Union for arms and, above all, to his decision to nationlise the Suez Canal in 1956. Eden claimed that British trade would be at risk if Egypt controlled the canal. His policy reflected the irrational and emotional attitude adopted by the British towards the canal; they saw it as peculiarly their property and ignored the fact that many other nations had the same interest in maintaining the flow of commerce. In collaboration with France and Israel, Eden ordered an invasion of Egypt. However, this provoked massive speculation against the pound, and when the American government refused to support the British currency, Eden was forced into a humiliating withdrawal.

What significance should be attributed to this crisis? In the short-term it was certainly a disaster for Britain. It undermined her influence throughout the Middle East and stimulated nationalist movements elsewhere. Indeed, apart from Australia and New Zealand, Britain stood wholly isolated when the issue came up at the United Nations. On the other hand, some of the damage was repaired fairly quickly; relations with the United States, for example, were restored by Macmillan. In the long term the question is how far Suez accelerated the trend towards decolonisation. Until 1956 it was widely assumed that independence was still a long way off for most colonies. Only the Sudan (1956) and Malaya and the Gold Coast (1957) were close to winning self-government. But by destroying Eden's premiership and bringing Harold Macmillan to power the Suez Crisis had a major *indirect* effect. Once he had established his authority and won an election in 1959 Macmillan transformed British policy. He abandoned trusteeship and began to grant independence to the colonies almost regardless of whether they were prepared for it. Altogether 27 territories were lost between 1960 and 1969, so that by the mid-1970s all that remained of a once great empire was a scattering of islands in the Pacific and Latin America, in addition to Hong Kong, Gibraltar and the Falkland Islands.

During the 1960s even the Commonwealth began to lose its appeal. This was partly because Canada, Australia and New Zealand looked increasingly to the United States to assist them with defence. But the Commonwealth also became rather divided over

Britain's imposition of restrictions on immigration in 1962 and over her failure to tackle effectively the illegal declaration of independence by the white supremacists in Southern Rhodesia in 1965. In this way Britain's traditional role had collapsed by the mid-1960s; not surprisingly some of her leaders had already begun to search for an alternative.

THE DISCOVERY OF EUROPE

In the aftermath of 1945 the British regarded Europe as an area of devastation that would take many years to recover. Not surprisingly, therefore, they dropped their co-operation with France, rather as they had done after 1918, and chose instead to concentrate on consolidating relations with the United States and the Commonwealth. In the words of the Foreign Secretary, Ernest Bevin, Britain was simply 'not part of Europe'. Consequently, governments of both parties rebuffed the efforts made by Jean Monnet to interest Britain in greater European unity in 1949; they tried to avoid taking part in the formation of the European Coal and Steel Community in 1950–52, and in the talks about integration by the six founders of the EEC after 1955. In fact the British were surprised that, despite their attitude, the six signed the Treaty of Rome in 1957.

While Britain's attitude immediately after 1945 is understandable, her reluctance to seize the opportunities to participate in European developments during the 1950s requires more explanation. Many politicians on both left and right believed that a new supra-national organisation would be a threat to sovereignty and to the role of the British parliament. They also argued that British trade was still heavily biased towards the Commonwealth, and it would be unwise to throw away the advantages of cheap food supplies. In addition, the British people were culturally very insular; such links as they had with the wider world were largely through emigration over many decades to America, Australia and Canada. The emotional ties arising from these connections outlived the formal demise of the Empire. Above all, many politicians felt that an attempt to join with Europe in the 1950s would have been an admission that the bid to retain the status of a great power had failed; they were not yet ready for this.

By 1960 informed opinion had certainly begun to change. The Liberal Party led the way in urging Britain to join the EEC, supported by some rising Labour figures such as Roy Jenkins, and Conservatives such as Edward Heath. The Prime Minister, Macmillan, recognised the success of the six EEC members in stimulating their economies by reducing tariffs and harmonising external duties. Like most of those who supported British entry into the EEC, Macmillan expressed the case largely in terms of the *economic* advantages. By the 1960s it had become clear that the old markets of the Commonwealth were too small and that Britain must sell her manufactured goods in the wealthy west European markets instead. In fact, trade had already begun to shift in that direction. However, the unspoken motivation for joining was more a *political* one. Neither the special relationship with America, nor the nuclear deterrent, nor the Commonwealth looked likely to maintain Britain's influence or status in world affairs. Europe offered the only viable alternative.

Thus, despite opposition amongst Conservatives, Macmillan applied for British entry into the EEC in 1961. Negotiations proceeded well until vetoed by President de Gaulle who correctly felt that the British had not yet given up their older commitment to the American alliance. When Harold Wilson became Prime Minister in 1964 he pursued the special relationship with the United States and showed little interest in Europe. This pleased many Socialists who regarded the EEC as essentially a club for capitalists at this time. But, like Macmillan, Wilson was gradually forced by his own failures with the economy to seek a fresh role for Britain. As younger men like Jenkins rose through the party hierarchy, so the pressure to join Europe grew stronger. Thus a second application was made in 1967, only to be vetoed once again by France. Not until the election of 1970 did a genuinely pro-European prime minister, Edward Heath, come to power. Heath believed that as Germany became stronger the United States would inevitably place less and less importance on her relationship with Britain. Also, the French began to regard Britain as a potentially useful counterweight to the dominance of Germany within the EEC. Negotiations commenced again in January 1970 and concluded in June 1971. In October the House of Commons approved British entry by 356 votes to 244. The Treaty was signed in January 1972 and Britain actually joined in January 1973.

However, for the British people the argument was only just beginning. The opposition or indifference of the public towards British membership of the EEC remained strong, partly because the terms on which she had joined seemed unfavourable. Britain lost the advantages of cheap food supplies from the Commonwealth and made disproportionate contributions to the EEC budget. By 1978 she paid 20 per cent of the total revenue but received only 8 per cent of the expenditure. It was also unfortunate that Britain's entry coincided with a severe economic depression in western Europe. As a result, the benefits, in terms of higher economic growth and living standards, proved to be elusive. In addition, the Labour Party capitalised upon the unpopularity of the EEC by arguing that Heath had achieved a very poor deal. Consequently when Wilson recovered office in 1974 he set out to renegotiate the terms and offered the people a referendum in June 1975 to decide whether they wished to remain members. In fact 67 per cent voted in favour of EEC membership, though more out of fear of the consequences of leaving than out of enthusiasm for remaining in. As unemployment increased and the balance of payments worsened it was tempting for critics of both right and left to blame all the country's problems on Europe. This paved the way for the vigorous anti-Europeanism adopted by the new Tory leader, Mrs Margaret Thatcher, when she became Prime Minister in 1979.

28

Affluence and Decline, 1960–75

The 1960s began in a mood of confidence and well-being personified by the relaxed, Edwardian style of Harold Macmillan. The prosperity of the previous decade appeared likely to continue; the Prime Minister's well-publicised visits to the USA and the USSR preserved the illusion that Britain remained one of the world's great powers; and the decade saw an explosion of cultural achievements especially in popular music, fiction and fashion. However, the underlying problems in British society could no longer by ignored. A younger and well-educated generation, accustomed to expect prosperity and a lifetime's employment, adopted a critical view of the institutions and leaders of their society. The two conventional political parties began to lose support to a range of alternatives, from a resurgent Liberal Party, to the Nationalist parties in Scotland and Wales, and extreme right-wing organisations campaigning against Commonwealth immigration. These were all symptoms of Britain's economic decline, which developed into an obsession during the 1960s. As the Empire finally disappeared the British tentatively began to consider an alternative role in the world, but most were, as yet, not convinced about the necessity to join the EEC.

THE 'SICK MAN OF EUROPE'

The rapid rise in living standards during the 1950s had been based on insecure foundations. With an annual average growth rate of 2.2 per cent the British economy performed markedly less well than those of her rivals; West Germany, for example, enjoyed an average

4.9 per cent growth rate. Unfortunately, workers and trade unions had come to expect wage increases which were far beyond any improvements in productivity. As a result, industry suffered from inflation, its goods became less competitive, and Britain developed a serious balance of payments problem. Governments had acquired the habit of stimulating the economy only to apply the brakes shortly afterwards. For example, the tax cuts prior to the 1959 election led to inflation and a rise in imports. The Chancellor then intervened to check this by raising interest rates, but this had the effect of deterring investment and weakening manufacturers' competitiveness even further. Foreign investors believed that the weakness of the economy made a devaluation of the pound inevitable. However, as the government continued to regard devaluation as a political impossibility, its only alternative was severe deflationary measures designed to check domestic consumption. During 1961–2 this policy led the Chancellor to impose a complete freeze on pay increases, but the ensuing unpopularity prompted Macmillan to sack him along with one-third of his cabinet in 1962. In spite of this, the new Chancellor repeated the same errors. In an attempt to restore the government's fortunes in time for a general election in 1964 he began expansionist policies during 1963. In the process he helped to create a balance of payments deficit of £800 million by the end of 1964 as consumers bought foreign goods rather than British.

Not surprisingly this cycle of economic failure engendered a mood of pessimism; it became commonplace to describe Britain as the 'Sick Man of Europe' – an ironical reference to the prolonged decline of the Turkish Empire in the nineteenth century. The question arose, how to cure the malaise? Some blamed the greed and power of organised trade unions. Others saw the problem in terms of Britain's inflexible class system, which created bad industrial relations and restricted the rise in able men and women who lacked the advantage of wealth and private education. An increasingly fashionable remedy was entry into the EEC on the assumption that this would give Britain the stimulus of a larger export market and higher economic growth. Macmillan was by no means unresponsive to this thinking. Unfortunately, his application to join the EEC was vetoed by President de Gaulle. Moreover, by 1962 the Conservative leaders had become so afraid of losing votes to the revived Liberal Party that they continued to try to boost living standards beyond what was justified by economic performance.

HAROLD WILSON AND THE LABOUR RECOVERY

The three successive defeats suffered by the Labour Party in 1951, 1955 and 1959 had caused a crisis of confidence in British Socialism. One symptom of this was the publication of *The Future of Socialism* by Anthony Crosland in 1956, in which he argued that socialism in the form of state ownership of industry should go no further; the key question was how to distribute the products of the mixed economy, not change the ownership of industry. Yet while the party remained officially committed to socialism in its constitution, there could be no acceptance of Crosland's thesis. Meanwhile the steady fall in the Labour vote suggested that the party was being undermined by fundamental social changes. In particular, working-class prosperity seemed to have led many voters to identify with middle-class aspirations such as home-ownership, and thus to support the Conservatives.

However, Labour was rescued from its dilemma partly by the collapse of Conservative support after 1961 and also by the election of a new leader, Harold Wilson, in 1963. Wilson showed immense skill in suppressing the ideological divisions within the party, in exploiting Macmillan's difficulties, and in appealing to the middle classes. Wilson was himself a reassuringly middle-class professional who formulated an appeal in terms of applying new technology to the British economy. But in spite of all this, Wilson only narrowly managed to recapture power in 1964, when Labour won 44 per cent of the vote compared with 43 per cent in 1959.

After thirteen years of Conservative government, expectations were very high when Labour took office once again. Wilson was a professional economist with experience in the civil service during wartime and a much greater awareness of the need to modernise British economic and political institutions. Unfortunately the new Prime Minister devoted himself more to short-term political survival and to presentation rather than to the substantive problems faced by the country. Having inherited a large balance of payments deficit from the Conservatives, Wilson and his colleagues proved to be conservatives themselves rather than the bold modernisers they were believed to be. They soon adopted a deflationary policy designed to dampen speculation against the pound. But the effects of raising the bank rate, increasing taxation and restricting imports were to kill off the prospects of fast economic growth on which Labour's social policies depended. The alternative lay in a devaluation of the currency so as to restore the competitiveness of exports and stimulate output. But Wilson remembered the Labour government's experience of devaluation in 1949, and shrank from a repetition.

This proved to be a crucial miscalculation which affected the whole of the government's record. In order to defend the value of the pound the Prime Minister desperately required American co-operation. President Johnson agreed on the need to avoid a British devaluation, but in return for his support he insisted that she should maintain her costly and anachronistic defence role in the Far East and support the Americans in their war against Communism in Vietnam. Wilson largely accepted this, though Britain avoided any direct military involvement in Vietnam. This expedient succeeded in maintaining the government in the short-term, so that it managed to win a second election with a much increased majority in March 1966. But in effect Wilson had surrendered control of British economic policy. Short-term political expedients could not guarantee the indefinite survival of the government. By 1967 the worsening trade deficit forced the cabinet once again to consider whether the currency was over-valued. In November of that year the long-awaited devaluation finally took place. At the same time it was decided to begin withdrawing from the imperial defence role and to make another application to join the European Economic Community. But another dose of deflation improved the balance of payments at the cost of economic growth. During the period from 1964 to 1970 output increased by only 2.7 per cent per year on average. Britain continued to fall behind the rest of western Europe.

By the later 1960s the failures of the Wilson government had generated a wide-ranging political revolt. One symptom of this, which took conventional politicians by surprise, was the upsurge of nationalism in Wales and Scotland. Since the establishment of Plaid Cymru (the Welsh Nationalist Party) in 1925 and the Scottish National Party (SNP) in 1934, the English politicians had regarded nationalism as a marginal and even eccentric phenomenon. However, the prolonged decline of heavy industry in Wales and Scotland and the perceived neglect by London-based governments of both parties eventually made the idea of a devolution of power to the regions seem attractive. As a result the Labour Party began to lose by-elections to the two nationalist parties in 1966 and

1967. Although both Conservative and Labour leaders found it hard to recognise that so small a country as Britain had always been a multi-nation state, they were forced to come to terms with the long-term loss of confidence in the very idea of the United Kingdom.

In dealing with external affairs the Wilson government largely alienated its own left-wing. Labour already faced pressure from the Campaign for Nuclear Disarmament, in which many of its own members were active, to give up Britain's claim to an independent nuclear weapon. Wilson flatly refused to do this, though he managed slight reductions in spending. But during the 1960s much of the energy that had gone into the Campaign for Nuclear Disarmament was diverted into attempts to reverse the British government's support for the American policy in Vietnam. Young, well-educated, middle-class people were especially appalled by the sustained bombing of Vietnam and disillusioned by Wilson's failure to recognise the moral case against it. In this way the government presided over a steady demoralisation of its most idealistic supporters and the alienation of its left wing.

As if the economic and foreign issues were not enough, the government also disappointed expectations by failing to achieve significant reforms of Britain's political institutions. Though the case for changing the working of parliament and the civil service had been widely argued and investigated, Labour retained the old system largely intact; the cabinet drew up a bill to modernise the House of Lords, which still enjoyed a largely hereditary membership, but abandoned it in embarrassing circumstances. Most damaging of all was the abortive attempt to modernise the trade unions during 1968–9. The way had been prepared by a Royal Commission, and since the public blamed the unions for Britain's economic problems, the political risk involved was undoubtedly worth taking. But when a bill was drawn up Wilson backed down in the face of opposition from union leaders and some cabinet colleagues. His humiliating retreat symbolised the dilemma of a government unable to control policy in spite of its large majority. The immediate result of these failures was the defeat of the Labour Party at the 1970 election; and in the longer run the effect was to cause a sharp move to the left among ordinary members who felt betrayed by Wilson's record in office.

THE CONSENSUS CRACKS, 1970-5

The inability of the Labour government to check Britain's economic decline between 1964 and 1970 proved to be a disillusioning experience. But when the same fate overtook its successor the result was to call into question the whole political system and the economic thinking that had prevailed since the Second World War. Like Wilson, the new Conservative Prime Minister, Edward Heath, aroused expectations that he was unable to satisfy. He gave the impression that he would abandon consensus policies and revert to a non-interventionist style of Conservatism. Yet Heath was himself a product of the Macmillan era, committed to full employment and social welfare. Above all, he believed passionately in the cause of Europe. Thus, it was never part of Heath's plan to introduce a more right-wing or 'Thatcherite' brand of Conservatism; indeed after a few initial concessions to right-wing opinion he reverted to what some of his colleagues regarded as the errors of Keynesianism. As unemployment rose towards a million the Chancellor attempted to stimulate the economy into rapid growth. Soon employers were conceding wage rises of 15 per cent; inflation accelerated and the trade gap widened. Yet Heath showed himself unwilling to allow the free market to destroy vital British industries; he therefore offered subsidies in several cases, and in 1971 he nationalised Rolls Royce, the prestigious motor car manufacturer.

In spite of these comparatively liberal policies, however, Heath acquired a reputation for inflexibility. This was largely because of his Industrial Relations Act, which restricted the trade unions' ability to hold strikes. The unions, who had always assumed that they were beyond the scope of the law, reacted ferociously to the legislation. By 1972, 23 million working days were being lost in strikes – more than in any year since the General Strike of 1926. The challenge to the government was led by the National Union of Mineworkers, which used a system of co-ordinated pickets to stop the movement of coal in 1972. After rejecting an offer of an 8 per cent wage increase the miners eventually won a 21 per cent increase in 1973. In the process the militant leaders of the union gained the initiative and believed that they could totally discredit the government's trade union legislation. Thus, by the end of 1973 they had rejected another wage increase and forced Heath to declare a state of emergency and impose a three-day working week upon industry. In this way the industrial problem turned into a political crisis, for the elected government was virtually being prevented from governing by the trade unions.

In this situation some of the Prime Minister's advisors urged him to call a general election on the assumption that the voters had been antagonised by the overbearing behaviour of the unions and would therefore support the government. Heath hesitated but eventually agreed to hold an election at the end of February 1974. This proved to be a major miscalculation for the electorate had largely lost sympathy with the government because of the unemployment and inflation created by its economic policies. In fact, the electorate had become disillusioned with both the major parties. At the election the Liberals contested every constituency and won a fifth of the votes, a level of support not achieved since 1929. In Scotland the discovery of oil gave fresh credibility to the Scottish national Party's claim that an independent Scotland would be economically feasible. In 1974, 30 per cent of Scots voters supported the SNP and, by implication, endorsed its policy of independence. The effect of the Liberal and Nationalist advance was to terminate the era of two-party dominance in British politics. In the process it created major pressures for constitutional changes, including the devolution of power from London to the regions, and the introduction of proportional representation in place of the traditional single-member electoral system. In the short term the election destroyed Heath's government and restored the Labour Party to power until 1979.

Not surprisingly these events generated a bitter backlash against Heath, who had led his party to three election defeats and only one victory. At the time this was not primarily an ideological reaction. However, it created the opportunity for the right-wing of the Conservative Party, led initially by Sir Keith Jospeh and later by Margaret Thatcher, to challenge the leadership. When a ballot took place in February 1975 many MPs supported Mrs Thatcher, not because they wanted or expected her to become leader, but simply in order to punish Heath. In the event, Thatcher polled so many votes that she forced Heath to resign and went on to seize the Leadership in a second ballot. Her victory dealt a fatal blow to the politics of consensus, though at the time this was not obvious.

29

Thatcher and the End of Consensus Politics, 1975–97

During the late 1970s, the inability of British governments to deal with the country's economic problems finally discredited the political consensus that had prevailed since 1945. The underlying economic malaise manifested itself in a loss of popular confidence in the conventional political system. An obvious symptom of this was the fall in support for the two main political parties. At the two elections of 1974, Labour won 37–9 per cent of the vote, while the Conservatives took only 34–5 per cent. As a result, although the Labour Party held office under Harold Wilson and James Callaghan until 1979, it lived a precarious existence; long before 1979 its small majority in parliament had disappeared, thus forcing the Prime Minister to seek pacts first with the Liberals and then with the Scottish Nationalists. In spite of these expedients the Labour government was never really in control, partly because much of its energy was devoted to party management. Wilson skilfully placated his left-wing critics by holding a referendum on British membership of the EEC in 1975. But the left's dissatisfaction went far wider. Under the leadership of Tony Benn the left pressed hard for the radical reforms that Wilson had avoided ever since coming to power in 1964: wider nationalisation of industry, unilateral nuclear disarmament, abolition of the House of Lords, and greater democracy within the Labour Party itself. In fact, the ordinary members succeeded in opening up the Leadership to election by trade unions and party members as well as by the MPs; and it also forced the

MPs to submit to regular re-selection by their local constituency parties, a change which put pressure on the more right-wing figures.

But as Labour began to move sharply to the left, other parts of the political system moved to the right. The election of Margaret Thatcher as Conservative Party leader in 1975 was an obvious sign of this. But the move away from consensus became evident in the policies of the Labour government. By the end of 1976 the Chancellor of the Exchequer was forced to deal with a balance of payments crisis by seeking a large loan from the International Monetary Fund. The price for this support, however, was a series of cuts in government spending, an increase in the cost of living, and higher unemployment. In effect, Labour had abandoned Keynesianism in favour of what later came to be known as monetarism two and a half years before Mrs Thatcher came to power.

THATCHERISM AND ECONOMIC DECLINE

The political creed known as monetarism – the belief that governments could reduce inflation by controlling the money supply – had long been advocated by economists such as Friedman and von Hayek. But in Britain its only adherents had been marginal figures within the Conservatives such as Enoch Powell and Sir Keith Joseph. When Mrs Thatcher took up this idea she largely obscured it beneath the familiar list of Conservative cries; governments, she argued, should stop trying to achieve Socialism, accept that Keynesianism had failed, and abandon subsidies, incomes policies and high taxation even if the short-term effects were to allow inefficient businesses to collapse and unemployment to rise. As a result, even her own ministers did not fully appreciate that their new leader intended to apply monetarist doctrines quite literally and accept the short-term political risks.

After her election victory in 1979 Thatcher took care to appoint one of her supporters, Sir Geoffrey Howe, as Chancellor of the Exchequer. His first test came in 1981, by which time the economy had fallen into a serious depression. He responded to this, not in traditional fashion with counter-cyclical measures, but by increasing taxation and reducing government borrowing. Although many Conservative ministers opposed this because they knew it would lead to massive unemployment, they reluctantly acquiesced.

However, their fears proved to be more than justified. Soon the British economy suffered its worst slump since the 1930s. During 1981 alone the gross national product diminished by 3.2 per cent and unemployment rose to 2.7 million, a level not experienced previously by any but the oldest British people. Eventually a quarter of all British manufacturing capacity was destroyed during the first depression of the Thatcher years. One result of this was a huge and long-term balance of payments deficit. For its part, the government argued that inefficient businesses must go under. Unfortunately it proved difficult to replace them with new businesses because the government's determination to defend the value of the pound meant that they kept interest rates high, and consequently, investment was inhibited. In this way economic and political doctrine trapped the government in a cycle of low growth and high unemployment. It was claimed that lost manufacturing jobs would be replaced by new employment in the service sector. To some extent this was true. However, the new jobs also proved to be vulnerable to the depression; many were only part-time and low-paid jobs for women workers; and, as a result, no fewer than 3.2 million people were officially unemployed by 1985.

Significantly, this very high level of unemployment was recorded in the middle of a period of economic *recovery* from 1983 to 1988. This was an indication that Britain had now moved into a new and dangerous phase of her decline, in the sense that a large balance of payments deficit and large-scale unemployment amongst men had become permanent features of her society.

Such recovery as did take place in the mid-1980s was largely stimulated by financial de-regulation. Banks and building societies offered generous loans to their customers, much of which was actually spent on imported goods. As a result, householders' debts rose from £16 billion in 1980 to £47 billion in 1989. This artificial boom pushed Britain's trade deficit to an unprecedented £15 billion in 1988–9. Tax cuts, designed to help win further elections in 1983 and 1987, only exacerbated the situation. By 1990 this boom collapsed as the economy fell into a second depression. The effect was that Britain's rate of economic growth was only 1.75 per cent per annum between 1979 and 1990, an average well below that of the 1950s, 1960s and 1970s which the Thatcherites had so derided. The chief effect of Thatcherism had been to accelerate Britain's economic decline.

THE ATTACK ON THE STATE

Perhaps the most central object of the Conservative government during the 1980s was to curtail the role of the state and to set free the individual enterprise of the people. The most immediate means of accomplishing this was to cut the rate of income tax, which Mrs Thatcher regarded as a deterrent to British businessmen. However, the huge increase in unemployment, and the social costs it involved, put great pressure on public spending. As a result, the reductions in direct taxes had to be compensated for by increases in indirect taxes on consumption. The effect, contrary to original claims, was to *increase* the tax burden on the British people; whereas under the pre-1979 governments the state had taken 35 per cent of gross domestic product, it took 37–8 per cent under Mrs Thatcher. Moreover, the changes in taxation simply shifted the burden from rich people onto poor people and those on average incomes, thereby reversing the historic trend towards the redistribution of incomes.

Their inability to reduce government spending preoccupied the Conservative ministers throughout the 1980s. They introduced a series of measures designed to curtail the costs of old age pensions, unemployment benefits, child benefits, housing benefits and student grants. However, the Conservatives hesitated to attack popular forms of state welfare such as the National Health Service. They attempted to deal with this by stages, for example, by closing down hospital beds and hospitals on the grounds of promoting efficiency; but the introduction of what were called 'market forces' into health care only resulted in a large increase in spending on administration, and the gradual exclusion of certain categories of people, such as the elderly and those requiring dental treatment, from the system. An easier target of attack was the local authorities. Local councils' expenditure was strictly regulated by the government so that they gradually lost effective control. They were also compelled to sell council houses but prevented from building new homes. As a result, by 1987 there were 370,000 people officially homeless in Britain; beggars began to reappear on the streets of the large towns; the number of people living in poverty increased by 1.6 million by 1989 according to EEC figures; and crime rose by 79 per cent between 1979 and 1990. By the end of the Thatcher premiership British society had begun to break down under social strains of a kind and an extent not witnessed since the industrial revolution.

As the difficulties involved in attacking the welfare state became clearer, the Conservatives identified an alternative target in the form of the nationalised industries. Little mention had been made of them in the original version of Thatcherism, but it became clear that sales of state assets could be a means of paying for tax cuts. Consequently gas, water, electricity, telephones and several other industries were 'privatised', or returned to private ownership, largely in the face of public opposition. Harold Macmillan, now elevated to the House of Lords, was sufficiently antagonised by these sales to denounce the whole policy as one of 'selling the family silver'. However, at first the privatisation programme brought some political compensation to the government because the state assets were sold at far below their real value and thus yielded an immediate profit to the new shareholders. Subsequently, however, it emerged that the new management was making huge profits at the expense of customers, and at the cost of workers, many of whom were sacked. Thus, by the beginning of the 1990s the policy of privatisation had begun to be more of a liability than an asset.

THE REDISCOVERY OF ENGLISH NATIONALISM

Since the end of the nineteenth century Conservatives had gradually ceased to exploit patriotism as a political weapon. One of Mrs Thatcher's most important contributions to politics was the resurrection of this weapon in the service of her party. As the first female party leader she probably felt vulnerable to accusations of weakness in foreign affairs, and thus began to compensate by adopting an exaggerated patriotic posture. This became clear in the early days of her leadership in her extreme attacks on the Soviet Union. As Prime Minister she chose to criticise the views of the African and Asian members of the Commonwealth, an institution with which she had no sympathy and of which she had little knowledge. Above all, Thatcher's experience of life and politics had given her no comprehension of Europe; she failed to understand how her predecessors, Heath and Macmillan, had become so enthusiastic about the cause of European unity. Instead she chose to glory in Britain's isolation within the EEC. In this sense her foreign policy represented a throwback to an earlier era; she tried to restore the special relationship with the United States and exploit the popular dislike for European bureaucracy.

Mrs Thatcher's close relationship with the American President Ronald Reagan was not just a matter of ideological sympathy; she also wanted American support to help maintain Britain's status as a nuclear power. Now that the polaris submarines were becoming obsolete, Britain relied upon the United States to supply Trident submarines as the replacement. Unfortunately, the government's belief in the importance of nuclear weapons somewhat blinded it to the dangers of reducing conventional forces. It was the withdrawal of Royal Navy ships form the South Atlantic which almost destroyed Thatcher's premiership in 1982 when it encouraged the Argentine government to seize the Falkland Islands. In fact, like all its predecessors, the Thatcher government planned to withdraw British control from the Falklands gradually over a period of years. But the invasion placed the Prime Minister in an awkward dilemma. She resolved it by dispatching a 28,000-strong task force which recaptured the islands and rescued her premiership at the same time. This external triumph, combined with a recovery from the economic depression, and the leftward turn of the Labour Party, allowed Thatcher to win an easy victory at the general election of 1983. But a long-term price had to be paid; once regarded as virtually worthless, the Falklands were now seen as an asset to be retained despite the costs to the British government.

The Prime Minister's belligerent stance in foreign affairs led many of her followers to claim that she had restored Britain's standing in the world. However, this suggestion conflicted embarrassingly with what the Thatcherites regarded as Britain's humiliating role in Europe. In domestic politics Thatcher effectively exploited popular hostility towards the EEC, and in the process she diverted her party from its course. Since the 1960s, Conservative opposition to the EEC had been forced underground, but had never disappeared; Thatcher made it respectable once again. Anti-Europeanism was not just an expression of frustrated English nationalism, it also reflected the ideology of the Conservative right-wing; from this perspective the EEC appeared as a new form of socialism because it involved an extension of state intervention and regulation in economic affairs. Her populist instincts prompted Thatcher to claim that Britain paid too much into the Community's budget; from 1979 onwards she demanded repayment of £1000 million of 'our money'.

For the entire decade British ministers opposed and obstructed EEC legislation on the grounds that it was a threat to British national interests. However, though this policy proved to be popular with a good many people, it was ultimately a vain attempt to turn the clock back to 1970. Even Mrs Thatcher dared not try to withdraw from Europe for fear of wholly alienating the business community, which was strongly pro-European. In fact, she committed Britain to the single European market in 1992, and to membership of the Exchange Rate Mechanism. For all her Churchillian posturing, Thatcher had effectively surrendered British sovereignty, at least as it was traditionally understood.

THE FALL OF THATCHERISM

Although the Conservatives won three successive elections under Mrs Thatcher, in 1979, 1983 and 1987, they owed as much to luck and to the electoral system, as to popular support for their policies. Each victory was won with a minority of votes – around 42–3 per cent. This was sufficient partly because the opposition was now evenly divided between the Labour Party and an alliance between the Liberals and the Social Democratic Party, which had broken away from Labour in 1981. In 1983 when this alliance won 25 per cent of the vote it seemed about to displace Labour, which received only 27 per cent, its lowest poll since 1918. Although Labour recovered slightly in 1987, it remained far below its usual level. This was to some extent attributable to long-term social changes which had reduced the party's natural base, as well as its policy shifts in the 1980s. By the late 1980s the manual working-class voters comprised only 45 per cent of the British electorate; only a little over one employee in three belonged to a trade union; and 58 per cent of all manual workers were now buying their own homes. Thus, while Labour's traditional working-class support was shrinking, some of those who remained working-class were becoming upwardly mobile, and thus being won over to Conservatism.

In spite of this, the opinion polls showed that the majority of voters had not been converted to Thatcherism. The British continued to favour the welfare state and Keynesian economic policies; and some characteristic Thatcherite policies such as the privatisation of water were overwhelmingly unpopular. But above all, it was the Prime Minister's insistence on replacing the local rates with a new 'poll tax' in 1987 which precipitated her downfall. First applied in Scotland, the poll tax was widely perceived as unfair because poor people paid as much as wealthy ones. Within two years of its introduction the tax was almost impossible to collect in many parts of the country.

The poll tax symbolised the arrogance engendered by years of unfettered power. Although many of her ministers believed the tax to be a mistake, almost none of them were prepared to oppose it in cabinet. When combined with the evident failure of Thatcher's economic policies by 1990, the issue fatally undermined her standing within her own party. In that year inflation rose again to over 10 per cent and the trade deficit to £16 billion. During 1991-3 a full-scale economic recession was under way for a second time in a decade. But it was, ironically, Europe that finally forced her from office. Two of her leading ministers had succeeded in manoeuvring her into agreeing to join the Exchange Rate Mechanism, much against her wishes. Thatcher took her revenge eventually by sacking one of them, Sir Geoffrey Howe, in July 1989. She went on to denounce the whole idea of economic and monetary union at the European summit conference at Rome. However, Howe struck back in a famous speech in the House of Commons in November 1990, accusing the Prime Minister of sabotaging Britain's interests in Europe. His initiative forced a leadership contest on Mrs Thatcher in which, on the first ballot, she narrowly failed to win enough votes to retain her position. Subsequently she withdrew and the Conservatives elected John Major in her place. The explanation for this extraordinary repudiation of a leader who had won three general elections lay in the fact that most Conservative MPs had never been fully converted to Thatcherism; they had tolerated her as long as she delivered victory, but by 1990 it seemed certain that she would lead them to defeat next time.

In the short run this ruthless manoeuvre succeeded, as similar coups had in the past. Mr Major escaped the blame for the economic depression and managed to win a narrow victory at the 1992 election. Yet this did nothing to resolve the underlying problems that had shipwrecked Thatcher. She had left behind her a country suffering from a rapidly declining manufacturing base, an industry still short of investment, and a dangerous ambivalence towards Europe.

Owing to the perceived weakness of the Britian economy, the pound lost value within the Exchange Rate Mechanism during the early 1990s. Although the government and the Bank of England attempted to defend the currency by raising interest rates as high as 15 per cent, the almost inevitable result was a humiliating failure. In September 1992 Britain abandoned the ERM and allowed sterling to float – in effect a 15 per cent devaluation. This had the beneficial effect of strengthening exports and reducing unemployment; but the Major government never recovered from the blow to its reputation for economic competence. Though the Prime Minister hung on until 1997, his authority had been largely destroyed by attacks by fellow Conservatives over his pro-European views, and his small majority almost disappeared through by-election defeats.

Meanwhile, the Labour Party recovered the popular advantage under a new and relatively young leader, Tony Blair, who completed the work of Neil Kinnock by scrapping left-wing policies and adopting large parts of the social and economic programme of Thatcherism. 'New Labour', as it became known, made crime a major priority, repudiated 'tax-and-spend' policies, abandoned full employment as a goal, accepted the privatisation of industry and offered no proposals to restore the power lost by trade unions. By 1997 the Conservatives had become so unpopular that it was unclear whether Blair's revisionism was really necessary. In the event, his party won a huge victory of 419 seats and a majority of 179, though with a modest 43 per cent share of the vote. The Conservatives' share dropped to an unprecedented 31 per cent and 165 seats, and they were eliminated entirely from Scotland and Wales. For the Liberal Democrats 1997 brought the triumphant return of 46 MPs, their highest since 1929.

In this sense 1997 appeared to mark a major turning-point. Whether it had really brought an end to Thatcherism in economic and social affairs remained uncertain, however, since the new government committed itself to its predecessor's strategy in taxation and expenditure. Its rigid emphasis on maintaining low inflation above all other economic objectives led 'New Labour' into a familiar pattern of high interest rates, dwindling exports and rising unemployment within a year of taking office. On the other hand, in political–constitutional affairs a real turning-point had been reached. Elected parliaments were quickly established for Scotland

and Wales, which, in view of the rise in support for the Scottish National Party, portended further threats to the Union. Elections for both the Welsh and Scottish assemblies and for the European Parliament were to be conducted by proportional representation. The government also prepared to abolish the hereditary element in the House of Lords. At Westminster the return of no fewer than 119 women MPs made little immediate impact but suggested long-term changes in the conduct of parliamentary business. In the country the loosening of the traditional ties between Labour and the trade unions foreshadowed a fundamental alteration in the character of the party. It was widely understood that Blair intended to edge towards some form of coalition with the Liberal Democrats with a view to keeping the centre-left in power during the twenty-first century.

Bibliography

Addison, P., *The Road to 1945* (London: Cape, 1975).

Addison, P., *Churchill on the Home Front, 1900–1950* (London: Cape, 1992).

Bartlett, C., *British Foreign Policy in the Twentieth Century* (London: Macmillan, 1989).

Bedarida, F., *A Social History of England, 1851–1975* (London: Methuen, 1979).

Blake, R., *Disraeli* (London: Methuen, 1966).

Blake, R., *The Conservative Party from Peel to Thatcher* (London: Fontana, 1985).

Bourne, K., *The Foreign Policy of Victorian England, 1830–1902* (Oxford: Oxford University Press, 1970).

Briggs, A., *The Age of Improvement, 1783–1867* (London: Longman, 1959).

Brooke, J., *King George III* (London: Constable, 1972).

Burridge, T., *Clement Attlee* (London: Cape, 1985).

Calder, A., *The People's War: Britain, 1939–45* (London: Cape, 1969).

Cannon, J., *Parliamentary Reform, 1640–1832* (Cambridge: Cambridge University Press, 1973).

Chambers, J. A. and Mingay, G. E., *The Agricultural Revolution, 1750–1880* (London: Batsford, 1966).

Christie, I., *Wars and Revolutions: Britain, 1760–1815* (London: Arnold, 1982).

Clarke, P., *Lancashire and the New Liberalism* (Cambridge: Cambridge University Press, 1971).

Clarke, P., *Hope and Glory: Britain, 1900–1990* (London: Allen Lane, 1996).

Colley, L., *Britons: Forging the Nation, 1707–1837* (Yale: Yale University Press, 1992).

Constantine, S. (ed.), *The First World War in British History* (London: Arnold, 1995).

Dean, P., *The First Industrial Nation* (Cambridge: Cambridge University Press, 1967).

Derry, J. W., *Castlereagh* (London: Allen Lane, 1976).

245

Derry, J. W., *British Politics in the Age of Pitt* (London: Macmillan, 1993).
Dickinson, H. T., *British Radicalism and the French Revolution, 1789–1815* (Oxford: Blackwell, 1985).
Evans, E., *The Forging of the Modern State: Early Industrial Britain, 1783–1870* (London: Longman, 1983; 2nd edn London: Addison Wesley, Longman, 1996).
Feuchtwanger, E. J., *Democracy and Empire: Britain, 1865–1914* (London: Arnold, 1985).
Fraser, D., *The Evolution of the British Welfare State* (London: Macmillan, 1984).
French, D., *The British Way in Warfare, 1688–2000* (London: Unwin, l990).
Gamble, A., *Britain in Decline* (London: Macmillan, 1981).
Gash, N., *Sir Robert Peel* (London: Longman, 1972).
Gash, N., *Politics in the Age of Peel* (Brighton: Harvester, 1977).
Glynn, S. and Booth, A., *Modern Britain: An Economic and Social History* (London: Routledge, 1996).
Golby, J. M. and Purdue, A. W., *The Monarchy and the British People: 1760 to the Present* (London: Batsford, 1988).
Greenleaf, W. H., *The British Political Tradition*, vol. I: *The Rise of Collectivism* (London: Methuen, 1983).
Greenleaf, W. H., *The British Political Tradition*, vol. II: *The Ideological Heritage* (London: Methuen, 1983).
Harrison, J. F. C., *The Early Victorians, 1832–51* (London: Weidenfeld and Nicolson, 1971).
Harvie, C., *Scotland and Nationalism: Scottish Society and Politics, 1703–1977* (London: Routledge, 1977).
Hinton, J., *Labour and Socialism: A History of the British Labour Movement, 1867–1974* (Brighton: Wheatsheaf, 1983).
Hunt, E. H., *British Labour History, 1815–1914* (London: Weidenfeld and Nicolson, 1981).
Hyam, R., *Britain's Imperial Century, 1815–1914* (London: Hutchinson, 1976).
Jenkins, R., *Gladstone* (London: Macmillan, 1995).
Jenkins, T. A., *The Liberal Ascendancy, 1830–1886* (London: Macmillan, 1994).
Jenkins, T. A., *Party and Politics in Victorian Britain* (Manchester: Manchester University Press, 1996).
Kavanagh, D. and Morris, P., *Consensus Politics from Attlee to Thatcher* (Oxford: Blackwell, 1989).
Kennedy, P., *The Rise of the Anglo-German Antagonism, 1860–1914* (London: Allen and Unwin, 1980).
Levine, P., *Victorian Feminism* (London: Hutchinson, 1987).
Lewis, J., *Women in England, 1870–1950* (Brighton: Wheatsheaf, 1984).
Lovell, J., *British Trade Unions, 1875–1933* (London: Macmillan, 1977).
MacLeod, H., *Religion and Society in England, 1850–1914* (London: Macmillan, 1996).
Marquand, D., *Ramsay MacDonald* (London: Cape, 1977).

Marsh, P., *Joseph Chamberlain* (Yale: Yale University Press, 1994).
Matthew, C., *Gladstone, 1875–1898* (Oxford: Oxford University Press, 1995).
McCord, N., *The Anti-Corn Law League* (London: Unwin, 1958).
McCord, N., *British History, 1815–1906* (Oxford: Oxford University Press, 1991).
Morgan, K. O., *The People's Peace, 1945–1990* (Oxford: Oxford University Press, 1992).
Panayi, P., *Immigration, Ethnicity and Racism in Britain, 1815–1945* (Manchester: Manchester University Press, 1994).
Peden, G. C., *British Economic and Social Policy: Lloyd George to Margaret Thatcher* (London: Philip Allan, 1985).
Pelling, H., *Origins of the Labour Party* (London: Macmillan, 1954).
Pelling, H., *A History of British Trade Unionism* (London: Penguin, 1963).
Pelling, H., *Social Geography of British Elections, 1885–1910* (London: Macmillan, 1967).
Pelling, H., *Britain and the Second World War* (London: Fontana, 1970).
Perkin, H., *The Origins of Modern English Society, 1780–1880* (London: Routledge, 1969).
Pimlott, B., *Harold Wilson* (London: HarperCollins, 1992).
Pollard, S., *Britain's Prime and Britain's Decline: The British Economy, 1870–1914* (London: Arnold, 1989).
Porter, B., *The Lion's Share: A Short History of British Imperialism, 1850–1970* (London: Longman, 1975).
Pugh, M., *The Making of Modern British Politics, 1867–1939* (Oxford: Blackwell, 1982).
Pugh, M., *Lloyd George* (London: Longman, 1988).
Pugh, M., *State and Society: British Political and Social History, 1870–1992* (London: Arnold, 1994).
Reynolds, D., *Britannia Overruled: British Policy and World Power in the Twentieth Century* (London: Longman, 1991).
Robbins, K., *Nineteenth Century Britain: Integration and Diversity* (Oxford: Clarendon Press, 1988).
Rose, M. E., *The Relief of Poverty, 1834–1914* (London: Macmillan, 1972).
Rose, N., *Churchill: An Unruly Life* (London: Simon and Schuster, 1994).
Royle, E., *Modern Britain: A Social History, 1750–1985* (London: Arnold, 1987).
Rubinstein, D. W., *Capitalism, Culture and Decline in Britain, 1750–1990* (London: Routledge, 1993).
Searle, G. R., *The Liberal Party: Triumph and Disunity, 1886–1929* (London: Macmillan, 1992).
Smith, E. A., *Earl Grey, 1764–1845* (Oxford: Oxford University Press, 1990).
Stevenson, J., *British Society, 1914–1945* (London: Allen Lane, 1984).
Stevenson, J. and Cook, C., *The Slump* (London: Cape, 1977).
Stewart, R., *Parties and Politics, 1830–1852* (London: Macmillan, 1989).
Thompson, D., *The Chartists* (London: Temple Smith, 1984).
Thompson, E. P., *The Making of the English Working Class* (London: Penguin, 1968).

Thompson, F. M. L., *The Rise of Respectable Society: A Social History of Victorian Britain, 1830–1900* (London: Fontana, 1988).
Thompson, F. L. M. (ed), *The Cambridge Social History of Britain, 1750–1950* (Cambridge: Cambridge University Press, 1990).
Thompson, P., *The Edwardians* (London: Routledge, 1992).
Thurlow, R., *Fascism in Britain, 1918–1985* (Oxford: Blackwell, 1987).
Turner, J., *Macmillan* (London: Longman, 1994).
Vincent, J. R., *The Formation of the Liberal Party, 1857–1868* (London: Penguin, 1972).
Walvin, J., *Leisure and Society, 1830–1950* (London: Longman, 1978).
Walvin, J., *Victorian Values* (London: Cardinal, 1987).
Weiner, M., *English Culture and the Decline of the Industrial Spirit, 1850–1980* (Cambridge: Cambridge University Press, 1981).
Winter, J. M., *The Great War and the British People* (London: Macmillan, 1985).
Young, J. W., *Britain and European Unity, 1945–1992* (London: Macmillan, 1993).

Index

Aberdeen, Earl of, 69, 85, 94–5
Act of Settlement (1701), 11
Act of Union (1707), 13
agriculture, 3–5, 6–7, 28, 35, 39, 64, 73
air force, 197, 201
Anglicanism, *see* Church of England
Anti-Corn Law League, 63, 65–7
appeasement, 198–200, 201–3
army, 22, 83–4, 100, 165, 196–7, 200–1,
   220, 233
   reform of, 121, 156, 160
Ashley, Lord, 56, 65
Asquith, H. H., 141–2, 151, 163–5
Attlee, Clement, 191, 210, 211, 216
Attwood, Thomas, 47
Auckland, Lord, 88

Bagehot, Walter, 71
Baldwin, Stanley, 183, 184–5, 188, 197
Balfour, A. J., 112, 150, 156
banks, 35, 116, 237
Beach, Sir Michael Hicks, 112
Belgium, 85, 160, 161
Bentham, Jeremy, 41–2
Bevan, Aneurin, 213
Beveridge, Sir William, 118, 140, 207, 210
Bevin, Ernest, 177, 185, 207, 210, 220,
   222, 225
Bill of Rights (1689), 8
Birmingham, 47, 105
birth rates, 1, 119, 194, 207
Blair, Tony, 243–4
Boer War, *see* South African War

Booth, William, 118
Boy Scout movement, 121, 159
Bright, John, 65
Bristol, 2
British Union of Fascists, 189–90
   see also Sir Oswald Mosley
Brittain, Vera, 198
Brunner, Sir John, 117
Burke, Edmund, 23, 26
Burt, Thomas, 126
Butler, R. A., 207, 216

canals, 31–2
Canning, George, 84–5, 95
Cartwright, John, 22
Castlereagh, Viscount, 24, 84
Catholics, 11–12, 68, 79, 94
   emancipation of, 47–8
Chamberlain, Joseph, 105–6, 108, 113,
   132, 134, 138, 155
Chamberlain, Neville, 177, 199, 201,
   202–3, 205
Chartism, 59–62
Christian Socialism, 79
Church Liberation Society, 79
Church of England, 11–12, 13, 27, 77,
   100–1
Churchill, Winston, 120, 135, 140, 173,
   199–200
   as prime minister, 204–6, 210–11,
   216–17
Clive, Robert, 4
Cobbett, William, 39

249

Cobden, Richard, 62, 65–7, 71–2, 87
Cold War, 216, 222
Colquhoun, Patrick, 2–3
Commonwealth, 221, 224–5, 239
Communist Party, 191
Conservative Party, origins of, 15, 17–18,
    26–7, 44–5
  divisions in, 47–7
  under Peel, 52–3, 55, 63–5, 70, 91
  revival of, 99–100, 103–5, 108–10
  Edwardian problems of, 150–1
  in wartime, 168–9
  between the wars, 180, 183
  post-1945, 216–17, 243
  see also Margaret Thatcher
Corn Laws, 39, 69–70
  see also Anti-Corn Law League
Cornwallis, Lord, 25
Corporation Acts, 11–12, 23, 47
cotton textiles, 5, 28–9, 115, 189
Crimean War, 85–7, 94–5
Cripps, Sir Stafford, 209, 215, 216
Crosland, Anthony, 230
Curragh Mutiny, 151

Dalton, Hugh, 210, 214, 215
Darwin, Charles, 79
Defence Requirements Committee, 201
devaluation, 174, 176, 177–8, 215, 231,
    243
disarmament, 197–8
Disraeli, Benjamin, 55, 64, 99, 103–5,
    109, 129
Dissenters, see Nonconformists
Dreadnought (battleship), 156, 159
drink, 78

East India Company, 4, 14, 42–3, 87, 88
Eden, Sir Anthony, 200, 217–18, 224
Edinburgh, 2
education, 51
  1870 Act, 101
  1902 Act, 121
  1918 Act, 167
  1944 Act, 207, 213
Egypt, 105, 129, 130, 224

electoral system, 10–11
  see also parliamentary reform
Empire, 14–15, 21, 38, 87–9, 123, 178,
    196, 209, 223, 224
  and New Imperialism, 129–33
  and Imperial Federation, 134
  popularity of, 134–5, 136
  see also Commonwealth; India
eugenics, 119–20
European Economic Community, 218,
    225–7, 229, 239, 240–1, 242–3
exports, 5, 15, 29, 73, 115, 172–3, 215,
    229

Fabian Society, 126, 128, 138, 166
factory legislation, 56, 65
Falklands War, 240
family allowances, 207–8, 213
fascism, see British Union of Fascists
Fielden, John, 56
Fisher, Admiral Sir John, 156
food, 35, 123, 135, 165, 193, 225
Fox, Charles James, 24, 26
France, 15, 84–5, 89–90
  war with, 20–2, 25, 38
  entente with, 157, 159, 160, 161
free trade, 41, 44, 45, 64, 116, 123, 178,
    183
  see also Corn Laws; Anti-Corn Law
    League; tariffs
Friendly Societies, 77, 80, 81, 124
Frost, John, 60, 61

Gaitskell, Hugh, 215
General Strike, 174, 184–6
George III, King, 8, 15, 17, 43
George V, King, 183, 188
Germany, attitudes towards, 15, 21, 130,
    155
  naval rivalry, 155–6
  hostility towards, 157, 159, 161
  inter-war, 198–200, 201, 202
Gladstone, W. E., 68, 90, 130
  becomes a Liberal, 91, 94
  and reform, 80, 97, 98–102, 105–6,
    110–11
  and Ireland, 103, 107–8

Gold Standard, 45, 173–4, 176, 184
Graham, Sir James, 65, 69
Graves, Robert, 198
Great Exhibition, 72–3
Greece, 84–5, 89
Grey, Charles Earl, 26, 48, 50
Grey, Sir Edward, 157, 159, 161, 163

Haig, Sir Douglas, 164
Haldane, Richard, 160, 161, 182
Halifax, Earl of, 203
Harcourt, Sir William, 111
Hardie, James Keir, 110, 127
Hardy, Thomas, 22, 24
Harmsworth, Alfred, 117
health insurance, 140
  see also National Health Service
Heath, Edward, 226–7, 233–4
Henderson, Arthur, 110, 168
Hetherington, Henry, 47, 60
Hoare, Sir Samuel, 201–2
Hobhouse, L.T., 111
Hobson, J. A., 111, 132
honours, 117, 180
House of Commons, 9–10
House of Lords, see peerage
housing, 34, 165, 167, 193, 214, 218, 238
Howe, Sir Geoffrey, 236, 242
Hubt, Henry, 40

Independent Labour Party, 126–8, 176
India, 42, 172, 209, 221
  mutiny, 88–9
  national movement, 180, 209
  see also East India Company
industrial revolution, 5–7, 28, 36–7
  social impact of, 55
Ireland, 4
  population, 2
  Act of Union, 25
  politics of, 13–14, 24–6, 111–12, 180
  the famine, 68–9
  religion and nationalism, 25–6, 45, 52, 67–9, 102–3
  Home Rule bills, 107–8, 150–1
  Home Rule Party, 103, 106
iron and steel, 5, 29–31

Italy, 198, 201–2
  unification of, 89–90, 96

Japan, 121, 157, 198, 200, 209
Jarrow, 175
  March, 191
Jenkins, Roy, 226
Jones, Ernest, 62

Keynes, J. M., 174, 176–7, 186, 236
King, Gregory, 2
Kipling, Rudyard, 120, 133
Kitchener, Earl, 135, 163

Labour Party, 125, 139, 143, 146–7, 180–2, 182–4, 185, 191, 194, 230, 232, 235–6, 241
  formation of, 127–8
  in First World War, 164, 170–1
  in Second World War, 210–11
  in government, 182–4, 187–8, 213–16, 230–2, 235–6, 243–4
  see also Fabian Society; Independent Labour Party; Socialism
Lancashire, 40, 46, 59, 65, 73, 127, 189
Lansbury, George, 191
Law, Andrew, Bonar, 150–1, 164, 168, 180
League of Nations, 197–8, 202
Lever, William, 117
Liberal Party, 61, 66–7, 91, 92–7, 100–2, 105–6, 126, 145–7, 152, 153, 177, 184, 186, 226
  and New Liberalism, 110–11, 138, 139, 143–4
  and war, 161–2, 163–5, 171
  revival of, 229, 234, 241, 243
  see also Whigs
Lipton, Sir Thomas, 117
Liverpool, Lord, 27, 38–9, 40, 43–5
Lloyd George, David, 142, 143, 144, 148, 149, 159, 177, 186, 187, 188
  as prime minister, 164–5, 168–9, 171, 179–80
local government, 9–10, 51, 76, 112, 125, 238, 242
Locke, John, 8

London Corresponding Society, 22–3
Lovett, William, 47, 60

Macaulay, T. B., 71
MacDonald, James Ramsay, 110, 127,
  146–7, 164, 181–2, 183–4, 187–8
Macmillan, Harold, 177, 217–19, 223,
  224, 226, 229
Major, John, 242–3
Manchester, 60, 63
Mann, Tom, 148
Manning, Henry, 79
marriage, 4, 119, 167–8, 207
Marx, Karl, 71–2, 180
Maternity and Child Welfare Act, 167
Mayhew, Henry, 80
Maynooth Grant, 68
Means Test, 192, 207
Melbourne, Lord, 52, 53, 92
Methodists, 11, 40, 62, 107
middle classes, 2–4, 47–8, 65–6, 69, 72,
  76–8, 117
Mill, J. S., 91, 101, 125–6
Milner, Sir Alfred, 136
miners, 59, 126, 143, 184–5, 233
Ministry of Munitions, 165
monarchy, 8–9, 11
Mond, Sir Alfred, 117
monetarism, 236–7
Morrison, Herbert, 210
Mosley, Sir Oswald, 182, 187, 189–90
Mountbatten, Earl, 221
Munich Agreement, 202–3

national debt, 19–20, 44–5, 136, 173,
  182, 208
National Government, 177–8, 188, 189
National Health Service, 213–14, 238
National Service League, 156
National Unemployed Workers'
  Movement, 192
nationalisation, 214, 215, 217, 233, 239
navy, 83–4, 155, 159–60, 164, 200, 240
Nelson, Admiral Horatio, 21
Newman, John Henry, 67–8, 79
Nonconformists, 6, 11–12, 22, 52, 66, 68,
  77, 79, 100–1

Norwich, 2
nuclear deterrent, 212, 222–3

Oastler, Richard, 54, 56
O'Brien, Bronterre, 60
O'Connell, Daniel, 45, 47, 67
O'Connor, Feargus, 60,61
old-age pensions, 138, 139, 140, 141,
  193, 214
Opium War, 87–8, 89
Orange Society, 24
Orwell, George, 192
Owen, Robert, 58
Oxford Movement, 67–8

pacifism, 198
Paine, Tom, 23–4
Palmerston, Lord, 85, 88, 89–90, 95–7
Pankhurst, Emmeline, 151–2
Parliament Act (1911), 150
parliamentary reform, 22–4, 26, 38–40,
  44, 45
  in 1832, 46–9, 49–50, 54
  and Chartism, 62
  in 1866–7, 98–100
  in 1884–5, 100, 106
  in 1918, 169
Peace Ballot, 198
Peel, Sir Robert, 42, 52–3, 55, 63–5, 67–70
peerage, 9–10, 48–9, 81–2, 149–50, 232,
  244
'Peterloo Massacre', 40
Pitt, William, 17–18, 19–20, 20–1, 23–4,
  25, 26
Place, Francis, 44, 60
police, 42
poor law, 3, 42, 118–19, 138
  1834 reform, 51, 56–8
population, 1–2, 74
Post Office, 76, 77, 80, 140
privatisation see nationalisation
Privy Council, 10

railways, 32–3, 74–6, 214
rearmament, 200–1
Rhodes, Cecil, 133, 136
Ricardo, David, 41

Roosevelt, F. D., 177, 220
Rosebery, Earl, 132, 134
Rowntree, B. S., 118
Russell, Lord John, 45, 67, 69, 93–4, 95
Russia, 15, 83, 84, 86–7, 104, 157, 199–200

Sadler, Michael, 56
Salisbury, Marquess of, 107, 109, 111–13, 130, 133, 136, 154–5
Samuel, Herbert, 111, 188
Sassoon, Seigfried, 198
Scotland, population, 2
    politics of, 12–13, 59, 102, 127
    and nationalism, 231, 234, 244
Septennial Act, 9
servants, 3, 77, 166, 167, 175
Shaftesbury, Lord see Ashley
Six Acts, 40
slavery, 50
Smiles, Samuel, 77
Smith, Adam, 41
Snowden, Philip, 182, 183
Social Democratic Federation, 126, 128
Socialism, 125, 126–8, 143, 181–2, 190–1, 230
Society for Constitutional Information, 22–3
South African War (1899–1902), 112, 114, 120, 135–6, 138, 155–6
Stopes, Marie, 194
Stresa Front, 201
strikes, 124–5, 128, 147–8, 170, 181, 185, 233
    see also General Strike
Suez Canal, 130
    crisis over, 217, 223–4
suffragettes see women

Taff Vale Dispute, 128, 148
Tamworth Manifesto, 52–3
tariff reform, 115–16, 134, 138–9, 178, 183
taxation, 19, 41, 44–5, 64–5, 101–2, 111, 112–13, 217, 219, 238
    and 'People's Budget', 141–2
    in wartime, 20, 34, 166, 208

Test Act, 11–12, 23, 47
Thatcher, Margaret, 227, 234, 236–7, 239 41, 241 2
Thorne, Will, 127
Thorneycroft, Peter, 218–19
Tillett, Ben, 127
Tolpuddle Martyrs, 55
Tone, Wolfe, 24
Tories see Conservative Party
Trade Boards Act, 144
trade unions, 44, 55, 58–9, 80–1, 100, 123–6, 127, 128, 147, 181, 185, 188, 191–2, 232, 233
    in wartime, 165, 170, 212
    see also General Strike; strikes; Triple Alliance
Trades Disputes Act, 185
Triple Alliance (industrial), 148, 181
Triple Entente, 157–9
Turkey, 84–5, 86, 195

Ulster, 25, 150–1
unemployment, 138, 140–1, 174–6, 177, 186, 187, 192, 216, 233, 237
Union of Democratic Control, 164
United States of America, 14–15, 17, 19, 90, 208, 215, 216, 222, 224, 231, 240
upper classes, 2–3, 13, 50, 81–2
    see also peerage
Utilitarianism, 41–2

Versailles, Treaty of, 195, 198
Victoria, Queen, 52, 96, 104, 114
Vincent, Henry, 60

Wales, population of, 2
    politics of, 12, 61, 102, 231
Washington Naval Conference, 200
Webb, Beatrice, 118, 126, 138
Webb, Sidney, 170
welfare state, 213–14
Wellington, Duke of, 22, 47–8
Whigs, 15, 17, 23, 26–7, 50–3, 92, 108
Wilberforce, William, 12
William IV, King, 48
Wilson, Harold, 215, 223, 226, 230–2

women, 77–8, 119, 124, 138, 140, 175,
193–4
  enfranchisement of, 101, 151–2, 169,
244
  wartime role of, 159, 167–8, 206–7
working classes, 2–3, 54, 74, 77
  living standards, 33–5, 80–1, 122–3,
193–4

  in wartime, 169–71, 206–8
  see also Chartism; trade unions
Wyvill, Christopher, 22

Yorkshire, 10, 40, 49, 59, 127